Zones of Rebellion

Zones of Rebellion

*Kurdish Insurgents and
the Turkish State*

Aysegul Aydin and Cem Emrence

Cornell University Press
Ithaca and London

First published 2015 by Cornell University Press
Printed in the United States of America

Library of Congress Cataloging-in-Publication Data

Aydin, Aysegul, 1973– author.
   Zones of rebellion : Kurdish insurgents and the Turkish state / Aysegul
Aydin and Cem Emrence.
      pages cm
   Includes bibliographical references and index.
   ISBN 978-0-8014-5354-0 (cloth : alk. paper)
   1. Kurds—Turkey—History—Autonomy and independence
movements. 2. Ethnic conflict—Turkey. 3. Partiya Karkerên Kurdistani.
I. Emrence, Cem, author. II. Title.
   DR435.K87A917   2015
   956.103—dc23   2014044848

Cornell University Press strives to use environmentally responsible
suppliers and materials to the fullest extent possible in the publishing of
its books. Such materials include vegetable-based, low-VOC inks and
acid-free papers that are recycled, totally chlorine-free, or partly composed
of nonwood fibers. For further information, visit our website at
www.cornellpress.cornell.edu.

Cloth printing   10 9 8 7 6 5 4 3 2 1

Contents

PREFACE

This book is the result of five years of research on the Kurdish conflict in Turkey. It is a story about continuity and resistance to change. Just like individuals, organizations do not make decisions unencumbered by the past. They carry a historical burden, one that surfaces each time they have to cope with changing times. Such is the story of civil wars with no end. Both victorious governments and defeated insurgencies find themselves repeating the same strategies for survival. They do not invent new ways to connect with the masses: instead, they continue to rely on divisions created by the conflict, perfecting them at every turn, in order to hold on to their support base.

The reader will find two central points about political violence in this book. First, we argue that the nature of violence varies according to time and space. Distinct zones of rebellion gradually emerge in civil wars. Once formed, these zones acquire a legacy that defines the relations of combatants with the masses for years to come. The reason is simple: conflicts are resource-dependent processes. Combatants fight conflicts based on their interactions with territory and people. However, these interactions do not develop randomly and cannot be reset overnight. Second, this book shows why this is the case. We explore the combatants' long-term choices that inform their interactions with territory and people and explain the production of violence along these fault lines.

Our methodology reflects a growing trend in social sciences today that unsettles the boundaries between qualitative and quantitative research. We tried to write an accessible book that has a powerful narrative and an analytical framework. We also strove to combine a strong empirical foundation with arguments driven by major theoretical bodies of work. The result, we hope, is a well-rounded story of the Turkish civil war. Yet the book does not present a survey of the Kurdish conflict or use the Turkish context to test a general argument. It is this new intellectual terrain that makes the book a case study about Turkey and a general study of conflict processes at the same time. It is our hope that colleagues at both ends of the spectrum will find something well worth reading.

The Kurdish conflict has been one of the few issues that has managed to occupy headlines in Turkey throughout the last thirty years. The conflict led to tremendous human suffering and cost billions of dollars. It has also shaken up the political field in irreversible ways. A politicized Kurdish identity was born at the intersection of state repression and insurgent violence. Scholarly studies typically have approached the Kurdish issue as a function of pre-conflict grievances. True as it might be, this view does not tell us much about what went on during the conflict and, perhaps more critically, almost ignores the transformative role of violence. We believe that a narrative that relies on a quantification of violence and a nuanced reading of political processes in Turkish history has something to offer beyond this framework.

This book has been in the making for a long time. Its preparation took more time than originally planned, as we continued for years to work on it during the hot summers of Istanbul and the snowy winters of Colorado. Our priorities shifted along the way. Just like a pebble washed away by the waves, we chased the manuscript as it required a new round of attention of each time we thought we were done. The process of collecting data was exhaustive but innovative, writing and revisions took countless hours but proved rewarding, and the review process was challenging but improved the book in almost every way. This has been an exceptional journey that was well worth the effort.

Our editor, Roger Haydon, has been involved in this project from its inception. He put endless time and energy into turning the manuscript into a book that the reader can actually enjoy reading. He helped us present the most complex ideas about violence in digestible forms. He knows how books work, and we had the pleasure and privilege of learning from his insights and feedback for several years. The attention to detail of one of our reviewers pushed us to cover an extensive literature as we interpreted civil war violence against the background of modern Turkish history since the nineteenth century. His or her extensive knowledge of Turkey was also instrumental in helping us rethink friends and foes in the Turkish civil war.

Our colleagues provided motivation and guidance throughout this journey. Stathis Kalyvas invited us to share our work at the Program on Order, Conflict, and Violence. This book benefited from his ideas and pointed comments in many ways. Will Moore, Daniel Chard and Eric Schoon generously devoted their time to reading and commenting on parts of the manuscript. At the University of Massachusetts-Amherst, David Mednicoff provided a hospitable environment for thinking about the manuscript in its early stages. Several colleagues at the Center for Public Policy and Administration gave useful feedback. We had insightful conversations with Kemal Kirişçi, a friend with a long tenure in Turkish studies. Throughout the years, Şevket Pamuk, Hasan Kayalı, and Çağlar Keyder engrained one of the authors with a deep appreciation of Ottoman-Turkish history from social scientific angles. The University of Colorado's Innovative Seed Grant Program funded the fieldwork that turned our new intellectual direction into a book and set the stage for a research program.

We also had silent partners: Family and friends were the guideposts as we slowly found our way. Necla, Münir, Leman, Gülümser, Halil, and Ali İsmail taught us the value of determination, freedom of choice, and tolerance. We are grateful to each of them.

Abbreviations

AKP	Justice and Development Party
ARGK	Kurdistan Peoples' Salvation Army
BDP	Peace and Democracy Party
DDKD	Revolutionary Democratic Culture Association
DDKO	Revolutionary Cultural Society of the East
DEP	Democracy Party
Dev-Sol	Revolutionary Left
DHKP-C	Revolutionary People's Party-Front
DTP	Democratic Society Party
DYP	True Path Party
ERNK	National Liberation Front of Kurdistan
FBIS-WEU	Foreign Broadcast Information Service, West Europe
GAM	Free Aceh Movement
GAP	Southeast Anatolia Project
HADEP	People's Democracy Party
HEP	People's Labor Party
HRK	Kurdistan Salvation Union

IED	improvised explosive device
KCK	Union of Kurdistan Communities
KUK	Kurdistan National Liberationists
MİT	Metropole Revenge Teams
MGK	National Security Council
OHAL	Emergency rule
PKK	Kurdistan Workers' Party
RP	Welfare Party
RPG	rocket-propelled grenade
SHP	Social Democratic People's Party
TAK	Freedom Falcons of Kurdistan
TBMM	The Turkish Grand National Assembly
TDP	Revolutionary Party of Turkey
TDKP	Revolutionary Communist Party of Turkey
TIKKO	Turkish Workers and Peasants Liberation Army
TIP	Turkish Workers Party
TKP/ML	Turkish Communist Party/Marxist-Leninist
TKSP	Turkish Kurdistan Socialist Party
YCK	Youth Council of Kurdistan

Chronology: Three Phases of the Turkish Civil War

Transforming the Community, 1984–1990

November 1978: The Kurdistan Workers' Party (PKK) is launched and its ideological program is announced.

September 1980: A military coup bans all leftist groups, including Kurdish organizations. The PKK settles abroad and sets up rebel camps in northern Iraq and Syria.

August 1984: The first successful guerrilla attacks take place in the remote districts of Eruh and Şemdinli.

September 1984: The first reported village raids take place in the Hakkari province. Rebels target state-allied Kurds in hundreds of village raids.

March 1985: The political wing of the PKK, the National Liberation Front of Kurdistan (ERNK), is founded to propagandize for the rebel cause in urban settings and across Europe.

September 1985: The Turkish state starts recruiting and arming coethnics (village guards) to slow down insurgents in the countryside.

October 1986:   The PKK's Third Party Congress calls for a forced recruitment campaign.

July 1987:   The state responds to the security challenge by putting several provinces under emergency rule (Olağanüstü Hâl Bölgesi; OHAL) and expanding the village guard system.

September 1989: The first act of civilian unrest takes place in the Silopi district (Mardin province). The state employs widespread political repression, particularly mass detentions, in an effort to stop political mobilizations.

Competition with the State, 1991–1999

August 1991:   Regional wars over Iraq increase the military capacity of the PKK. Weapons found in PKK's rural hideouts show that the rebel organization has acquired advanced weapons after the Gulf War.

March 1992:   Civilian unrest engulfs border towns. Protestors clash with security forces in mass Nevrouz celebrations leading to hundreds of civilian deaths and injuries. The People's Labor Party (HEP), a recently founded pro-Kurdish party, ends its partnership with the incumbent Social Democratic People's Party (SHP) in protest.

August 1992:   The PKK raids Şırnak, a province on the Iraqi border, clashing with security forces for fifty-two hours.

May-June 1993:   Both sides announce total war after rebels kill thirty-three unarmed military personnel in a single attack in Bingöl.

May 1993:   With voluntary recruits, the rebel army grows to include thousands of militants. OHAL governor Ünal Erkan announces that there are 2,000 rebel soldiers inside the country and 4,000 in northern Iraq.

June 1993:   The Tansu Çiller government is formed and counterinsurgency operations expand.

October 1993:   The PKK announces that it has banned all political parties in the OHAL region.

October 1994:   The number of insurgent attacks begins to fall dramatically after peaking in 1993.

January 1995:   The PKK's Fifth Party Congress acknowledges the one-man rule of rebel leader Abdullah Öcalan in order to reverse military decline.

March 1995:	Operation Steel eliminates hundreds of rebels in northern Iraq camps. Security forces engage in cross-border operations, organize massive security sweeps, and target rebel strongholds.
April 1995:	Under heavy military pressure, the ERNK organizes the Kurdish Parliament-in-Exile in Lahey to find political support in Europe.
February 1999:	After leaving Syria in 1998 and being shuttled back and forth between European countries, Öcalan is captured in Kenya with U.S. assistance outside the Greek embassy.

Deadlock, 2000–

August 1999:	Öcalan calls for a cease-fire from prison and the PKK leaves Turkey.
March 2000:	The PKK's Extraordinary Seventh Party Congress follows the lead of Öcalan. It advocates the "Democratic Republic" project and promises to use violence more selectively.
May 2003:	From its new base in Kandil mountain in northern Iraq, the PKK renews its military activity. A rebel ambush in Yayladere, Bingöl, kills one soldier and wounds eight others.
July 2007:	After the general elections, Recep Tayyip Erdoğan, the prime minister and leader of Islamic-leaning Justice and Development Party (AKP), claims that the AKP and not the Kurdish nationalist party represents Kurds. Islamic charities and civic society organizations are mobilized by the government to emphasize Muslim solidarity and downplay ethnic nationalism in the region.
October 2008:	Dramatic upsurge in insurgent attacks. The PKK targets military posts on the Iraqi border. Major clashes leave forty dead and another twenty wounded on both sides after militants attack the Aktütün military post in the border district of Şemdinli.
June 2011:	Election results demonstrate that the defunct OHAL region is now politically divided between the ethnic project and state hegemony.
July 2011:	In an extraordinary meeting in Diyarbakır, the Democratic Society Congress (DTK), an umbrella organization under the influence of the Kurdish nationalist party, demands democratic decentralization to end the Kurdish problem.

Zones of Rebellion

INTRODUCTION

After years of training, the rebels were ready. The Eruh raid was based on an elaborate and well-prepared plan. Prior to the attack, the group staged mock attacks on a model of the target site and became familiar with roads and buildings. Each member of the group was given specific tasks to perform during the attack. On August 15, 1984, around 9:00 p.m., the rebels reached their destination. They assaulted the army compound and set the government building on fire. They also stole guns from the armory and spread propaganda from the mosque's loudspeaker mounted on the minaret. The organizer of the attack was Mahsun Korkmaz, who would later become a legendary military commander. In his report to the rebel headquarters, he concluded that the Eruh incident demonstrated the vulnerabilities of the Turkish army and boosted the confidence of rebel forces.[1]

The rebels soon began to exert their influence in rural areas. The villagers of Taraklı watched as a firing squad shot their neighbors, who were accused of collaborating with the Turkish state and its tribal allies, the Babats.[2] Violence in the countryside improved rebel prospects, turning the small group into a mass organization. On its thirteenth anniversary (1991), rebel supporters vandalized banks in Istanbul and clashed with police in Adana and Izmir. The following year, the rebels tried to capture Şırnak province to create a liberated zone on the Iraqi border. When rebel fortunes began to decline, Leyla Kaplan was only seventeen years old. Code-named Pınar, she had grown up in Dağlıoğlu, a poor neighborhood of Adana populated by Kurdish migrants. Pınar became a suicide bomber in 1996. On October 25, she blew herself up, causing several casualties.[3]

War also changed life for those on the other side. Mesut Taner Genç was a district governor in 1993.[4] He was assigned to Beytüşşebap, a strategic border district where pro-state village guards enjoyed a prominent presence. Travel between the provincial center of Şırnak and the district was dangerous: The road was heavily mined and the rebels frequently installed roadblocks. When he began his new assignment, the district governor had to wait for days for an open seat in an army helicopter, which was crowded with security forces, bureaucrats, and their families. In the mid-1990s, the military situation began to improve: Operation Sparrow (1996) destroyed key rebel camps inside Turkey, and the army periodically conducted cross-border operations into northern Iraq. In 1999, Ankara's military victory was confirmed: the rebel leader was captured in Kenya and later imprisoned for life. Public jubilation followed, a strong indication that the insurgency was to disappear into history with no chance of return. A decade later, however, thousands in Diyarbakır would disagree. In the fall of 2009, they gathered to salute a group of militants who had surrendered to the Turkish state as a sign of goodwill by the rebel organization.

Kurdish armed contention in Turkey has a long and complicated history. The conflict has spanned three decades and cost more than 40,000 lives. It has destroyed state infrastructure, brought the regional economy to a halt, and resulted in forced migration. The military contestation has also generated a wave of civilian unrest in urban centers that evolved into a Kurdish nationalist platform. The origins of the conflict go back to the 1970s, when the Kurdistan Workers' Party (PKK) was founded by a handful of university students. The PKK's goal was to create an independent Kurdistan by transforming the Kurdish community and destroying state institutions in southeastern Anatolia. Rebel hopes were soon dashed. The Turkish state decisively defeated the PKK on the battlefield and found political allies in the Kurdish community. Since the capture of the rebel leader, Abdullah Öcalan, the conflict has taken a new turn. The rebels are now staging fewer attacks to win political concessions from the government, and, like Sinn Fein in Northern Ireland, a legal Kurdish nationalist party has emerged as a major political force in the region.[5]

The fortunes of the combatants followed a strange path. Each side started from a disadvantaged position, later gained momentum, and yet failed to capitalize on its battleground gains. On the insurgency side, how did a small group of students turn into a mass guerrilla force? In the early 1990s, the rebel group carried out multiple attacks on any given day and operated across a large territory. It commanded a propaganda machine in Europe, urban cells in border towns, and ample resources in the countryside. In a few years, most of this infrastructure was destroyed. The performance of the counterinsurgent followed a strikingly similar trajectory. Despite the earlier dismal record, security forces largely eliminated Kurdish rebels in the second half of the 1990s. Military success did not, however, deliver political peace. Both sides failed to translate military gains into political solutions at critical junctures in the conflict.

The key issue was the combatants' failure to unite the Kurdish people and territory around their political agendas. Since the late nineteenth century, the Turkish state had set up special administrative regions and excluded "troubled" areas from the nation-building process. The state further fragmented the Kurdish society by encouraging ethnic defections in the special region. Local allies received economic and political rewards for fulfilling security functions. The insurgency did not fare any better. Heavy-handed rule mismanaged the territorial expansion that followed military success. Similarly, the PKK's nominal definition of Kurdish identity failed to win the loyalties of many in its target community. The end result has been a form of resource partitioning:[6] Civil war parties divided civilian loyalties and territory in the Kurdish universe. These boundary making efforts have had a formative impact on violence and shaped its distribution.[7]

This book tracks the long causal chain in the Turkish civil war. We explain variation in violence as an outcome of the combatants' long-term policies. Our argument has two parts. First, we propose an ecological reading of war that focuses on the interaction between combatants and resources.[8] Combatants have had varying levels of civilian support and territorial control across space, and these differences in turn form distinct zones of violence. Second, we explain why combatants have enjoyed different levels of access to territory and people. Adopting a historical institutionalist approach, we unveil the historical processes behind zone formation and show how combatants' earlier choices have informed patterns of violence.

Zone Making

We divide the civil war geography into three zones, which emerge asymmetrically for each side: a zone under control, a contested zone, and a zone beyond reach.[9] In areas where combatants are most successful in transforming the community and uniting it around their political agenda, a zone under control emerges. Examples include the Ayacucho department for the Shining Path in Peru, the North Aceh district for the Free Aceh Movement (GAM) in Indonesia, and Mindanao Island for Muslim rebels in the Philippines. In the zone beyond reach, by contrast, this mobilization is least successful. The contested zone includes areas where neither side is capable of establishing hegemonic control; each combatant faces a unique challenge that prevents it from imposing its political project on territory and people.

Zones reflect the strength of ties between combatants and resources. To understand these dynamics, we turn to organizational analysis, the ecology school in particular, which examines issues of survival and competition from a resource standpoint.[10] This school studies organizations in relation to their resource bases (niches) and argues that competition emerges when resource bases overlap.[11] We take a similar approach and suggest that civil war violence varies according to the combatants' access to resources. When resources are secured by one side, violence is selective and both sides rely on a single tactic. States can close off central political markets to insurgents, whereas the latter can carve out new distant markets in outlying areas. Indiscriminate targeting then becomes the main strategy to enter a rival's home court. Competition over the same resource base generates a different type of encounter. It diversifies violence in a contested zone and forces combatants to adopt multiple tactics in order to cultivate civilian loyalties and achieve territorial control.

The establishment of emergency rule by the Turkish state was instrumental in zone making during the Turkish civil war. Building on historical precedents, the state carved out a special administrative region in south-eastern Anatolia (Olağanüstü Hâl Bölgesi, OHAL, 1987–2002) to contain insurgent violence. This decision was the main difference maker in the distribution of violence. Special rule allowed the combatants to approach civilians and territory differently than it was in the rest of the country. This form of governance put the rule of law aside, escalated the armed conflict to new heights, and opened the door for civilian victimization and social resistance. Accordingly, violence took different forms inside and outside the OHAL region. Still, within this special region, there were fundamental differences depending on combatants' interactions with territory and people. Civil war sides enjoyed hegemony in certain areas and ran into major difficulty in others.

We identify distinct zones of violence in the Turkish civil war. Outside the OHAL region, the state was hegemonic. We named this area Zone 3, the state's stronghold. OHAL, however, presented distinct advantages and challenges for each combatant. For the insurgents, the OHAL meant two zones: Zone 1, the insurgency's stronghold, where the PKK could easily survive and was most effective; and Zone 2, where the PKK faced rivals, a less enthusiastic clientele and considerable state presence. Consistent with its past experience, the Turkish state's record in the OHAL region was different. Most of this region was a battlefield where the state responded to insurgent violence with military operations. We call this area the Battle Zone. Elsewhere, the state faced a more complex problem. We refer to this section of OHAL as the Transition Zone. Here ethnic mobilizations challenged the state and forced the counterinsurgent to diversify its methods and targets.

In the initial years of guerrilla struggle (1984–1990), the PKK turned a number of border districts into an insurgent stronghold, Zone 1. To accomplish this, the rebel group used village raids and waged war against its own community. Punishing state-allied coethnics brought about a community transformation. In the second phase (1991–1999), the PKK expanded beyond the border area and operated across the entire region under emergency rule. It used multiple tactics to destroy state infrastructure and assault its rivals. Insurgents frequently targeted schools, businesses, and highways in order to sever the region's ties with the rest of Turkey. Expansion toward this contested site, Zone 2, however, did not bring Kurdistan under rebel control. Despite the increasing scale of violence, the outcomes remained uncertain. With the capture of Öcalan in 1999, the PKK returned to the border. In this third phase (2000–2008), rebels stopped targeting co-ethnics and the national infrastructure. Instead, they used improvised explosive devices (IEDs) to target security forces in Zone 1 and organized spectacular attacks against civilians in large cities. Indiscriminate targeting aimed to bring public pressure to bear on the government.

The Turkish state employed distinct tactics across space. In areas outside the OHAL region, where rebels had only a sporadic presence, the state could easily identify operatives and monitor networks that were sympathetic to the rebels' cause. Arrests were used to preempt the group's infiltration into the rest of Turkey, Zone 3, and limited the participation of coethnics in the Kurdish nationalist movement. The counterinsurgent operated with a different set of priorities inside the OHAL region. In the Transition Zone, a political question defined the Turkish state's experience. The Transition Zone was comprised of select urban settings, which held the key for political leadership in the Kurdish universe. The state employed multiple repertoires in this contested site, relying on mass arrests to curb popular mobilizations and military encounters to eliminate insurgents. It regarded the rest of the OHAL region as a battlefield. After cutting off the rebels' logistical support in the countryside, the state responded to PKK violence with military encounters in the Battle Zone.

What do these Turkish patterns tell us about violence? First, they show that tactics follow a reverse U-shaped pattern during the course of a civil war. Combatants start with a single tactic, switch to multiple repertoires at their peak, and revert back to a single form when they experience military decline. In spatial terms, we observe a similar pattern. Civil war sides rely on a single method at home and in their opponent's territory, yet employ multiple methods of waging violence in contested sites. Second, the Turkish case is instructive for thinking about the efficiency of violence. We believe that the most productive tactics are those adopted in the zone under control. Because the combatant has established strong ties with resources, its method of violence is more interactive and multifaceted than in other zones. For instance, village raids put the PKK rebels instantly in touch with villagers, allowing them to punish foes and recruit for the rebel army. These raids also had a preemptive function: They severed ties between locals and the Turkish state. Third, the choice of targets is a resource-dependent process. Targets become indiscriminate as the combatants' military capacity wanes. The PKK primarily targeted state-allied coethnics in its stronghold, whereas civilians were key targets in the zone beyond reach.

Midfield Wars

When the PKK expanded beyond its stronghold in the early 1990s, it encountered a reality that it was not prepared for. It proved difficult to attract the support of the Kurdish community in the newly contested sites, Zone 2. There were locally embedded rival organizations, a heterogeneous clientele, and a credible state presence. In these contested sites, the rebel group was unable to forge coalitions and missed the chance to unite the Kurdish community around its nationalist agenda. The firm boundaries of Kurdish Islam and the partial support that Kurdish Alevites gave to the rebel project were strong signs that territorial control would not materialize in the form of an ethnic homeland.[12] Even worse, outside the OHAL region, millions of Kurds were simply beyond rebel reach. Facing state power at its height, the PKK tried to enter these political markets through the use of indiscriminate violence.

Meanwhile, the Turkish state had to deal with a different problem in contested sites. The Transition Zone became the scene of competition between the ethnic project and state hegemony. The state feared that a group of political entrepreneurs acting as brokers might ignite popular revolts in the Transition Zone and lower the threshold of rebellion in other parts of the country.[13] Civilian unrest demonstrated the capabilities of these brokers. Acts of resistance wove together a network of towns (1989–1993) and highlighted the centrality of these sites in Kurdish politics. A harsh counterinsurgency response soon helped transform civilian unrest into an ethnic platform. The Kurdish nationalist party emerged as a contender in the region and intensified the rivalry with the Turkish state in contested sites.[14] Subsequently, a long-lasting opposition consolidated against the state.

"Midfield wars" kept combatants trapped in their strongholds, and the resistance to change at the height of their military success further contributed to deadlock (see figure I.1). Insurgencies are especially prone to a competency trap: a rebel group succeeds in securing territory through armed struggle and thereafter insists on continuing the same strategy.

Expectations rise, especially among sons-of-the-soil movements that claim an ethnic homeland. After gaining control over the border area, the PKK stepped up its military activity to consolidate the Kurdish universe. A window of opportunity opened for the rebels. They could either switch to a political platform or continue the guerrilla struggle. The former strategy would have required rallying the masses behind them. Indeed, civilian unrest was engulfing Kurdish towns and had the potential to turn into popular revolts. But the PKK made a tactical mistake similar to that made by the Communist Party of the Philippines in the wake of Ferdinand Marcos's fall (1983–1986). The rebels invested their energies in the guerrilla struggle, only to discover their opponents' superior capabilities on the battlefield. Eventually, military defeat in the second half of the 1990s forced the rebels back into the border sanctuaries where they had started out as a small group.

The Turkish state's military strategy worked. Its effective use of space first pushed the rebels into sanctuaries and then eliminated them in these

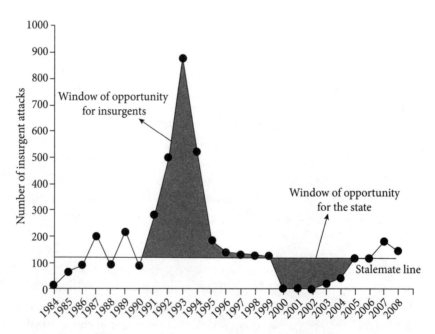

Figure I.1. Kurdish armed contention in Turkey, 1984–2008

hot spots. Beyond military solutions, however, the state's political choices precluded any long-lasting solution. Since the state had already committed itself to special interests such as tribal allies, village guards, and religious orders, it failed to integrate the region and win the hearts and minds of the people. After its military peak in 1999, the state also shied away from political solutions that involved group recognition; a matter that became all the more urgent as an ethnic party sympathetic to the rebel cause had emerged during the war. The end result was a military victory with no political agenda to back it up. Once again, combatants missed a window of opportunity to eliminate fault lines in Kurdish society.

How can we explain the mixed record of the combatants in the Turkish civil war? Why was it difficult to change the course of the war even when one side seized the advantage on the battlefield? Why did their tactics lead to a contested zone and fail to unite the Kurdish people? We believe that preconflict interactions between the combatants and resources made the Kurdish conflict exceptionally resistant to any form of settlement. In the next section, we show that the combatants' long-term ties with territory and people configured the violence and created distinct zones of rebellion.

Origins of Violence

States have long historical records that provide them with a unique set of tools and fairly stable ideas for cementing a relationship with a territory and its people. Similarly, the long-term experience of insurgencies most often reflects the early decisions they make regarding survival. Once the combatants are set on track, different options are foreclosed until the next turning point. For example, writing on the Aceh conflict in Indonesia, Jacques Bertrand suggests that the decision of Indonesian elites to politically exclude Aceh at a critical time laid the foundations of the region's troubles in the last quarter of the twentieth century (1976–2005).[15]

The rigidity of policies stems from combatants' earlier choices.[16] Historical institutionalism illuminates these choices and informs our arguments in two ways.[17] First, it shows how institutions/policies distribute power and exclude certain constituencies from the political process.[18] Second, it suggests that policy choices are path-dependent: They are embedded in history and can be revealed by studying key processes over time.[19] In the Turkish example, three episodes have been critical: (1) the late Ottoman period, from 1878 to 1922; (2) the early Republican period, from 1923 to 1945; and (3) the Kurdish conflict in contemporary Turkey, starting in 1984 and continuing to the present day. Insurgencies have shorter life cycles. The PKK's institutional memory and experimentation with ideas and strategies can be effectively traced back to the revolutionary protest cycle that engulfed Turkey in the 1970s.

Early experience was reinforced through organization and ideology. Both sets of policies displayed strong continuity over time and shaped combatants' preferences in the Turkish civil war. They worked as feedback mechanisms to secure territorial control and produce civilian support. Organizational setup determines how much territorial control can be achieved. Questions about ordering space and territorial governance are directly linked to the nature of the organization. On the other hand, ideology promotes loyalty and discourages noncompliance. By promising to reward friends and punish foes, it sets the terms of a one-way contract a political actor imposes on the civilian population. Viewed together, both mechanisms define the physical and mental boundaries of combatants' imagined political community.

In the Turkish civil war, organizational policies were critical for combatants' ability to control territory. The state viewed ethnic contention in spatial terms and responded accordingly. Building on historical memory, it set up a special administrative region (the OHAL) to contain Kurdish insurgency and used redistricting to isolate the rebels. Its administrative practices put several provinces under emergency rule for decades and carved out new units for security purposes. This manipulation of the target territory through administrative arrangements is a common state practice. For example, faced with multiple insurgencies in the 1990s, the Indonesian state planned to divide East Timor and Papua into several provinces and invented new districts in Aceh to block independence movements and defend loyalist enclaves.[20]

The state's organizational response has far-reaching consequences, as the situation in Ireland illustrates. The British decision to keep loyalist districts attached to the empire redistributed violence, destroyed the unity of Ireland, and made integration an unattainable dream. Similarly, while the establishment of the OHAL region in Turkey contained the PKK violence, it also created a de facto Kurdistan on the national map. This was a historic outcome. Unlike in Iraq and Iran, Kurdistan has never denoted a territory with specific boundaries in the Turkish context. As such, and contrary to the intended purpose, the state policy contributed to the rise of an ethnic consciousness within the Kurdish community by detaching the region from the rest of the country.

Kurdish rebels had their own organizational puzzle. First came success, with the cult of leadership surrounding Öcalan. The PKK acquired resources from the Kurdish community through forced recruitment campaigns and later turned these recruits into high trusters in training camps.[21] The early prize was increased rebel control on the Iraqi border. Soon after, community transformation and widespread state repression gave the PKK the status of a mass organization. But capturing Kurdistan required an efficient administration that allocated resources, coordinated units, and ensured common goals in the organization. In the mid-1990s, Öcalan single-handedly controlled insurgent careers, the party bureaucracy, and the PKK's military strategy. However, the one-man rule that had generated early success later became an obstacle to territorial expansion. The rebels were unable to set up a modern bureaucracy and solve their principal-agent problems.[22] Organizational dilemmas kept the PKK trapped on the border despite its significant efforts to achieve geographical expansion.[23]

If the combatants' organizational choices kept the target territory divided, ideology played a similar role in splintering the loyalty of the Kurdish people. Insurgencies have historically thrived on a single clientele and have had a hard time addressing multiple societal cleavages. This is especially the case for revolutionary groups that see themselves as having a self-proclaimed mission and act with a religious zeal. The PKK fits this description. Programmatic in character, its nationalist call found a warm reception in areas with weak ties to the central state. Sharing the experience of GAM in Indonesia, the PKK's ideology had a major downside: it rejected religious-based programs, which had informed previous Kurdish revolts in the region.[24] Accordingly, insurgent ideology allowed no room for hyphenated identities in the Kurdish community. It fiercely competed against Kurdish Islam, ignored Alevite identity, and hardly mentioned Zazas, the last two being distinct ethno-confessional groups within the Kurdish community.[25] As the Shining Path learned in Peru, this ideological exclusivity turned local differences into major obstacles to winning people's allegiance.[26]

The Turkish state fared no better in consolidating the target group. The state's ideological position on Kurds rested on two principles. It sought transformation and modernization of Kurdish areas during peaceful times and reverted to co-optation when there was a security threat. The co-optation framework was fully installed when the state viewed insurgents as political bandits with international allies. Informed by history, this cyclical ideology shaped the way the Turkish state responded to the PKK challenge.[27] Kurdish insurgents were no longer understood as tribal malcontents resisting centralization. Accordingly, the state responded to the PKK's community transformation efforts by recruiting its own allies. The key arrangement was the institution of village guards. As corporate units, the tribe and the village formed the basis of recruitment. Replicating the experience of their late Ottoman predecessors, village guards slowed down insurgents. The co-optation model, however, had a major flaw. It prevented the central state from reaching out to all members of the Kurdish community. Instead, the state legitimized the power of its allies, provided them with resources, and subcontracted various security functions.

Distinctions between friend and foe bred new divisions in the Kurdish community. Most critically, boundary making efforts consolidated an ethnic platform. The temporal evolution and spatial origins of the Kurdish nationalist party validate this claim. When the Turkish state mobilized rival local identities, in particular Kurdish Islam, and repressed civilian dissent in contested sites, it unintentionally contributed to the making of a new political identity: Kurdish nationalism with a mass following. Built at the interstices of state repression and insurgent violence, the nationalist movement proved to be resilient. It defended contested sites against the political monopoly of the Turkish state.

What eventually happened? The Turkish state won the military struggle and sent the insurgents back to where they first started. Like their Colombian counterparts, Kurdish rebels returned to the border under pressure from the military.[28] Still, the political question that emerged during the war remains unsolved. Because the Kurdish community is now divided, each civil war side has to rely on its support base. The partitioning of resources in contested sites leaves no room for a negotiated political settlement. Entrenched in path-dependent choices, the combatants have failed to break the political stalemate. The fault lines in contemporary

Kurdish society cannot be undone by foreign intervention or new institutional commitments that address rebel demands.[29]

Looking Ahead

The book is divided into two parts. In the first part, we explore the record of the PKK. Chapter 1 suggests that organizational choices enabled early group success but became obstacles to victory in later stages. Most important, heavy-handed rule curtailed the rise of a managerial class, paving the way for internal struggles and a dysfunctional bureaucracy. Chapter 2 traces the rebel group's ideological journey. The PKK campaigned for independence early in its existence, invited foreign pressure in the 1990s, and more recently has become interested in political bargains with the Turkish state. The transformation of rebel discourse closely followed changes in military performance, failing to promote an inclusive Kurdish identity. Chapter 3 examines the military record of the insurgent group. It shows that civilian commitment to the rebel cause varied greatly along spatial lines, which in turn shaped three zones with distinct records of violence. In particular, the chapter unveils PKK's origins on the border and its declining fortunes with geographical expansion.

We then examine the same mechanisms from the vantage point of counterinsurgency. We find strong path dependency in state behavior, which divided the territory and loyalties of its Kurdish citizens. Chapter 4 reveals the organizational response of the Turkish state to the PKK insurgency. It shows how this historically embedded response viewed insurgency in spatial terms and was put to use each time the Turkish state faced ethnic demands. Special administrative solutions consolidated a contentious universe and resulted in boundary making. Chapter 5 demonstrates that the boundary making effort was not merely geographical. The Turkish state tried regional transformation in peaceful times and reverted to the co-optation model whenever it faced a security threat. This cyclical ideology split people's loyalties, especially during times of rebellion. Chapter 6 brings to light the state's counterinsurgency strategy. Underlining its organizational and ideological origins, we document distinct tactics in three counterinsurgency zones. While military campaigns isolated the insurgents in the Battle Zone, widespread political arrests consolidated an ethnic opposition in contested sites.

The conclusion has two tasks. Most important, it suggests that there is no easy fix to end protracted civil wars. Unless civil war parties change the way they interact with resources (territory and people), a negotiated settlement will not guarantee peace in the long run. We observe that civil wars are incomplete group-making projects. Political brokers play a critical role for mobilization, forms of claim making are diverse across space and time, and collective identities are forged and challenged in a civil war environment.

Part I

Insurgency

1

Organization

In the contemporary world, guerrilla movements have to operate as modern organizations. They need to secure internal commitment and public legitimacy, and function efficiently with a complex division of labor to achieve their goals. The experience of the PKK was no different. It had to find ways to win the trust of its members and the public, eliminate outside competition, and create a bureaucratic body for an independent Kurdistan. This chapter discusses the organizational evolution of the PKK. We show that the organizational strategies that turned a small student group into a mass guerrilla organization became major obstacles to success in later stages. The PKK's failure to manage rebellion in organizational terms derailed its chances of territorial control.

We document the PKK's managerial success in the early stages of rebellion and its inefficiency in the later period. The first two sections show that, for early survival, the PKK used collective action to dampen competitive pressures and relied on organizational myths to build trust among its members. Once rivals had been defeated and the loyalty of its members had been secured, the rebel group turned to resource extraction and outside legitimacy. The third section discusses how these twin processes enabled the PKK to reach a critical mass. Despite ample resources and support from the international community, the rebel group failed to take control of and consolidate the Kurdish territory. Why this unexpected outcome? The last two sections demonstrate that the PKK's bureaucratic inefficiency blocked its path to military success and prevented it from transforming into a political actor.

Competitive Origins

The PKK emerged with the transformation of the revolutionary left into an organizational field in the 1970s.[1] A generation of student-entrepreneurs at top universities successfully turned socialism into a political product for consumption by the masses. Using elements of Marxist-Leninist scholarship, young revolutionaries presented socialism as the ultimate idea for defeating imperialism and establishing a people's democracy in Turkey. The primary target audience was their fellow students. The revolutionaries held heated debates on university campuses, organized several student groups, and worked tirelessly to recruit members from each other's organizations. Their connectedness and spatial proximity gave birth to a political industry that was characterized by competition among revolutionary organizations. State surveillance soon became a problem.[2] Despite constitutional freedoms, the Turkish state banned these organizations and pushed the revolutionary left outside the legal sphere. Stripped of legality and legitimacy, the revolutionaries went underground. They were no longer constrained by formal rules and political routines. The propaganda techniques grew more radicalized as the revolutionary field grew smaller in size and became increasingly divided from within.

In this vein, the Turkish revolutionary left underwent a full protest cycle from 1968 to 1980.[3] First, it brought fresh resources, tactics, and legitimacy to contentious politics in Turkey. The Turkish Workers Party (TIP), which was founded in 1968, was instrumental in this regard. It hosted the majority of political activists, organized mass demonstrations and introduced socialism to the public.[4] Revolutionary Youth (Dev-Genç) played a similar role at colleges, where it brought university youth into its fold. The honeymoon of the Turkish left ended abruptly in 1971 when the military convinced the government to suppress leftist organizations. The second episode of the Turkish protest cycle was characterized by increasing competition among revolutionary organizations. Political parties and student organizations multiplied and tactics became more radical. This led to an overcrowding of the political field, and several organizations began to compete for the same resource base.[5] Political violence between left and right and among leftist movements escalated. Splinter groups were especially prone to violence. Turkey's military coup in 1980 brought the competition to an end and eliminated the Turkish left from the political scene.

Leftist Kurdish politics closely followed the Turkish protest cycle. In the early 1970s, the Revolutionary Cultural Society of the East (DDKO), which originated in the TIP, became the main political platform for voicing Kurdish demands.[6] As an umbrella organization, it established several branches in Kurdish-populated towns and cities. Debates on the backwardness of Kurdish regions, bans on Kurdish language, and revolutionary change were the hot topics of the day. Kurdish politics became more radical, violent, and fragmented after 1975. Ideological differences about varieties of socialism (Soviet, Chinese, and Albanian) became more pronounced, and activists who believed that violence should be used as a political strategy soon got the upper hand. New organizational foundings also reflected the changing fortunes of the Kurdish movement. Between 1976 and 1978 there were twice as many new Kurdish organizations as had been established since 1965. Competitive pressures peaked in 1978 with the birth of eight different Kurdish organizations, the highest number since World War II. The Kurdish political universe had reached its carrying capacity (see figure 1.1).[7]

The PKK emerged in the capital city of Ankara as a student group under the influence of the Turkish revolutionary left (1973–1978). Its core members were university students, mostly from teachers' colleges. Uprooted and idealistic, these individuals were a product of Turkish modernization. They were often talented youngsters who had no social status or economic resources in Kurdish society, and modern education gave them a chance to claim leadership in their community. The revolutionary wave of the 1970s provided the opportunity. Idealistic students were transformed into revolutionaries as they gained access to resources, discovered new ideological frameworks, and borrowed the contentious repertoires of the Turkish revolutionary left. As early recruits, students could easily dedicate

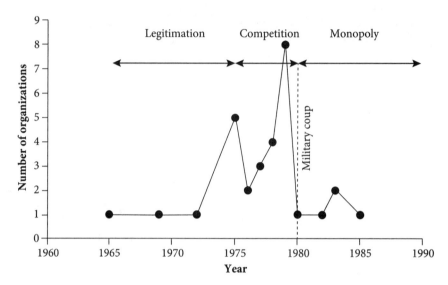

Figure 1.1. Kurdish protest cycle

themselves to a higher cause. Socialism provided the necessary mental map.[8] While its popularity made it a legitimate medium, its secular content and class-based discourse enabled the aspiring revolutionaries to introduce novel ideas into Kurdish politics. Members of the early PKK group also realized the importance of strategy in their struggle. They embraced the political record of the Turkish left, which had successfully challenged the Turkish state through organized violence. This attention to strategy contrasted starkly with previous Kurdish revolts, which had been tribal and spontaneous and had been easily crushed by the central state.

With these lessons in mind, the PKK turned into a political organization in 1978 under competitive pressures. At the time at least nine other political groups were engaging in armed struggle in the name of Kurdistan. As one PKK founder later put it, the group realized that they would either form an organization or disappear from history.[9] This harsh reality defined the short-term goal of the PKK: to survive politically by overcoming the liability of newness problem.[10] For this purpose, the PKK needed to eliminate its rivals and become the only revolutionary group that was pursuing the Kurdish cause. Doing so would attract new members and confer legitimacy on the organization. The PKK's first strategy was a niche shift: The organization abandoned the central political markets, such as Ankara and Istanbul, and attempted to weave itself a political network in Kurdish areas.[11] Its high-ranking members made several trips to southeastern Anatolia, trying to assess the political potential in more developed cities such as Gaziantep, Şanlıurfa, and Kahramanmaraş.[12] Their main objective was to organize the semi-educated urban youth who shared a similar background with that of the party's founders. The PKK's eastern campaign had one major advantage over other organizations that were making similar claims: It had a plain message that was sharp, focused, and authentic.[13] Its members were armed men from the region who wanted to eliminate the rich and powerful in the name of Kurdistan.[14]

Collective action delivered the message. In a few years' time, the PKK earned the reputation of being the most violent and ruthless organization in the region.[15] This strategy lowered barriers to entry, increased the organization's legitimacy, and dampened competition.[16] Unlike other organizations, the PKK did not subject its members to endless debates about socialism or spend its energies on discussing revolutionary publications. The rebel group realized the need for tactical specialization and chose armed struggle to make its point. Its main target was other revolutionary groups, which had already established strong bases in the region. The PKK fought against six different Kurdish-leftist organizations in four different cities.[17] Under competitive pressures, the PKK worked to create its own insurgent niche in Şanlıurfa in 1977–1978. The rebels did so by showcasing their "antifeudal" ideology. They took sides in tribal warfare and tried unsuccessfully to assassinate an influential regional politician, Mehmet Celal Bucak, who came from a powerful landlord family in Siverek, Şanlıurfa.[18] Judging by the number of court cases it faced, the PKK became the largest separatist organization in Turkey in the late 1970s.[19] The rebels' political victory was later sealed when the military coup of 1980 completed what they had set out to do: eliminate rivals and leave the PKK as the only surviving organization that would work for the Kurdish cause.

Building Trust

Once the state had unintentionally eliminated its competitors, the PKK turned within to increase its chances of survival. The first order of business

was winning the trust of its members. For this purpose, the rebel group relied on organizational myths.[20] Rituals of trust-building would ensure unwavering support for the organization. These were especially critical in the
1980–1984 period, when the PKK fled abroad and was not capable of waging violence in Turkey. Selahattin Çelik, a longtime PKK member, rightly
assessed the situation: "In reality, we were finished as an organization after
1980. We had no strength in Europe; in Turkey, we were in prison."[21]
What saved the day for the PKK was the suicide of three senior PKK cap-
tives in the Diyarbakır prison in 1982.[22] Calling it the "Diyarbakır prison
struggle," the rebel organization used this incident to secure its members'
commitment to the cause. A discursive strategy facilitated such commitment. Instead of blaming the inhumane conditions inside the Diyarbakır
prison, the PKK presented the incident as a heroic act that confirmed the
correctness of the party line.

If political martyrdom was an effective strategy for keeping the group
together in its early years, group cohesion provided the organization with
new blood in the longer run. Training camps in particular created closed
societies that separated members from the outside world and helped them
become fully invested in the organization's routines. Members, most of
whom were young adults, were not allowed to see their families and were
expected to give their complete allegiance to the rebel organization. Their
social ties were replaced with carefully planned routines and centrally
administered social interactions. As Doğu Ergil observed, "Group pressure in such an organization was second to none."[23] Members became fully
dependent on the PKK for all aspects of life and increasingly identified
themselves with the group. The rebel organization gave them new (code)
names, articulated a nationalistic message that was previously unknown to
them, and fostered a common identity at the expense of individuals' past
histories.[24] In this respect, the PKK successfully acquired the trust of its
members by creating a closed network with rigid boundaries.[25]

The PKK also obtained the faith of its members in the organization
by building a leadership cult. At a time when the PKK's political future
looked bleak, strong leadership solidified the party line. Although Abdullah Öcalan was a charismatic leader, he did not always enjoy absolute
authority in the organization. In the early days, the rebel group was insignificant in the revolutionary universe of Ankara. In addition, Öcalan
had no proven political track record and was known to be a fiery and

uncompromising personality. Toward the end of the 1970s, Öcalan began to emerge as the theoretican and leader of the newly founded PKK, which gathered together a small group of university students with provincial backgrounds. Even at that point, his authority was far from unchecked: He could neither dictate the party line nor remove other party organizers from power. After the military coup, however, things changed. Organizational myths and training camps turned Öcalan into the supreme leader of the PKK and kept the group united around his choices.

The leadership cult was created in several ways. First came the organizational ideology that viewed domestic opposition as the ultimate threat to the party. Öcalan eliminated political dissidents as "traitors" who questioned his unchecked powers, authoritarian style, and ruthless guerrilla tactics. At the Second Party Congress (1982), the head of PKK operations in Europe was assassinated for demanding a party line that would grant more resources and organizational autonomy to the European propaganda effort.[26] Mehmet Cahit Şener, another high-ranking member who had served time in prison, had to flee the party after the Fourth Party Congress (1990), where he had requested an investigation of civilian and political killings and asked for a central committee with genuine powers. As he later noted, Öcalan knew well that the real debate was about the PKK's future and his own practices.[27]

Second, the rebel leader created a trust deficit among party members. He turned the "criticism–self-criticism mechanism" into a political weapon for downgrading party members with high reputations and preventing alliances from being formed against him. Group approval gave the impression that political persecutions were not the leader's individual decisions but reflected a consensus. No fewer than sixty-one members, including military commanders who organized PKK's initial attacks, were detained or executed in the 1980s. An additional fifty militants escaped this fate by taking refuge with Massoud Barzani's Kurdistan Democratic Party (KDP) in northern Iraq.[28] Third, Öcalan controlled access to power and authority in the organization. His unchecked power enabled him to make and break political careers, turning yesterday's hero into today's traitor. For example, Şahin Baliç, the coordinator of the strategic Mahsun Korkmaz Academy, and Halil Kaya, an influential military commander were killed for carrying out internal executions and forced recruitment campaigns despite the fact that both of them had been acting under Öcalan's orders.[29]

Finally, the rebel leader developed an organizational language that separated him from the PKK.[30] He objectified his position by calling himself the "Leadership," blamed militants for military failures, and threatened to leave if the organization could not meet his standards. As one influential military commander, Selim Çürükkaya, rightly put it, Öcalan was what the ordinary members of the organization could not be.[31] The rebel leader idealized his life experience as a model for insurgents, presented the PKK as their savior, and assigned unrealistic tasks to the militants. In this view, the qualities of the rebel leader appeared as supreme from day one, and insurgents were depicted as lost souls without a cause who could not satisfy their leader regardless of how hard they tried. Öcalan was the sole driving force behind the PKK, the insurgents, and Kurdish society. He invented a new identity for insurgents, established the PKK to change the Kurds' misfortune, and built a Kurdish nation despite many obstacles. As such, he was the embodiment of Kurdistan and an unattainable role model for all Kurds.

The PKK survived the early years by building trust among its members.[32] It did so, ironically, by eliminating domestic and external competitors. The PKK made defection costly and associated party commitment with loyalty to the party leader. The main beneficiary and architect of this model was Öcalan himself, who succeeded in this enterprise by transforming rebels into a closed group of high trusters. In-group and out-group distinctions were strictly imposed, and power asymmetries between the rank and file and the leader became unbridgeable over time. However, cohesion was not sufficient to transform the PKK into a full-fledged guerrilla movement with mass support. To reach critical mass, the insurgency had to walk the intricate path of expansion.

Extracting Resources

The organizational expansion of the PKK rested on the idea of extracting resources from the Kurdish community. The main strategy was the recruitment drive. Although the rebel organization predicted a long war from its inception, it barely survived in the mountains in its early days. The rebels were too few to sustain the conflict even though they had undergone years of military training. This was the plain reality from 1984 to

1987, when a successful year of insurgency was followed by major military losses. The PKK concluded that it would cease to exist as an organization unless it significantly expanded its mountain units. To remedy the problem, the Third Party Congress (1986) made it mandatory for Kurdish families to give their sons to the organization.[33] Forced conscription provided the PKK with new members, increasing the number of insurgents to 1,500 by 1989.[34] Forced recruits had shared characteristics—most of them were under eighteen years old, had been abducted in village raids, and came from border villages close to Iraq and Iran.

Under heavy state pressure and increased rebel activity, the number of volunteers picked up significantly in the early 1990s. In Diyarbakır alone, more than thirty recruits were joining the rebel ranks each day.[35] New guerrillas were from a different cohort than the founders. Most of them were youth from towns and villages in Kurdish areas and university students from large cities. Others who joined the struggle were Syrian Kurds from villages scattered along the Turkish border or members of the Kurdish diaspora in Europe. Each group earned a different place in the organizational hierarchy. Like the teenagers of Caqueta who fought for the Revolutionary Armed Forces of Colombia (FARC), youth from the Kurdish region formed the backbone of the guerrilla army.[36] Most often, their social background was similar to that of forced recruits, and despite their bravery, they survived on the battlefield only for a few years. University graduates with exceptional credentials and a strong commitment to revolutionary ideals were assigned to military commander positions. Diasporic Kurds were scarce in the rebel ranks and left the mountains when romanticized notions of military struggle were replaced by the hard facts of guerrilla life. Finally, Syrian Kurds solved the loyalty problem for the rebel leader. As a small group operating among Turkish Kurds, the Syrians were trusted by Öcalan. He employed them as personal bodyguards and entrusted them with key military positions.

The network effect successfully transformed the PKK into a mass guerrilla force. The preexisting social ties of PKK members were instrumental for passing information, building trust, and winning allies since the organization recruited heavily from a limited segment of the community.[37] Friendship played a critical role in attracting university students to the organization, and kinship helped villagers choose sides in the conflict. In addition, large Kurdish households proved to be the perfect venue for recruiting new members. Circumstantial evidence suggests that the PKK had no difficulty in enrolling people who were biologically related to or had social ties with PKK members.[38] The recruitment drive was most successful in the war-torn Botan region, indicating the importance of spatial proximity in Kurdish mobilization.[39]

If social ties made mobilization possible, changing cultural frames provided the incentive. As civilian unrest engulfed border towns from 1989 to 1993, new recruits joined the struggle to protect Kurdish honor. Mass arrests and deadly crackdowns on protestors facilitated such mental transformation and turned the tide in favor of the insurgency. Group-specific motivations were also important.[40] Educated groups were convinced that the historical moment for Kurdish independence was finally here, young women from rural areas imagined the PKK as a way to escape the Kurdish gender hierarchy, and local youth wanted to resolve generational conflicts and change traditional power relations with the help of the rebel organization.

Recruiting new members was not the PKK's only intention. It also needed to extract economic resources from the Kurdish community to finance its military operations. Relying on its organizational strength in Europe, the PKK collected millions of dollars from the diaspora. Part of this money was donated voluntarily in fund-raising drives that attracted thousands to festivals, mass demonstrations, and other activities. In addition, as the PKK's presence grew inside Turkey, criminal activities emerged as a significant source of financing for the rebels. Road-building contractors especially became vulnerable to coercion and blackmail. Taking advantage of its presence on both sides of the border, the PKK also controlled smuggling between Turkey and northern Iraq, collecting "customs dues" from smugglers. Finally, contraband financing was an attractive source of revenue as the PKK became increasingly drawn to the drug trade between Turkey and Europe.[41]

Simultaneously, the PKK invented new ways to boost its legitimacy. It initiated a serious public relations campaign in Europe to promote its political cause. Following the Ottoman-Turkish tradition, its main strategy rested on negative campaigning against the Turkish state. The rebel group organized street demonstrations and attacked Turkish businesses and consulate buildings to protest human rights violations in Turkey.[42] This high-profile response familiarized European publics with the Kurdish issue. Leftist parties and certain nongovernmental organizations were especially drawn to the Kurdish cause. PKK mobilizations also built trust in the diasporic Kurdish community, securing material support to the organization. While the rebel group mainly relied on rallying public support in Europe, its strategy in Kurdish areas was coercive. At the peak of guerrilla fighting and civilian unrest, the PKK penetrated into border towns. In places such as İdil, Cizre, and Nusaybin, the rebels established local courts and enforced a moral code.[43] Pornography and drinking were banned in order to save the energies of the locals for the struggle. Still, like the GAM in Indonesia, the PKK was unmoved by the demographic dislocation and economic distress that engulfed Kurdish areas.

Front organizations were instrumental in mobilizing resources for the rebel cause. In 1985, the PKK set up the National Liberation Front of Kurdistan (ERNK) to operate in urban settings and establish a political network in Europe.[44] The ERNK played a supportive role in the armed struggle by coordinating logistics, finding new recruits, and raising funds. Ideological and material support, recruitment and demonstrations, intelligence gathering and political assassinations all fell under the ERNK's jurisdiction. At the height of its success, it had branches in several European countries, with Germany having a pivotal position.[45] The ERNK also exerted considerable influence in the urban areas of Turkey, where its main mission in the early 1990s was to give political direction to civilian unrest.

The ERNK created a new niche, a novel resource base for the organization. It grew into a mass movement in urban locations and mobilized the Kurdish diaspora for political purposes. The source of its success was organizational branching, This enabled the PKK to reach out to different political audiences with relative ease. The rebel organization used the same approach to connect with social groups that it considered to be vital to its military performance, although this initiative is less well known. It set up the Youth Council of Kurdistan (YCK) to target university students, and built a vibrant women's organization, both of which were innovative rebel strategies for bolstering guerrilla units.[46]

At its peak, the PKK became a powerful organization with ample resources and a legitimate cause. It had money and personnel, and no rivals. Its efficiency in borrowing resources from the public and spreading the word created trust within the Kurdish community and brought legitimacy in the European sphere. Yet such efficiency came with a price. Before long, the PKK had to face the unintended consequences of its dramatic expansion.

The Weberian Experiment Failed

With 10,000 fighters in the mountains and a close-knit political community in urban areas, the PKK had a historic opportunity in the early 1990s. The rebel organization could now evolve into a regular army and form a political front in the cities.[47] Regular warfare and mass revolt would lead to the creation of an independent Kurdistan. The earlier strategies of trust building and resource extraction were not suitable for this task. While the former was most effective with small groups, the latter did not necessarily provide guidelines about how to use newly acquired resources efficiently. Meanwhile, new challenges arose with expansion. The growing size of guerrilla units made troop movement and logistics cumbersome.[48] The ERNK was also having major difficulty with transforming civilian unrest into an organized revolt against the state. It soon became clear that the deeper issue facing the PKK was managing the rebellion.

The most urgent problem was the absence of a managerial class. The PKK had concluded as early as 1990 that it lacked a group of people with leadership skills to run the organization on a daily basis. A managerial class was particularly needed in the military sphere. Öcalan had a different view. At the Fifth Party Congress (1995), he argued that military commanders were major obstacles to organizational and tactical unity. He blamed them for military failures and promised the congress to set up a mechanism to train a new generation of military cadres.[49] The rebel leader insisted that commanders run their regions like small fiefdoms, in keeping with the feudal nature of Kurdish areas. However, it was the leadership cult that prevented a middle stratum from developing and moving up in the organization. Öcalan periodically eliminated party members who had achieved high levels of prestige. He also created an informal setting that firmly tied the careers of insurgents to his personal choices. Accordingly, meritocracy and formal channels of mobility did not play a major role in the workings of the rebel organization.

Another challenge for the PKK was the waning capacity of insurgents to accomplish new tasks. Öcalan warned rebel soldiers that the next phase of the rebellion was not simply about armed struggle. The insurgent had to arm himself with the right ideology in order to become a true party member and convince others to join the party's cause. Mostly of village origins, new recruits had a less sophisticated understanding of insurgency. Primitive rebels approached the problem from their own anthropological universe. They were willing to fight long and hard, but their commitment yielded few political results. Öcalan called this attitude "villager's revenge," which fell squarely into traditions of honor and tribe.[50] Similarly, new recruits tried to preserve their social loyalties inside the organization. Tribe, kinship, and regionalism became signposts about militants' attitude toward party tasks.[51] The rebel leader later lamented the fact that he had flooded the organization with too many people in the early 1990s.[52] Despite the challenges the new recruits posed for the organization, he promised to transform "armed Don Quixotes" into professionals through job training.[53] He was a strong believer in the transformation of individual's consciousness, and his biggest weapons were education and ideological indoctrination.[54] However, PKK training camps could not deliver the expected results this time. At the peak of the war, the number of rebel trainees was too large and the window of opportunity too short for the PKK to seal its military success with political transformation.

With the elimination of the middle stratum and in the face of mounting military losses, the would-be managerial class turned to a decentralist alternative. This created a typical principal-agent problem for the PKK. Military commanders ignored the requirement to report to rebel headquarters and developed distinct party cultures in their provinces. The Botan region was notorious in this regard.[55] The center for resistance, though, was Tunceli (Dersim).[56] A hotbed of insurgency, the Dersim region is populated by Zazas, a religiously and linguisticly distinct group within the Kurdish community. Şemdin Sakık, a Zaza who had fought in the mountains for more than a decade, posed the most serious threat to the PKK's leadership in the second half of the 1990s. He was not necessarily interested in democratizing the PKK, but he found out the hard way that there was no place for a second man in the organization. Öcalan could not easily crush him either. Instead, he stripped him of his authority and made him "confess" his mistakes. Sakık later escaped and became a whistle-blower in the hands of the state. His story, although exceptional, reflected the political vision of several military commanders.[57]

Faced with "feudal fiefdoms," Öcalan decided to step up his attempts at centralization. His goal was to gain access to information at the local level and limit the autonomy of commanders. He made it mandatory for teams and committee members to report to him personally at short intervals. Öcalan also tried to control military commanders by dividing their authority. While guerrilla teams were supervised by military commanders and political agents, a new position, that of zone commander, was created in the late 1990s to enforce the tactical priorities of the center. The most radical move came at the Fifth Party Congress (1995) at a time when the PKK faced an uphill battle against the Turkish military. The rebel leader made the cult of leadership official. The congress changed the PKK's party program and bylaws for the first time, transforming Öcalan's rule into a one-man regime. He was no longer the general secretary of the politburo; he was now the chairman of the party. Öcalan also set up new administrative branches to consolidate his power. The newly established Chairman's Council replaced the executive branch of the party (the Central Committee), and the Disciplinary Committee served as a perfect instrument for instantly eliminating political dissidents within the party.[58]

In addition to centralization measures, the PKK also established new units in an attempt to reverse its military failures. The special units idea was an emergency response that was designed to save the organization when routine action did not bring the intended outcomes. The PKK introduced suicide bombing in that spirit in 1996. The rebel leader praised the first suicide bomber and presented her as a great tactician with a strong commitment to the party.[59] The majority of suicide bombers were women in their twenties who aimed at security targets in major cities. Later, the rebel organization introduced another special unit. This was the Freedom Falcons of Kurdistan (TAK), a bombing squad that was formed to perpetrate indiscriminate violence against civilians in large cities. The TAK targeted shopping malls, town squares, and crowded areas, especially in Istanbul. In July 2008, this special unit planted two consecutive bombs that killed seventeen and injured hundreds in a single incident in Güngören, a neigborhood of Istanbul populated by recent migrants.[60] Meanwhile, the PKK tried the strategy of cooperation with other rebel groups without much success. The Revolutionary Party of Turkey (TDP), a PKK-trained insurgent group, failed to spread the conflict toward the Black Sea region, and a wave of political assassinations by the Revolutionary People's Party-Front (DHKP-C) in large cities proved to be unsuccessful.[61]

Ironically, organizational expansion brought about the PKK's demise on the military front in the 1994–1999 period. The PKK's earlier structure, which had been based on members' loyalty, was not sufficient for political success. In the quest for an independent Kurdistan, the rebel organization was unable to transform itself into a fully functioning bureaucratic body. No regular army materialized. Instead, a veiled decentralization set in indefinitely. In response, Öcalan formalized a leadership cult, consolidating the very mechanism that made bureaucratic transformation impossible for the organization. Special units were not enough to address the PKK's declining military fortunes, either. As had happened for Shining Path in the aftermath of Abimael Guzman's arrest, Abdullah Öcalan's capture was the last nail in the coffin. The PKK had to find new ways to survive.

Organizational Inertia

Öcalan was captured in Kenya in 1999 after European countries denied him political asylum. The rebel leader had controlled the Kurdish insurgency for many years from Syria but was forced to flee in 1998 because of the increasing diplomatic pressure Turkey brought on the Syrian government. A pragmatic man, Öcalan realized that times had changed. The PKK had lost the military conflict, neighboring countries could no longer tolerate the rebel organization, and European political intervention in favor of the Kurds had not materialized. He decided to steer the PKK in a new direction. His hours-long statement at his trial laid out the main principles of the organizational change he envisioned.[62] Öcalan asked the PKK to leave the country, announce a cease-fire, and, most important, transform itself into a political entity. Öcalan also called for a fundamental shift in the PKK's ideology. The PKK would no longer campaign for political independence or regional autonomy but would insist on securing constitutional rights for the Kurds. He formulated the "Democratic Republic" thesis, which rested on the idea of common land and political unity, yet he also highlighted the need to secure cultural rights for the Kurds. The rebel leader reinforced his new political position from prison. In a political report submitted to the Leadership Council of the PKK in 1999, he blamed Western imperialism for sustaining the Turkish-Kurdish conflict and called for a democratic solution to the Kurdish issue.[63]

Öcalan's road map for organizational change faced several challenges. Reaction was especially strong inside the PKK. Several members said that they had joined the PKK to win independence for the Kurds and threatened to leave the organization. The challenge was more serious on political grounds. Abandoning guerrilla tactics created a fierce debate within the organization from 1999 to 2003. The women's movement, military commanders from the Erzurum-Dersim region, and several political prisoners openly challenged this new vision at the Extraordinary Seventh Party Congress (2000).[64] The ERNK also resisted change: Öcalan's democratic solution promised to undercut its central role in the PKK's propaganda efforts. On the opposite end of the spectrum, Osman Öcalan, a high-ranking member of the PKK and Öcalan's elder brother, applauded the new direction and expressed his support for a political deal with Turkey.[65] The elder Öcalan concluded that the socialist experiment was over and that old-style politics should come to an end. Meanwhile, the majority of PKK members adopted a wait-and-see attitude, unsure what this new era would entail for the organization. Despite major disagreements, all agreed that abandoning the guerrilla struggle altogether and discontinuing the PKK would have tremendous sunk costs.

External factors also constrained the PKK's efforts for change. One such constraint was what Ezra Zuckerman called "illegitimacy costs." The PKK had become a mass organization through armed struggle. More than 30,000 insurgents had been killed in the conflict and thousands of people had been persecuted for being members of the PKK. As Öcalan rightly claimed, the PKK struck its heaviest blow at the Turkish state by creating a martyr within each Kurdish family.[66] This political impact was multiplied in Kurdish society, which was characterized by large households bound by strong kinship ties.[67] The risk of losing external legitimacy was coupled with an equally threatening prospect: the imprisonment of PKK members. Turkish law did not allow the PKK to turn into a legal political party overnight, and the public strongly opposed a general amnesty.[68] In practical terms, any step toward legality would mean political surrender and jail time for the majority of PKK members.

Despite domestic pressures and external constraints, the new PKK was launched by an inner circle that was loyal to the rebel leader. In this process, all sorts of domestic opposition were terminated a la Öcalan style. Yet, it still proved impossible to restructure the organization. The Chairman's Council complained at the Sixth Party Conference that newly established branches, such as Agitation and People's Struggle Centers, were not functioning; the women's movement was not participating in the daily routines of the party; and old cadres lacked the necessary skills for the new structure.[69] The closed-network character of the PKK that had once helped the organization to survive now became a barrier to change. Network externalities were so strong that only a handful of insurgents surrendered to the security forces, even after military defeat and attractive government incentives. According to Öcalan, it proved impossible to transform a follower (*mürid*) into a democrat.[70]

In the midst of uncertainty and failure, the PKK ended the armistice in 2003 and restarted its guerrilla campaign. The PKK had realized that organizations remember by doing. Its military performance from 2005 to 2008 was second only to its record in 1991–1994, the peak of its military activity. Returning to old ways of doing business successfully averted the challenge to the organizational core and silenced dissidents. Viewed from a broader perspective, this decision simply confirmed that the PKK was unable to escape organizational inertia.[71] Internal routines stifled change, yet they saved the organization from ultimate collapse. Meanwhile, Öcalan's proposal managed to bring about change at the periphery of the organization. Unlike tactics and organizational life, where there was strong continuity, the PKK's ideology shifted. Its official stand on the Kurdish issue became one of political compromise, stipulating a solution that would promote a democratized Turkish Republic.

The PKK's ability to systematically wage violence set it apart from other insurgent groups. Despite astonishing military success in the early 1990s, a free Kurdistan remained an unattainable dream. Indeed, the conditions that first facilitated military success were responsible for political failure in the later stages of the insurgency. Good faith and belief in the party's agenda held the organization together in its early years. Heavily recruiting from its community, the PKK became a mass organization by creating a powerful network effect that spread the word. Meanwhile, funding from the diaspora and legitimacy from abroad provided the necessary resources for the PKK to wage a "just war" in the name of an oppressed ethnic minority.

Yet this size advantage soon became a liability. In the political sphere, the PKK was a losing cause as it struggled to transform its military victories into political outcomes. At a time when the PKK needed a managerial class to achieve political goals, Öcalan's centralization efforts led to a dysfunctional bureaucracy. Neither territorial control nor mass revolts materialized. Because of internal struggles, the PKK missed a historic opportunity that few insurgencies would enjoy in their lifecycle. Change came late—after the war was lost—and had a limited scope. It was the discourse of the rebellion that changed from independence to peaceful coexistence with constitutional guarantees. Yet in its efforts to achieve that end, the PKK went back to its old way of doing business: guerrilla struggle. In the next chapter, we turn to rebel discourse and examine the PKK's ideological evolution.

2

IDEOLOGY

As the Iranian Revolution of 1979 demonstrated, cognitive frames are integral parts of social transformation.[1] Ideologies provide specific solutions to political problems and use a symbolic language that facilitates legitimate action.[2] In that respect, an ideology has two components. While its programmatic character offers a road map, its framing quality is essential for attracting and mobilizing potential adherents and constituents.[3] Revolutionary groups have a disappointing record of combining these elements: Radicals have produced elegant programs to foment change but have not situated these ideas in existing cultural frameworks. Their failure to do so has undermined civilian support for the revolutionary cause. This has occurred especially when an exclusive message has limited the opportunities to address multiple cleavages in a society.

The PKK attempted to "create" Kurds and Kurdistan by transforming people and consolidating territory. To achieve this goal, the rebel organization devised an ideology that worked in three steps. It first singled out the victim, then identified the culprit, and finally provided a road map to change the Kurds' fate. Rebels claimed that the Kurds have been victimized by imperialist powers, colonial states, and their local collaborators for centuries. Only the rebels' plan could reverse this misfortune. Still, the PKK's discourse changed over time. The rebel group campaigned for political independence early in the conflict, brought foreign pressure to bear on the Turkish government in the second half of the 1990s, and has become interested in bargaining directly with the Turkish state since 1999.

This chapter surveys the ideological evolution of the PKK. We suggest that the rebel group's ideology failed to promote an inclusive Kurdish political identity. This failure was the outcome of two processes. First, early on, insurgent ideology primarily operated as a political program. As discussed in chapter 1, this was a legacy of the 1970s, when the PKK competed against several rival groups and formulated a bold plan of action with socialist credentials. The revolutionary blueprint ignored intra-community dynamics and left confessional and religious groups out of the rebels' project. Second, the PKK refused to alter its relationship with the Kurdish community over time. Its ideology changed only after the rebels' military fortunes waned and could not mobilize fresh support for the rebel cause. Instead, ideological shifts served to secure certification from international actors. The end result has been the persistence of major divisions in Kurdish society, which in turn has weakened the rebels' nation-building efforts.

A Fight for Independence

The main premise of the PKK's ideology was its insistence on the Kurds' victim status. The Kurds have lived under Arab, Persian, and Turkish control since the tenth century, and foreigners have been invading and partitioning Kurdistan ever since. In 1978, Abdullah Öcalan openly stated in the PKK's manifesto that he was ashamed of the "cadaver status" of Kurdish society.[4] Victimhood was the outcome of internal divisions within Kurdistan.[5] Neither the Kurds nor Kurdistan could transform themselves into organic units. The Kurds had missed the opportunity to become a nation with a state of their own. The economic integration of Kurdistan had also suffered, and national classes had failed to take root in society. Cultural production and linguistic development had surfaced only when outside influence was relatively weak, in the sixteenth century. The end result was a perpetual colonization of the Kurds and Kurdistan. The PKK used two strategies to confirm this claim. First, it conflated identity with territory, associating the Kurds with an imaginary Kurdistan. Second, the PKK believed that an evolutionary path to modernization was denied for the Kurdish people. For the rebels, it was external forces that were responsible for the misfortunes of the Kurds.

One of the central claims of the PKK was that imperialism had systematically undermined Kurdish interests. The British colonial project was instrumental in dividing Kurdistan between Iraq and Turkey after World War I. In 1926, the Treaty of Mosul struck the final blow to the dream of an independent Kurdistan and confirmed political boundaries between the two states. The emerging hegemon, the United States, played a similar role in the region. It cemented an alliance among regional states that led to further colonization of Kurdistan. The Baghdad Pact (1955), which included Turkey, Iran, and Iraq, reflected this vision.[6] Yet the hegemon's plan faced a serious crisis in the 1970s as the United States lost one of the "Twin Pillars" in the Middle East. The Iranian Revolution turned Kurdistan into the weakest link in the imperialist camp. According to Öcalan, it was U.S. intervention that blocked the path to an independent Kurdistan in the 1990s. The United States gave Turkey military assistance during the PKK conflict and allowed a de facto Kurdish state to develop in northern Iraq. The rebel group viewed the latter development as an "imperialist trap" that was designed to stop its state-building efforts.[7]

Calling them colonialists, the PKK viewed Turkey, Iran, Iraq, and Syria as nation-states that suppressed Kurds and their identity. Yet, for practical reasons, the PKK decided to target only Turkey. The rebel soldiers were mostly Turkish citizens, the PKK received considerable support from other countries in the region, and Turkey's Kurdistan was by far the most developed of the various Kurdish areas. Rebel publications examined the evolution of the Turkish colonization project.[8] The Turkish army first occupied Kurdistan in the interwar era to suppress Kurdish rebellions. Successful counterinsurgency campaigns brought the region under state control. The Turkish Republic then improved its systems of tax collection and military conscription. More recently, the state has penetrated the region economically, building mines and dams to exploit its natural resources. The final stage of the Turkish colonization project was education. The PKK viewed state-sponsored education as the greatest threat to Kurdish identity.

According to the PKK, coethnics who collaborated with the Turkish state facilitated the colonization project, like no other. The influential leader of the Kurdish emirates, İdris Bitlisi, cooperated with the Ottoman Empire in Kurdistan (1514–1520), Hamidiye cavalry regiments fought against Armenians for the Ottomans (1890–1908), and village guards, also of Kurdish origins, have defended the Turkish Republic against the PKK since the 1980s. As such, colonizers have created a "feudal agent," whose interests and values are firmly attached to the colonialist power.[9] This comprador class consisted of large landlords, tribal leaders, and religious figures. They controlled economic resources, political representation, and ideological authority in Kurdistan. In doing so, they blocked economic development in the region and politically integrated it into the Turkish state. There was also a sociological element that kept local collaborators at the top of Kurdish hierarchy. This was the divided character of Kurdistan, which pitted tribe against tribe and region against region. The PKK considered divisions among coethnics to be a foreign (Turkish) product and targeted local actors who took advantage of such divisions.

Having identified the problem, the PKK's ideology involved a program of action to change Kurdistan's future. First, it was necessary to falsify competing proposals.[10] One such vision was the tribal resistance that had historically characterized Kurdish rebellions. The PKK suggested that the actors, methods, and goals of previous Kurdish revolts were not sufficient for a modern independence movement. These revolts, led by tribal and religious leaders, had a local perspective and promoted autonomy against a centralizing state. In the Şeyh Said (1925) and Dersim (1938) rebellions, the Turkish state quickly destroyed armed groups with the help of other tribes. The banditry that later characterized Kurdish dissent was not a political solution either. Accordingly, the Kurds failed to sustain a long-term insurgency with nationalist credentials until the PKK's emergence. To illustrate his point further, Öcalan compared the PKK's success in Botan (see chapter 3) with the brief resistance of Bedirhan Bey (1843–1848), who was often hailed as the modern hero of Kurdish resistance.[11]

The PKK also critiqued a different type of tribal resistance. The rebel organization claimed that Barzani-style opposition in northern Iraq would not lead Kurdistan to independence. Öcalan highlighted several negative features of what he called "limited nationalism" (*dar milliyetçilik*).[12] According to this view, Kurdish leaders in northern Iraq had never been interested in independence. They bargained for autonomy, first with Saddam Hussein's regime in 1974 and then with the United States in the aftermath of the Second Gulf War. Lacking a genuine political ideology, Kurdish leaders switched back and forth between popular ideas. The kind of socialism adopted by Massoud Barzani and Jalal Talabani failed to promise a program of change toward a classless society. For instance, Barzani created a fighting force (the Peshmerga) based on kinship, regionalism, and tribe. Öcalan suggested that without military and political training, the Peshmerga could not fight successfully against regular armies or politicize the Kurds for independence. Finally, the political survival of the Kurdish leaders rested solely on their alliance with imperialism. The PKK concluded that Iraqi Kurdish leaders were clients of Western powers and were promoting U.S. interests in the region.[13] Öcalan had ample evidence to support his claims. A U.S.-led military mission (Provide Comfort) protected Barzani and Talabani against Saddam Hussein's rage, and a federate Kurdish state was established in northern Iraq in 1992 with the approval of the United States.

The PKK also rejected the strategy of bargaining with the Turkish state. Early in its history, the rebel organization criticized political groups that pursued Kurdish rights without waging violence. Heavily invested in the socialist rhetoric of its time, the PKK called this passive stance the "propagandist character of the petty bourgeoisie." The PKK directed its primary criticisms at the TKSP, a leftist Kurdish organization that had a mass following in the second half of the 1970s.[14] The rebel leader also argued that neither economic improvements in the region nor political campaigning in Europe could address Kurdish demands. As the conflict escalated in the early 1990s, the PKK also rejected "political solutions" to the Kurdish issue. Öcalan viewed these as insincere attempts by the imperialist powers to shortchange the PKK after its military success.[15] In the same fashion, the PKK rejected calls for cultural rights or regional autonomy.

Having nullified competing proposals for change, the PKK strongly believed that the solution lay in political independence. Yet Kurdistan's independence was not simply a political matter. First and foremost, it was a sociological issue that involved a group-making project. The making of a Kurdish nation required eliminating foreign influences in the region by force. The PKK promised to sever the Kurds' political ties with imperialism, destroy colonial structures, and eliminate local collaborators. Such steps would foster a Kurdish identity and unify Kurdistan. In fact, this thinking became the blueprint for the PKK's military strategy for years to come.

The insurgents' political program failed to convince all Kurds. Like the Evangelicals who resisted the Shining Path in Peru, coethnics with Islamic loyalties were suspicious about the PKK's intentions. The rebel group promised to change social hierarchies in Kurdish society, viewed religion as superstition, and frequently employed women as fighters.[16] This rift, which fragmented Kurdish opposition, had historical precedents. Earlier Kurdish revolts were Islamic in nature and campaigned for autonomy rather than independence.[17] The two trajectories of dissent also had distinct geographical bases. Accordingly, the PKK ran into trouble in the north of Diyarbakır province, a Sunni stronghold that was the site of the largest Kurdish revolt (Şeyh Said Rebellion) in early Republican history.

In other parts of eastern Anatolia, the ethnic project also failed to win enough allies. In these areas, communal identity had evolved along confessional lines, forcing Alevite Kurds to identify themselves as Alevites rather than as Kurds.[18] The presence of a Zaza-Kirmanc identity in Tunceli further complicated community transformation in this important site of resistance. Paul White tells the story of Seyfi Cengiz, a guerrilla leader in the region who tried to convince villagers that they were Kurds. He was repeatedly told "We are Kirmanc. You are saying we are Kurdish. We are not Kurdish."[19] The 2012 kidnapping of Hüseyin Aygün, a member of the Turkish Grand National Assembly (TBMM) who was vocal about Zaza identity, further illustrates the tensions between the ethnic project and confessional groups.[20] In addition, Kurds who lived outside the OHAL region found the PKK's independence rhetoric unappealing. They were firmly connected to national structures, had a higher standard of living than their coethnics in the region, and did not face outright discrimination, especially in large cities.[21]

In sum, the PKK's ideology, which insisted on a nominal definition of Kurdish identity, became a major obstacle to rebel success. Its secular approach and involuntary nationalist discourse failed to win the loyalties of many in the Kurdish community.[22] Nonetheless, insurgent ideology changed over time. As its military power waned, the PKK shifted its political objective from pursuing independence to inviting foreign pressure. Inviting pressure from abroad was viewed as the right strategy to win the political struggle without having to adjust to multiple Kurdish realities. Kurdistan could be created and a Kurdish political identity could be forged with a little help from friends.

Inviting Pressure from Abroad

The early 1990s were the heyday of the PKK. The rebel organization was capable of staging multiple attacks on any given day and was preparing to set up a provisional government along the Turkish-Iraqi border. Around the same time, civilian unrest engulfed the Kurdish urban centers, raising hopes for political independence. In a matter of two years, it became clear that none of this would happen. Counterinsurgency picked up after 1993, forcing the PKK to stay on the defensive. Insurgent casualties rose rapidly, as the PKK announced several cease-fires in an attempt to halt counterinsurgency operations.[23] More important, though, the rebel organization decided to change its political ideology. Federation or regional autonomy became viable alternatives to independence. Confronted with military decline, Öcalan saw internationalization of the Kurdish question as a way to bring his demands to the bargaining table.[24] He increasingly relied on Europe to certify his claims and pressure Turkey for a favorable settlement. In Öcalan's view, Turkey would not be able to withstand pressure from the European Union, Russia, and the United States.

In inviting foreign pressure, the PKK's main strategy involved mobilizing European publics.[25] Acting with a moral imperative, foreign activists from European NGOs and intergovernmental organizations shared a deep concern about the growing violence in Turkey. Several high-profile international conferences were held that promoted the Kurds' right to self-determination.[26] As interest grew in the West, journalists, politicians, and diplomats began to pour into Turkey's Kurdish regions. One such group was the Helsinki Citizens' Assembly. After visiting the region in February 1992, the group demanded an armistice to stop the violence.[27] The following year, a group of European parliamentarians observed Nevrouz Day in Diyarbakır. Speaking for the visitors, Pieter Muller called for a political dialogue between Turkey and the PKK.[28] While the visit seemed symbolic, it had a far-reaching impact in Europe. The activists influenced Western policy and raised public awareness about the Kurdish question.[29]

Next, using its ideological credentials, the rebel organization established political connections with green, leftist, and communist parties in Europe. Members of the Italian, Greek, and German communist parties were eager to develop personal ties with the PKK.[30] Playing a major role in German politics, the Green Party also appeared on the front lines of promoting Kurdish rights. After bloody confrontations took place between the Turkish army and PKK sympathizers on Nevrouz Day in 1992, the Belgian Senate joined others in advocating Kurds' historic rights.[31] French socialists also showed an active interest in the Kurdish problem. Several prominent members of the Socialist Party defended the legality of the pro-Kurdish Democracy Party (DEP) in Turkey and abroad.[32] In a public letter, Mme. Mitterrand, the wife of the former French president, even accused Turkey of committing genocide against the Kurds.[33] The United States would also be dragged into the debate. A former member of the DEP briefed the U.S. Congress in 1994, arguing that Turkey's Kurds needed immediate international protection.[34] Stepping up its diplomatic efforts in 1995–1996, the PKK openly asked President Clinton and German Chancellor Kohl to intervene on behalf of the Kurds and find a diplomatic solution for the problem.[35]

The PKK seemed to have accomplished its goal by the second half of the 1990s. Turkey was penalized for its poor record with the Kurds and faced severe pressure in the international arena.[36] Germany decided to stop arms sales to Turkey in the period when the Turkish army was staging massive counterinsurgency operations. The United States, a longtime ally of Turkey, cut military aid and made future funds conditional on improvements in Turkey's human rights record. Turkey's relations with the European Union also suffered. The Customs Union agreement between Turkey and the European Union was suspended for a year. Turkey became the major country to blame in the European Parliament, and its Turkish members became increasingly isolated in international bodies. In 1994, the European Parliament formally asked Turkey to grant autonomy to the Kurds.[37] Similarly, a joint German-Italian proposal formulated in the wake of Öcalan's escape to Europe promised to resolve the Kurdish issue in an international conference.[38] These international developments created tremendous pressure for Turkey at a time when its economy was in shambles because of war spending, its military relied heavily on U.S. equipment, and its politics were attached to the European Union in important ways.

Equally instrumental in inviting foreign pressure was the idea of a Kurdish parliament-in-exile. After the Turkish Constitutional Court banned the DEP, a number of Kurdish parliamentarians fled to Europe. The PKK decided to use this opportunity to set up a Kurdish parliament in Europe. The rebel organization funded the initiative, supplied the majority of its members, and established political connections across Europe. The parliament met in several European cities from April 1995 to December 1996 but failed to produce concrete results. As Aliza Marcus put it, it was a "publicity stunt."[39] Nonetheless, the Kurdish parliament-in-exile served important purposes. First, it drew attention to the poor human rights record of Turkey and showed that the Kurds were barred from political representation. Second, it allowed the PKK to present itself as a legitimate body representing Turkey's Kurds. Third, the nonviolent character of the parliament, the PKK believed, would make the organization more acceptable to European publics. Finally, the Kurdish parliament-in-exile further contributed to the trust deficit between Europe and Turkey.

Toward the end of the 1990s, the PKK carved out another layer of international support, the "Orthodox camp." As a last resort, the rebel organization contacted Turkey's Orthodox neighbors, who had had rival claims in the past or had conflicting geopolitical interests in the present. Greece was at the top of the PKK's list. The Greek government allowed the ERNK to operate legally in the country and provided a safe haven for fleeing insurgents. PKK sympathizers were also given the opportunity to organize several fund-raising events in Athens.[40] The peak of Greek-PKK relations perhaps occured when several members of the Greek Parliament paid a personal visit to Öcalan in Lebanon in 1995. The meeting was planned for the purpose of developing a joint strategy against Turkey. Waving both PKK and Greek flags, Öcalan promised to defend the Greek position in its several conflicts with Turkey in return for Greece's support for PKK claims in Europe.[41] At the same time, the PKK strengthened its presence in Russia. It hosted an important conference in the Russian Duma in 1996 with the participation of the Russian nationalist and communist parties. The conference invited Turkey to find a peaceful solution to the Kurdish issue by granting autonomy to the Kurds. A few years later, the Duma reiterated its position on the issue by stating that the Kurds should

be given political status. The rebel organization reciprocated by supporting the Russian position on international energy conflicts. The PKK made
it clear that it would delay the construction of the Baku-Tbilisi-Ceyhan
pipeline, a politically sanctioned international investment to divert the
East-West energy corridor from Russian territory to the South Caucasus
and into Turkey.[42]

In less than a decade, however, the PKK found out that European certification had its limits. Throughout the 1990s, the rebels had tried to tap
international support for their cause. Yet the Europeans tended to back
down when the rebels threatened domestic order in their countries. The
PKK learned these lessons the hard way. After the rebel group announced
total war against the Turkish state in June 1993, the ERNK stormed Turkish consulates and businesses across Europe. Waves of violence by the PKK
convinced Germany to ban all PKK activity and thirty-five PKK-affiliated
organizations in November 1993.[43] France joined Germany in the same year
and announced that it now considered the PKK to be an illegal organization. Öcalan's capture in Kenya also illustrated the limits of European support. When the rebel leader fled Syria in 1998, enthusiastic majorities in the
Greek and Russian parliaments invited him to their countries. Öcalan was
shuttled back and forth between these countries, yet neither government
would grant him political asylum. After a brief time in Italy, he was once
again forced to leave. He was finally captured in Kenya immediately after
leaving the Greek embassy. After that, Öcalan was in Turkish custody.[44]

International attention allowed the PKK to shift its political ideology.
It abandoned the goal of an independent Kurdistan and instead looked
for ways to negotiate with the Turkish state. Imperialist powers were removed from the list of eternal foes, and local collaborators seemed risky
targets in this political environment. As the PKK became desperate on
the military front, pressure from abroad evolved in three distinct ways. It
started as a moral initiative, was later translated into a policy platform, and
finally became mixed with geopolitical interests. Throughout the 1990s,
the PKK tested the limits of European support. By 1999, it was clear that
the PKK's efforts in Europe had successfully internationalized the Kurdish question but had failed the rebel group as an organization. European
certification was no substitute for military success at home. Without any
prospect for military victory and having used up its opportunities in the
European arena, the PKK changed its ideological position once more. Left

to fend for itself, the PKK's next political move was bargaining directly with the Turkish state and convincing its formidable foe to grant concessions to the Kurds.

Bargaining with the State

The future of Kurdish insurgency seemed bleak at the turn of the twenty-first century. The rebel leader was in prison for life, and neither guerrilla struggle nor European pressure had created the intended political outcomes. As a solution, Öcalan prepared a new road map for the rebel organization, which, in practice, meant the overhaul of its ideology.[45] For the second time, the PKK revised its ideological position on the victim status of the Kurds and offered a new agenda for improving the Kurds' position in Turkish society. The rebel organization redefined its principal foes, devised new strategies, and presented more realistic goals for attaining Kurdish rights. This vision required a rethinking of the most fundamental arguments that had been in place since 1978.

The starting point for the PKK's ideological renewal program was a reinterpretation of the Kurds' history. The rebel group abandoned its age-old discourse about colonialism, which had been a key feature of its ideology. The Turkish state is no longer regarded as a foreign aggressor that occupied Kurdistan and colonized the Kurds. In this new version of history, the Kurds are elevated to the status of a founder nation. They are presented as equal partners with the Turks in founding the Republic. To celebrate the brotherhood between the two communities, the PKK emphasized social ties: The Kurds and the Turks had followed the same faith, intermarried, and shared similar customs for centuries. With its emphasis on unity, the PKK now explained the Kurds' victim status as a result of a specific historical pattern. Victimhood was the direct outcome of the rebellion-coercion cycle. The Kurds have been rebelling since the nineteenth century and Ottoman/Turkish armies have been suppressing them. Öcalan presented the PKK insurgency as the final rebellion in Kurdish history and claimed that it offered a historic opportunity to break this vicious cycle.[46]

The PKK still needed to identify the "evil forces" that victimized the Kurds. In the past, the PKK had viewed the Turkish colonial state through the lenses of oriental despotism and the Asiatic mode of production.[47] Both forces created a coercive state tradition that relied on military leadership, excessive centralization, and rent collection. Using careful language, the rebel organization now refrained from overt criticism of the Turkish state. The analytical solution that Öcalan found was to present the Turkish ruling class as a divided group. The rebel leader blamed the authoritarian wing of the Turkish political elite for suppressing Kurdish rebellions in the interwar era. Similarly, he highlighted the role of an oligarchy that consisted of ultranationalists and war profiteers who benefited from the Kurdish conflict in the 1990s. He contrasted this attitude with the fresh thinking of former president Turgut Özal. Özal's suspicious death in 1993 convinced Öcalan that internal political struggles were taking place within the Turkish political elite.[48]

The PKK returned to its anti-imperialist stand after 1999. This new reading of imperialism differed from its past version. The rebels now accused foreign powers of having a vested interest in sustaining the Turkish-Kurdish conflict. The United States, they argued, especially benefited from the situation because the end of the conflict would jeopardize the U.S.-built Turkish-Israeli alliance, threaten the Kurdish state in northern Iraq, and reduce Turkey's dependence on the United States. Öcalan's capture, too, was an international conspiracy organized by the United States, Britain, and Israel. To counter foreign influence on Turkish-Kurdish relations, the PKK promised to work with Turkey in northern Iraq and beyond.[49] The rebels also removed local collaborators from their list of enemies. Violence against civilians would damage the new image of the PKK in domestic and international arenas. More urgently, the cycle of relentless violence had politicized Kurdish areas and rendered this move unnecessary. A distinct Kurdish identity had already developed in the 1990s.[50]

Eager to negotiate with the Turkish state, the rebel organization ruled out several political scenarios that it had considered in the past. The PKK argued that independence was no longer a feasible plan. An independent Kurdistan would not be economically viable and would cut off Kurdish access to developed regions of Turkey. Demands for regional autonomy were also taken off the table. Millions of Kurds lived in the western parts of Turkey, Istanbul being the main site of attraction. Hence, dividing Turkey would not necessarily address the Kurds' grievances. The minority framework was similarly rejected.[51] This line of thought had been the favorite policy prescription of Western observers; it involved recognizing the Kurds as a minority and granting them group-specific rights. With a better sense of intercommunal relations in the region, the PKK did not subscribe to this vision. The rebels feared that if the Kurds were given minority status, they would be treated as second-class citizens, which in turn would create unforeseen challenges.

During the time when the PKK's future was most uncertain (1999–2003), the founding nation discourse allowed the organization to make a case for constitutional rights for the Kurds.[52] The rebel organization believed that three requests in particular would lead to the recognition of the Kurds as a distinct group without treating them as a minority. The first one was freedom of expression. The PKK argued that the state should facilitate and protect the Kurds' right to publish and broadcast in Kurdish. The second demand was native language education. The rebel group suggested that legal obstacles to education in Kurdish be revoked. Finally, the PKK demanded that Kurdish political actors of all stripes should have the freedom to voice their opinions. The first and third requests did not carry much political weight. While the Turkish public strongly opposed any move toward legalizing the PKK, adoption of the Kurdish language in the public sphere had already become a nonissue. With the exception of broadcasting, the language ban on Kurdish was lifted before 2002.[53]

The PKK was on target with its second demand, though. Education in the Kurdish language found some resonance in the society and was easily translated into a political issue. Its success, however, followed a strange path. When the central state allowed language training in Kurdish in the public sphere, there was great enthusiasm among Kurdish nationalists. Private language centers were opened with fanfare, but turned out to be a failure. Centers in Batman and Diyarbakır closed in less than a year for economic reasons—there was not enough demand. As a countermove, the rebels suggested what would have been unthinkable in the past: The PKK insisted that public schools should teach Kurdish to schoolchildren. Ironically, this was the very educational network that the PKK had destroyed in its heyday. It had targeted teachers and sabotaged schools, almost bringing education to a complete halt. Funded by the central state and dependent on taxpayers' contributions, the infrastructure that the PKK had once considered to be the vehicle of assimilation could now serve the rebels' nationalist goals.[54]

The PKK and its political ally, the Kurdish nationalist party, the Peace and Democracy Party (BDP), added another dimension to Kurdish claims in 2010: the "democratic decentralization project."[55] This project called for a redrawing of administrative boundaries in Turkey and the delegation of important government functions to local authorities. The intended outcome was no secret: the creation of a Kurdistan with ample resources and self-governing authority. While the PKK and its political allies would have the ultimate decision-making authority, the rest of Turkey would provide the bulk of revenues and institutions. As such, the rebels turned their strategy upside down in their efforts to found "Kurdistan." Instead of creating an independent political unit, the PKK now promoted the idea of building Kurdistan using state resources.

Both the democratic decentralization project and the promotion of constitutional rights required a new tactical approach. The rebel group began emphasizing propaganda activities and using violence more selectively. It believed that the more it could organize the Kurdish community, the more it would get from the Turkish state. However, political mobilization remained a formidable task for several years. Finally, in 2007, the PKK was able to forge a new organization, the Union of Kurdistan Communities (KCK). This new group was structured in the form of self-defense committees and found supporters, especially in the border towns that were PKK strongholds. However, the KCK was not a new idea.[56] It in fact embodied the ERNK with a new mission and involved promoting an organization within Kurdish society that would be an alternative to state rule.[57] The rebel organization also promised to forge new political alliances in line with its emerging ideology. Neither the revolutionary Turkish left nor European activists could offer the alliances that it needed in this political environment. The PKK became increasingly interested in establishing ties with political forces in Turkish society that could promote a peaceful solution to the Kurdish problem.

The new rebel ideology has yielded limited gains so far. Despite several overtures, the PKK neither found allies among the Turkish public nor bridged major divisions within Kurdish society. Timing was the major problem. Before this new vision took hold, sides in the conflict had already been chosen in Kurdish society. Kurds with hyphenated identities had already positioned themselves in the rival camp. While the Alevites continued to cherish the Republican ideals, the Islamists followed the lead of the conservative Turkish government. Meanwhile, Kurds in large cities continued to vote for national parties. Without mass support, the ethnic project was politically and geographically trapped. It is now shouldered by the Kurdish nationalist party, which represents the interests of the border towns and Kurdish areas that lie to the east of Diyarbakır. Once again, the PKK's shifting ideology has proved incapable of regrouping loyalties in Kurdish society.

Guided by a vision of history, the PKK envisioned the creation of Kurdistan through progressive change. In its early formulation, the PKK's ideology promised to free the Kurds and Kurdistan from imperial interests, colonial administration, and collaborationist coethnics. Yet the military success of counterinsurgency and the unwavering attitude of the state showed that independence was an unattainable dream. The second stage in the PKK's ideology took the reality on the battlefield into account. An ideological transformation began to take shape that involved scaling down demands and relying on European certification. The PKK internationalized the conflict to build pressure on Turkey for a favorable settlement. As the naming and shaming of Turkey in Europe failed to produce the desired outcomes, an agenda for domestic change took deeper root in the PKK's ideology. This shift involved bargaining with the Turkish state, beginning with moderate cultural claims and later evolving into a project that contradicted fundamental aspects of the PKK's founding ideology. Rebel demands now included a "democratic decentralization" scheme that would foster regional rule by the PKK and its political allies that would be funded by state revenues and institutions.

In the final analysis, ideology is the only aspect of the PKK that experienced transformation. However, the political alliances and loyalties that it garnered have become durable over time. Friends and foes of the rebel project were already set in Kurdish society during the 1990s. As such, ideology proved incapable of rallying the Kurds around a common political identity, while excessive centralization squandered the chances of territorial control. Both mechanisms in turn informed the PKK's military strategy. Chapter 3 will explain the PKK's strategy over time and show how the insurgents' military record followed these political choices.

3

STRATEGY

In civil war, survival is a function of long-term interactions with territory and people. Combatants develop a variety of strategies to secure territorial control and civilian loyalties. A pair of concepts borrowed from ecology, generalist and specialist, can help us explain why combatants have differential access to both resources.[1] As organizations, combatants connect with their environment in two distinct ways. Generalists survive in multiple environments, whereas specialists depend on a homogeneous clientele to thrive. States are typically generalists. They draw support from various segments of society and adopt similar policies across space. Yet, when faced with a resilient insurgency, state policies become targeted. States resort to specialist solutions tailored to the community that the insurgents seek to mobilize. Insurgencies have an opposite logic. As specialists, their survival strategy is to pursue policies catering to a specific clientele. Still, an insurgency needs to advance generalist policies if it is to expand its social and geographical reach. This is the only way to consolidate its target community, which is diverse and riddled with local divisions.

In pursuing independence, the PKK's main strategy was to delink Kurdistan from Turkey and consolidate it around its agenda. The former required severing the institutional ties of Kurdish areas to Turkey, whereas the latter meant penalizing local actors who were allied with the state. This ambitious political agenda required a generalist approach. The rebels tried to dominate every corner of Kurdistan, the fundamental niche, claimed by the organization.[2] A dramatic surge in guerrilla activity in the 1990s turned rebel rule into a realistic option.

The PKK's design of political monopoly, however, had an important drawback. Commitment to the rebel cause varied greatly along spatial lines. Three geographical zones emerged where the PKK enjoyed different levels of success. Zone 1 was a border area within the security framework of the OHAL region that presented several advantages for guerrilla action. Historically speaking, it was outside the state's target areas and provided optimal resources for insurgency. Zone 2 also fell within the OHAL framework, yet it provided less optimal conditions for the rebel organization. New tactics had to be invented to eliminate state institutions and rival rebel groups to gain access to resources. Zone 3 represented the rest of Turkey and remained beyond the mental boundaries of the insurgency. The PKK had a hard time reproducing itself in this area, where the Kurdish community was firmly embedded in national structures (see figure 3.1).

This chapter discusses the evolution of the PKK's strategy, using data on 4,299 attacks that the insurgency initiated from 1984 to 2008.[3] We demonstrate that the rebels' military record closely followed their long-term interactions with territory and people. Despite changing intensity, insurgent violence was waged in rigid zones with distinct forms. We note three separate patterns. First, the rebels' methods and targets were zone specific. Second, the PKK strategically calibrated methods of violence to targets according to its military capacity. Third, insurgent violence against civilians was selective in its stronghold and indiscriminate in the opponent's territory.

We start by tracing the specialist origins of the rebel organization on the border and explain how the PKK built such a strong influence in Zone 1. Once Zone 1 had been secured via community transformation, the PKK attempted to control Kurdish areas throughout the 1990s. We demonstrate that rebels' territorial expansion required tactical diversity as the insurgency came into contact with state institutions and a heterogeneous

Figure 3.1. Zones of rebellion

clientele. However, the rebel project failed to consolidate the contested Zone 2. During this phase, credible rivals and weaker ties with resources posed formidable challenges. We show in the final section that the PKK returned to the border after its military defeat in 1999. Since then the rebel group has targeted security forces in Zone 1 and resorted to indiscriminate violence in large cities.

A Border Specialist

The PKK was a specialist organization until the 1990s. It operated in a particular area, employed a single tactic, and aimed consistently at a specific target. Yet this was no revolutionary specialism of the 1970s that divided Turkey into several insurgent fiefdoms. Taking its cue from the Cuban Revolution, the PKK started a guerrilla war and challenged the state at its weakest point. As part of this ambitious plan, the rebels relocated to the border in the 1980s. This new environment was optimal for the rebel organization to thrive. Close-knit communities made recruitment easier, and weak competition from the state lowered the costs of military action.[4] Successful guerrilla attacks in Siirt and Hakkari provinces in 1984 convinced the rebel organization to turn the eastern borders of Turkey into a contentious area.[5]

Insurgent activity was heavily concentrated on the Turkish-Iraqi border. On its face, this seemed like an odd decision: The Turkish-Iraqi border was shorter than others and was the site of only six districts (subunits of provinces). Yet the Iraqi border offered a political opportunity space like no other. Its close proximity to safe havens located in northern Iraq provided a strategic advantage for hit-and-run tactics. Unlike the flat geography on the Syrian border, the mountainous terrain limited the state's ability to patrol the region and increased the insurgents' movement capabilities. Most critically, Cudi Mountain, where the Syrian, Iraqi, and Turkish borders meet, is connected to several mountain ranges. It served as a launching pad to reach destinations in Turkey without having to travel in lower elevations.[6]

The rebel organization called most of this border area Botan. A historical vision guided its choice. Like other nationalist movements, the rebels referred to age-old territorial claims and reinvented Botan in the 1980s.[7] In reality, Botan did not correspond to an actual administrative unit. Geographically speaking, it included all the districts on the Iraqi border and those adjacent to them (with the exception of Yüksekova) and incorporated Cizre on the west and Çatak on the east. Botan was the stronghold of the insurgency throughout the 1980s.[8] Botan was also special because of an administrative "hole" on the border. Şırnak, a low-profile district of Siirt in the 1980s, was several miles away from the border and the provincial center. The PKK used the so-called Şırnak corridor very efficiently: rebels would enter Turkey from the Iraqi border, travel along mountain ranges, and wage violence in Şırnak and its surrounding districts.[9] The Şırnak corridor allowed the PKK to attack targets deep inside the region without encountering security forces. As a result, three districts of Siirt, Şırnak, Eruh, and Pervari, accounted for one-fourth of all rebel attacks in the first six years of guerrilla warfare.[10]

Another critical factor in turning the border into a contentious area was the support the rebel group received from neighboring countries. Syria harbored the PKK and provided the organization with a head start in its initial years.[11] The PKK's most prominent military training camp, the Mahsun Korkmaz Academy (1986–1993), was named after a guerrilla leader killed in a counterinsurgency operation and was based in Lebanon's Bekaa Valley. Bekaa was a training safe haven for terrorist groups and was under heavy Syrian influence.[12] The camp was given to the PKK by the Democratic Front for the Liberation of Palestine (DPLP), the military wing of the Palestinian Liberation Organization (PLO). According to Öcalan, a total of 15,000 PKK militants were trained at the Korkmaz Academy, which received 300 to 350 young recruits every three months.[13] Another important function of Syria was its willingness to host the insurgency's leadership. Öcalan stayed safely in Damascus, holding meetings with guerrillas and hosting foreign visitors for several years.

Meanwhile, Kurdish leaders in northern Iraq allowed the PKK to operate in their areas. The absence of a credible political authority on the Iraqi side rendered Turkish diplomatic pressure ineffective. The PKK became a legitimate political actor in the region and forged a symbiotic relationship with other Kurdish groups. With the intervention of Syria, the rebel organization signed two separate protocols with Barzani and Talabani in the 1980s that secured freedom of action, political legitimacy, and rebel encampments in northern Iraq.[14] This arrangement allowed the PKK to settle on the border and launch guerrilla attacks from bases in Iraq's Kurdish areas. The first rebel base in northern Iraq was Lolan, which was followed by Haftanin and Lak-1. In 1987, there were twenty-seven camps in the area, mostly located within two to twenty kilometers of the Turkish border (see figure 3.2).[15]

The PKK successfully created a realized niche in districts close to the Iraqi border, namely the Botan area.[16] This was Zone 1, the stronghold of insurgency. The rebel organization was aware of Botan's special character and made plans to establish statehood in this area.[17] In 1992, the rebel journal *Serxwebun* promised its supporters a war government in Botan.[18] Because of its highly strategic location, Şırnak played a prominent role in this plan. The rebels organized an intense urban raid in downtown Şırnak in August 1992, when bullets and rockets rained down on the city for more than fifty-two hours.[19]

The rebel organization primarily focused on the countryside. Despite its failure to create liberated areas on the border, the PKK's capacity to wage violence in rural Botan was unequivocal. Most instrumental was

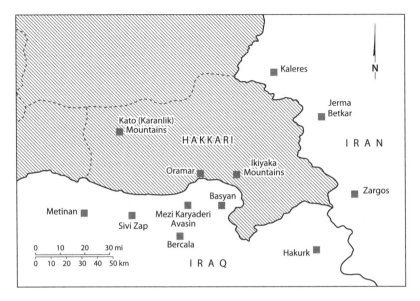

Figure 3.2. Rebel bases, Hakkari Province

selective violence against "collaborationists" and their families. After the Third Party Congress (1986), village raids became the main tactic for eliminating local allies of the state. More than half of all incidents in the 1984–1990 period consisted of raids on Kurdish villages.[20] In this regard, village raids played an important role in the PKK's group-making project: The organization aimed at fortifying intraethnic cleavages by waging violence on its own community.

The vulnerability of villages to outside attacks facilitated such violence. The villages targeted by the PKK were scattered across a sparsely populated land, had weak ties with urban centers, and were close to the border. In most cases, a raid would be over before security forces reached the village, and the insurgents would have already disappeared into the safety of the border. In more than 1,000 village raids over a 24-year period (1984–2008), 90 percent of the incidents took place in villages outside the jurisdiction of central districts (*merkez ilçe*), the administrative seats of provinces. These villages were far away from the provincial center and had inadequate communication and transportation infrastructures. The first governor of the OHAL administration, Hayri Kozakçıoğlu, was aware of the problem. In his first interview in 1987, he told the press that his most urgent task would be to build infrastructure for the region.[21]

The ritual aspects of village raids were remarkably similar. Coethnics who had sided with the state were systematically punished.[22] One such incident took place in the Nusaybin district of Mardin, where the PKK's firing squad killed thirteen civilians on May 8, 1988. The rebels came to Bahminin, a hamlet of Taşköy village, and gunned down all the members of the Çelik family. Each was called by name and was pronounced guilty of collaborating with the Turkish state.[23] Most prominent among the PKK's targets were village guards and village headmen. Their houses were singled out with special care, and ruthless attacks killed family members, burned houses to the ground, and destroyed livelihoods. An attack of this sort took place in the Ömerli district of Mardin in 1987. The rebels targeted Pınarcık village, the home of six village guards and a village headman. Forty insurgents entered the village from three directions. They had superior military technology (rocket-propelled grenades, RPGs) and easily outnumbered the guards. When they left, scores of villagers were dead.[24]

The PKK punished collaborationists in other ways as well. It sabotaged village infrastructure, burned harvests, and stole villagers' cattle. The organization also tracked down village headmen who migrated to urban centers. The former village headman of Derebaşı, Hacı Aydınlık, could not escape death even after he moved to Silopi. He was accused of helping a controversial counterinsurgency operation that led to the killing of innocent villagers.[25] Meanwhile, village guards were caught between the PKK and the state. Their decision to take sides with the state was guided by tribal allegiances, local power struggles, and economic incentives, if not by state pressure.[26] Their first successful clash with the insurgents occurred only when their numbers reached a critical threshold in 1987.[27] With the dramatic increase in insurgent attacks in the 1990s, thousands deserted their positions. A significant number frequently switched sides under pressure from both the state and the rebels.[28]

Village raids involved more than punishing those who were allied with the state. Neutralization was an important aspect: Village guards were called to lay down their weapons and stop resisting the organization. Insurgents adopted several tactics to get their message across. They sent respected members of the local community to the village, contacted village guards directly, or (more commonly) raided a neighboring village to spread rumors of an impending attack. In several incidents, village guards surrendered without a fight. In Kaval village of the Uludere district, the PKK collected the weapons of thirty village guards. In Mergi hamlet of the Eruh district, insurgents gathered the village guards inside the mosque and burned down the village headman's house to convince them that resistance would be futile.[29] In Cevizdibi village of the Beytüşşebap district, insurgents interrogated village guards for taking up arms against the organization.[30] Eager to eliminate them as a group, the PKK announced an armistice for village guards in 1992 and promised to spare their lives if they laid down their weapons.[31]

Another important aspect of village raids was propaganda. Typically, the PKK would gather residents at the village center and intimidate the villagers until they agreed to support their cause and denounce state institutions. These forced gatherings served other purposes as well. Most important, insurgents recruited local youth, targeting shepherds as well as sons of village guards and hostile tribes. Tekeli village of the Şemdinli district is located two miles away from the Iraqi border. On the first day of May 1987, insurgents came to the village and abducted thirteen teenagers. In June, they returned to abduct another forty-three from the same district.[32] Abduction was an important insurgent tactic facilitated by village raids. Almost all cases of abduction were recorded in conjunction with a village raid, and more than half of these incidents took place in the Botan area.[33] Raids also helped rebels identify suspected collaborationists and take them hostage. Some hostages were killed outside the village; some escaped, realizing that death was imminent; and some were young enough to be used as new recruits by the organization.

Despite the bloodshed, village raids played an important role for the rebel organization. They helped the PKK dominate the countryside and create a realized niche (a subset of the fundamental niche, where the organization is capable of sustaining itself) in Botan defined by strong ties to the community. Villages were social units where the state and insurgents competed fiercely for the same resource; the loyalty of Kurds. Insurgent rage against village guards and village headmen was intense. They were accused of providing the state with security, information, and resources. Violence in the countryside aimed at converting collaborationists where possible and eliminating them when they resisted.[34] In this respect, violence, facilitated by village raids, divided Kurdish society from within and resulted in boundary making.

Reaching Out

With increased manpower and better access to weapons, the rebels dreamed of reaching out to all parts of Kurdistan, the imagined ethnic homeland. Waging violence solely in the countryside was not adequate for this task. Territorial control across the OHAL region required tactical richness: Insurgents had to diversify their methods and learn to deal with new types of targets. Accordingly, the rebel organization used several new tactics to consolidate its military presence on the border and extend its geographical coverage. While tactics in Zone 1 aimed at carving out liberated areas along the border, the violence perpetrated beyond the insurgent stronghold mainly involved the destruction of state institutions.

In the 1990s, a key objective of the PKK was to consolidate its presence on the border. Despite a sixfold increase in insurgent attacks in this period, Zone 1 remained critical for guerrilla warfare. In an effort to liberate areas in Botan, rebels concentrated more than half of their attacks on military targets. They ambushed military convoys and planted roadside bombs. More critically, the PKK increasingly targeted military bases. Originally built to control contraband activity, military posts close to the border suffered the heaviest casualties. Guerrilla units crossed the border by the hundreds and attacked military posts at night, pounding them with gunfire for several hours and forcing the military to remain on the defensive.

Exogenous shocks helped the PKK on the border. As the Iraqi state withdrew from northern Iraq under international pressure, weak Kurdish rule created a hospitable environment for the rebels. Barzani and Talabani forces failed to assert control over the region despite the establishment of a no-fly zone in 1992 that barred the Iraqi army from entering northern Iraq.[35] In addition, northern Iraq was in social turmoil. Repression of the Kurds by the Iraqi state forced thousands to flee to Turkey and Iran. Political chaos allowed the PKK to roam freely on the border, recruit new members, and acquire weapons. Iran's role in the insurgency came to the forefront when the Iraqi border became less secure for the insurgents. Increasing attacks on Van, Hakkari, Iğdır, and Ağrı, located across the border from the Iranian cities of Mako and Urumiye, turned heads in Iran's direction. Intelligence reports indicated that Iran was hosting rebel camps; providing logistics, health services, and shelter; and allowing the PKK to operate in the country with false identification documents.[36]

Urban raids helped insurgent prospects on the border. Similar to attacks on military targets, half of urban raids in the 1991–1999 period occurred in Zone 1. Cizre, İdil, Yüksekova, and Silopi districts, which the rebel organization had high hopes of transforming into liberated areas, were hit the hardest. The goal of violence was less about damage and more about a show of force in urban settings. Raids demonstrated the organization's ability to challenge the state's institutional presence.[37] State buildings, including military and police headquarters, housing facilities for security forces, and administration buildings, became the main targets. Advanced weapons (especially RPG-7s) enabled the rebels to attack urban centers from a safe distance without clashing with security forces.

The PKK acquired the necessary capabilities to extend its geographical coverage in the 1990s. The number of insurgents grew from 1,500 to 10,000 in less than four years, which allowed the organization to penetrate other parts of the OHAL region.[38] Each armed unit now had 270–300 guerrillas who could easily attack military installations. The technology of violence also changed. Insurgent inventory now included RPGs, mortars, and even a few antiaircraft guns. The PKK's easy access to advanced technology was an unintended consequence of the regional conflicts engulfing northern Iraq in the early 1990s. During these years, rebels could easily acquire weapons from displaced Peshmergas and locals without having to pay dearly for them. A comparison of weapons captured from the rebel organization reveals the dramatic change in the PKK's arsenal in this period (see table 3.1).

Greater territorial control required tracking the movement of people in the OHAL region. Rebels set up roadblocks so they could kill state employees, take hostages, and destroy vehicles. The Lice-Genç road was a longtime favorite of insurgents. Over time, other major highways also became dangerous. In one incident, the rebels stopped hundreds of cars and collected valuables and identity cards in Erzincan, a province adjacent to the OHAL.[39] On another occasion, a bank branch manager, a customs official, and a bus driver were killed on June 6, 1993, when twenty insurgents stopped traffic in the Pülümür district of Tunceli province.[40] State

TABLE 3.1. The PKK's weapon technology[1]

Weapon type	1984–1992	1991	1994
Antiaircraft gun	4	—	19
Heavy machine gun	43	22	11
RPG launcher	260	260	747
Assault rifle[2]	6,150	7,743	4,655
IEDs	—	165	2,661
Hand grenade	1,750	1,719	4,741
Wireless radio	—	—	145

Source: Milliyet, April 1, 1992; October 30, 1992; February 26, 1995. The data for 1994 also cover January and February of 1995.
[1] Number of weapons captured in PKK hideouts.
[2] Includes Kalashnikovs (AK-47s).

employees and bus companies responded to the security threat in their own ways. The former began to travel less frequently and were forced to conceal their identity when they did. Soldiers were not allowed to use public transportation, police forces did not wear their uniforms during public travel, and high-ranking civil servants preferred air travel instead. Meanwhile, bus companies halted their service beyond Mardin province or agreed to give protection money to the PKK.[41]

The PKK disrupted the ties between Turkey and the OHAL region in other ways as well. Rebels systematically targeted road construction facilities (Karayolları Bakımevleri), which were run by a state institution. Railroads did not escape the attention of the rebel organization, either. Rebels attacked postal and passenger trains with trackside bombs and forced railroad workers to cut the tracks at gunpoint. This precarious security environment led the Turkish State Railways (TCDD) to halt most of its services in the region. Communication was also affected. As the PKK grew stronger, it became harder for the state to offer postal services in the countryside. Rebels also targeted radio-link stations, sabotaging them when they could. In September 1991, they burned down 10,000 trees in the Tatvan district of Bitlis province to prevent the extension of telephone lines.[42] Overall, more than three-quarters of the rebel attacks on transportation and communication targets occurred outside Zone 1. These attacks

TABLE 3.2. Expanding the conflict: The PKK's district coverage[1]

Target type	1984–1990	1991–1999
Transportation[2]	27	97
Economic	32	110
Education	31	58

[1] Number of districts attacked by the PKK.
[2] Includes communication targets.

increased the geographical coverage of insurgent violence to ninety-seven districts and gave the PKK a presence beyond the border (see table 3.2).

Another tactic to facilitate geographical expansion involved violence against economic targets. Attacks on economic units increased fourfold in the 1991–1999 period and occurred primarily in nonborder areas. The mounting violence served two purposes: to ensure the flight of capital from the region and to hurt the state on economic grounds. The PKK's top priority was economic enterprises controlled by the state. Insurgents attacked oil-drilling sites and oil storage facilities in Batman province and periodically sabotaged the Iraqi-Turkish oil pipeline.[43] Coal mines in Şırnak and tobacco-processing facilities throughout southeastern Anatolia shared a similar fate.[44] Small-scale mining companies and private contractors specializing in infrastructure projects also faced intense pressure from the organization. In other instances, rebels simply destroyed anything of economic value: They raided a chicken farm in the central district of Hakkari and did not hesitate to kill 13,000 chickens by burning them alive.[45]

The PKK gave economic enterprises, both state and private, two choices: pay a protection fee or leave the region.[46] By 1994, Chevron, Mobil, and Shell had canceled their oil-drilling licenses or had closed their oil sites.[47] The Village Services Division (Köy Hizmetleri Müdürlüğü), a state-funded institution that was responsible for ensuring the well-being of villages, could not fulfill any of its functions. It had no permanent personnel in key provinces such as Kars, Ardahan, and Ağrı, and workers refused to work in village projects. Others chose to strike a deal with the PKK. Private contractors paid up to 25,000 German marks per year for their safety.[48] Evidence also suggests that local administrators of large-scale state enterprises, such as the Turkish Petroleum Corporation (TPAO) and Tobacco, Tobacco Products, Salt and Alcohol Enterprises (TEKEL), also paid protection money to ward off violence.[49] Therefore, if roadblocks turned the PKK into a reality beyond Botan, economic targets allowed the rebel organization to extend its coverage into the rest of Turkey, Zone 3. In large cities, such as Istanbul and Adana, sabotage was the main method of violence: Low-risk attacks on businesses gave the PKK visibility without causing human casualties.

The rebel organization also halted the delivery of public services. Education targets received priority. The ERNK's Diyarbakır branch justified the attacks by arguing that national education was a state instrument that worked to assimilate Kurdish youth.[50] To destroy the education network, rebels killed teachers and burned schools, especially in central districts. The number of schools and students adversely affected by violence tripled from October 1991 to October 1993. At the peak of the PKK's military success, some 3,000 schools were closed down in the OHAL region, preventing 100,000 students from receiving a formal education. As the pressure on teachers mounted, many of them chose not to work in the region despite a wage incentive. In 1992, more than 2,000 teachers did not show up at the school to which they were assigned.[51] Others were not so lucky: They were gunned down on their way to their assignments or in village raids simply because they were teachers.

Education targets served the PKK's expansion agenda in two ways. First, rebels projected their influence on the most developed cities of the region. One-third of all incidents involving education targets took place in Diyarbakır and Tunceli. Diyarbakır had large districts away from the center and Tunceli's central district hosted several village schools. The majority of teacher deaths occurred in these two provinces. Second, the PKK aimed at education targets on the Iranian border. As the PKK's military success waned in the second half of the 1990s, rebels turned their attention to Turkey's eastern border. Located outside the northeast corner of OHAL, Kars, Ardahan, and Ağrı provinces seemed perfect targets. They were loosely integrated into Turkey, were located close to the Iranian and Armenian borders, and hosted competing communal groups (Azeris, Turks, Kurds, and Karapapaks). School burnings complemented village raids and increased sevenfold in this area.

The rebels also intervened in conventional politics in the 1990s. Several bombing incidents took place in large cities, which targeted political party offices. The PKK forced local politicians to resign from their political posts and switch to the newly founded Kurdish nationalist party (HEP and its successors). In the fall of 1993, the rebel organization officially announced that it had banned all national parties in Kurdistan.[52] Several local officials resigned from their parties. Politicians from Diyarbakır and Tunceli were kidnapped and interrogated by the rebels.[53] The pressure on local politicians was most intense in nonborder areas. The provinces of Diyarbakır, Mardin, and Tunceli alone accounted for one-fifth of the incidents involving local politicians. Yet, as the next section will demonstrate, political transformation remained the rebel's dream in the contested site, Zone 2. Regardless of how astute their repertoires were, rebel designs beyond Zone 1 would enjoy limited success.

Paying the Price

The PKK's efforts to consolidate Kurdish areas faced major obstacles. Most important, long-term interactions with territory and people would not allow for such a political outcome. The rebels' organizational structure and ideological discourse failed to garner civilian support and facilitate territorial control across the OHAL region. Attempts to reverse this outcome proved unsuccessful. The PKK decided to pay lip service to multiple Kurdish realities only when it ran into trouble after 1993. Similarly, its efforts to win community support were mostly pragmatic in nature. The PKK's opponents, the state and rival insurgent groups, capitalized on this trust deficit and divided resources in their favor. As a result, the rebel group wasted its energy with minimal gains in return as it moved away from the border area.[54]

Each zone presented different challenges to the rebel organization. In the state's stronghold, Zone 3, the PKK was unable to mobilize locals for the rebel cause. This had to do with the fact that the insurgency received only limited support from the community and could not breach the OHAL security framework. The PKK tried various strategies for surviving in Zone 3. The rebels organized widespread attacks in provinces adjacent to the OHAL region and engaged in community organizing in large cities such as Adana. They later shifted to a "selective expansion" mode, targeting areas where cultural cleavages mattered or there had been local support for revolutionary movements in the past.

The PKK initiative to reach the Alevites was such an attempt. The Alevites, who number in the millions, preach an Anatolian version of Shi'ite Islam and have historically faced an uphill battle against Sunnis. The massacre of Alevites in Sivas in 1992 by a religious mob provided the rebel organization with an opportunity to mobilize outside the OHAL region.[55] The PKK committed a similar tragedy against Sunni peasants in Erzincan, a multiconfessional city with a Sunni majority.[56] The rebel leader claimed that this was a response to the Sivas massacre and invited the Alevites to join the struggle.[57] The vigilant response of the Turkish state, however, kept the OHAL boundaries intact and forced the PKK to shift its focus to Sivas ("Koçgiri province"). Another multiconfessional city with critical importance, Sivas is located in east-central Anatolia. After 1996, the PKK targeted Sunni villages across the province with its Dersim units. However, this attempt to win supporters along confessional lines produced no tangible outcomes.

Similarly, the Mediterranean coastal expansion was designed to appeal to non-Sunni and non-Turkish populations. Hatay, a disputed territory between Syria and Turkey, is a cosmopolitan province that hosts Christians, Turks, and Arabs.[58] Rebels sporadically attacked this province in the second half of the 1990s. As had been the case in Sivas, the rebels had opportunistic goals. They killed villagers in the countryside and attacked military targets when they could. The PKK's expansion toward the Black Sea was different. Öcalan tried to mobilize the support the Turkish left had drawn from the region in the 1970s. The PKK provided military training to a Turkish rebel group, TDP, to prepare it for a guerrilla campaign in the Black Sea region.[59] Other than a few skirmishes with the military, however, this initiative also failed to extend the rebels' reach.

In large cities, the PKK's survival chances were limited. The rebels' favorite partner was another insurgent organization, the Revolutionary Left (Dev-Sol). In return for training camps in the Bekaa Valley, Dev-Sol cooperated with the PKK and struck against security forces, especially in Istanbul, in 1990–1992.[60] When military momentum was lost, rebel tactics in the cities had to change. The PKK turned to indiscriminate violence.[61] Bombing squads planned sensational incidents that claimed civilian lives.

Meanwhile, cities closer to the OHAL region presented new opportunities for the organization. Adana and Mersin received thousands of Kurdish migrants who were escaping from violence in the region. Displaced families settled in ghetto-type areas on the outskirts of these cities.[62] The PKK attempted to turn the despair and anger of recent migrants into collective action. The ERNK worked relentlessly to organize the Kurdish community around its political agenda and punished those who resisted. Political assassination was the most prevalent form of violence used to ensure communal conformity. The two cities accounted for one-fifth of all PKK assassinations during this period. Assassinations coincided with the PKK's military ascendancy and declined afterward.

While weak community support and poor military performance characterized the PKK's record in the rest of Turkey, rival rebel groups limited its chances of success in the contested Zone 2.[63] At the peak of its power, the PKK was involved in an intense rivalry with the Turkish Workers and Peasants Liberation Army (TIKKO, the military wing of Turkish Communist Party/Marxist-Leninist, TKP/ML) and the Revolutionary Communist Party of Turkey (TDKP) in Tunceli province, the home of Zaza-speaking and Alevite Kurdish populations.[64] Tunceli provided a perfect geography, a rich political tradition, and therefore a window of opportunity for Kurdish insurgency. The PKK's efforts to consolidate Kurdish dissent, however, met with severe resistance. Despite their small size, local groups were successfully tapping the resources of the province. A clash between the TDKP and the PKK in 1993 demonstrated the local dynamics at play: Shops were closed down in the city center of Tunceli and Hozat district to show locals' disapproval of the incident.[65] For a while, the PKK found a way to break this localism. It recruited influential Zazas into commander positions in Dersim. Code-named Dr. Baran, Müslüm Durgun played an instrumental role in opening up the province to the PKK: He came from a prestigious tribal family and was well known and respected in the area. His suspicious death and growing Zaza-Kurdish tensions inside the organization frustrated the PKK's hopes of turning Dersim into another Botan in the second half of the 1990s.

Another homegrown rebel group that presented a serious challenge to the PKK's monopoly was Hezbollah. Hezbollah promised to create an Islamic state in Kurdish areas and was most influential in Diyarbakır, Mardin, and Batman provinces.[66] The PKK had high hopes of staging popular revolts in the same provinces. Yet Hezbollah became a major obstacle for the ERNK, especially in Nusaybin, Batman, Silvan, and Diyarbakır.[67] Political murders reached record numbers in the 1991–1994 period. Most victims were killed in public places in broad daylight. With more than 600 unresolved cases in 1992 and 1993, the public strongly believed that Hezbollah was receiving support from the state. Rivalry between the two groups ended before 1995 with important consequences.[68] Most critically, preoccupied with Hezbollah, the PKK could not capitalize on Kurdish unrest and missed the opportunity to foment popular revolts.

Despite its political monopoly on the border, the PKK's major problem was a lack of institution building in Zone 1.[69] Although the rebel organization was able to eliminate state bureaucracy, it failed to replace it with a system of governance. Locals were trapped in their area with almost no access to public services such as health and education. The justice system also failed, as locals had a hard time finding a credible authority to resolve their disagreements. A few towns where the rebel organization tried to make a difference in public life remained committed to the PKK's cause. Cizre, İdil, Yüksekova, and Nusaybin have been hot spots for Kurdish unrest ever since. However, the broader meaning of Zone 1 did not change much for the PKK; it remained an insurgent stronghold where the rebels continued to have a strong military presence.

Back to Botan

The military legacy in Botan shaped Kurdish insurgency in the post-1999 period. The PKK returned to the border where it had begun the guerrilla struggle fifteen years earlier. Yet this was not merely a replication of its past experience. Throughout the 1990s, the PKK tried to dominate the OHAL region and expand beyond it. Rebel methods and targets became highly diversified. Economic targets and political assassinations in large cities, education and transportation targets in Zone 2, and military targets in Zone 1 were tactical choices that served the purpose. Despite these efforts, the rebels realized in 1999 that not only had they lost the war, they were also left without a leader. After four years of armistice, the PKK reappeared on the scene in 2003. It pulled back from the areas where it had once operated and went back to its specialist origins. Trapped on the border like its counterpart in Chechnya, the PKK now had a predominant tactic and a single target.

Since 2000, the PKK's main area of activity has been the border. Half of all insurgent attacks have occurred in border districts or in districts immediately adjacent to them. This figure represents a greater concentration on the border than was the case in the 1990s. The rebels revitalized their presence in Zone 1 of the now-defunct OHAL region while muting their attacks on the Iranian and Syrian borders. Accordingly, the PKK's military capacity in Zone 1 peaked between 2000 and 2008, accounting for 43 percent of all incidents in this period. The center of attraction was the Iraqi border with its rough terrain, cross-border advantages, and sympathetic local Kurdish groups. Moreover, the PKK found its main target and implemented its most effective tactic in this area.

In this final phase of the conflict, the rebels considered the Turkish military their principal enemy. The PKK no longer possesses the capacity to attack national facilities and refrains from waging violence against the local allies of the state. Thus, close to two-thirds of incidents in the 2000–2008 period were directed against security forces.[70] This figure illustrates the increasing importance of the military as a PKK target. Since the first phase of insurgency, the share of attacks on the military increased by 35 percent in the 2000–2008 period.[71] These attacks were concentrated in the PKK's stronghold. Approximately half of the incidents involving the military took place here. Şırnak and Hakkari, in particular, presented major challenges for the Turkish army.

Increasing violence against the military was facilitated by means of a new tactic: IEDs have become the killing tool of insurgents. Two-fifths of insurgent attacks involved roadside explosions in this period. This was an unprecedented tactical move. The PKK had rarely used roadside bombs in the past (5 percent on average before 2000). Since 2000, the use of improvised bombs became widespread, especially in Zone 1.[72] They have been the largest threat to mobile military forces. With the exception of two assault incidents, the military experienced its heaviest losses in IED-related cases. For instance, three separate incidents in the Güçlükonak district of Şırnak left thirteen members of the armed forces dead and wounded twenty-eight from December 2006 to June 2007.[73]

The robust use of IEDs highlights another fact. The PKK has recently shifted its focus from immobile to mobile military targets. During the first phase of the conflict (1984–1990), the rebels had neither the capacity nor the interest to assault army positions. As the PKK grew stronger in the second phase (1991–1999), it felt confident enough to systematically attack military bases. A countertrend has set in since 1999. The increasing use of ambushes and roadside bombs supports this observation: as the PKK's military strength declined, these rebel methods increased from 28 percent in the second period to 66 percent in the final phase of the conflict (2000–2008).

The rebel organization's recent attraction to mobile targets has a major downside. It does not promote the image of a strong insurgency that can take on the military in hot confrontations. To boost its public image, the PKK launched two strikes on military posts on the border. Both incidents occured at the peak of insurgent activity, in May and October of 2008. Hundreds of rebels crossed the border and stormed the Aktütün military post in the Şemdinli district of Hakkari.[74] They used rockets, Russian-made missiles, antiaircraft guns, and mortars. The balance sheet of the two incidents was horrifying. When the hours of fighting ended, the insurgents had lost forty-two militants. Casualties on the military side were also high: twenty-three were dead, and another twenty-eight soldiers were wounded. After ten years, the PKK had demonstrated that it could still strike military bases. In doing so, the rebel organization successfully boosted its image among its supporters, infuriated the public, and provoked the Turkish army to launch a cross-border attack into northern Iraq.

During this period, the rebel organization also stepped up its attacks on civilians. Two trends confirm the spatial and temporal change in indiscriminate violence. First, half of these incidents occured in the state's stronghold, Zone 3. Second, Zone 3 became more much prominent after 1997, when Öcalan was forced to leave Syria and the PKK's collapse seemed imminent. In addition to tourist destinations, the main theaters of violence were Ankara, Istanbul, and Izmir. Insurgents planted bombs in the downtowns of large cities to boost the PKK's image and force the government to a settlement. One such incident took place in May 2007, in a shopping center in Ankara when an A-4 bomb explosion killed nine and injured 118 civilians.[75]

In sum, the PKK lost its military capacity after 1999 and refashioned itself as a specialist group. It now operates in a limited market, has a dominant tactic, and can aim efficiently at only a single target. To overcome its specialist limitations, the PKK has staged a few spectacular attacks on the border and in large cities. Recently, the rebel group has adopted another tactic. Since 2008, insurgents have begun to use violence strategically to pressure the government. The PKK now refrains from violence for longer periods of time and expects the government to meet its demands. It insists that the Kurdish nationalist party can act on its behalf in negotiations with the government and threatens to ramp up violence in critical moments (such as during elections). Time will tell whether the PKK can successfully play this waiting game in the future or will once again resort to widespread violence in Turkey.[76]

This chapter has shown that insurgent repertoires have evolved across time and space. Our evidence from 4,299 insurgent attacks demonstrated that PKK's success was bounded both geographically and chronologically. The PKK emerged as a specialist in the Botan area where village raids ensured the organization's political ascendancy. The rebel group left a military legacy in Zone 1 that still defines state-insurgent interactions today. The ultimate challenge for the rebel organization was to expand beyond Botan and shift its focus from the countryside to urban locations. The PKK has employed multiple tactics to consolidate its presence on the border and expand its geographical coverage.

Despite the increasing scale of violence, outcomes have remained uncertain beyond Zone 1. Violent tactics and intense propaganda efforts have had only limited success in politicizing the contested sites and have failed to breach the OHAL security framework. Outside Zone 1, weaker communal support and the presence of formidable rivals have forced the rebel group to pay a heavy price for military confrontation. Since 2000, the PKK has returned to the border. It now concentrates its efforts in the Botan area, where it limits itself to military targets.

Part II

Counterinsurgency

4

ORGANIZATION

States fight insurgencies in several ways. The most common strategy has been a military response. State leaders believe that eliminating an insurgent threat first and foremost requires a victory on the battlefield. It is not a coincidence that, in the age of imperialism (1881–1914), the United States in the Philippines, the Russians in the Caucasus, and the Ottomans in Yemen, along with the Germans and British in Africa, were busy chasing insurgents in bloody intrastate wars.[1] More recently, states have increasingly deployed new tools to pacify armed contention. Gaining knowledge about the contentious territory and the social organization of discontented groups became states' top priorities. Modern states have studied landscapes, imposed boundaries, and classified populations. This new approach was most evident in the fields of cartography and anthropology, where knowledge production provided state bureaucrats with the necessary technical information and ideological discourses to assist counterinsurgency efforts.[2]

These second-order measures were available to practitioners in a path-dependent fashion. Historically speaking, Western states were in a unique position to make use of the most advanced techniques. With efficient bureaucratic structures in place and ample resources at their disposal, they fared better than their counterparts in acquiring access to local information, putting it into policy use, and eliminating principal-agent problems. The European experience in the colonies and the U.S. war effort in Vietnam are cases in point. Other states had limited access to these capabilities and chose to work with other tools. For example, a demographic solution proved to be the most successful strategy in dissolving regional leaderships in Central Asia: waves of Russian and Chinese migration displaced local populations in favor of colonizers who aligned firmly with the central state.[3] At the bottom of the international hierarchy, fragile states of the Third World had neither the capacity nor the experience to deal with insurgent movements. With the exception of intricate bargains, they relied on the use of force to resolve internal conflicts. Saddam Hussein's Iraq and Muammar Qaddafi's Libya responded to opposition groups in this fashion, thereby opening a window of opportunity for third-party intervention.

The Ottoman-Turkish experience fell somewhere between those of efficient Western polities and weak Third World states. Turkish rulers consistently updated their institutions in order to block European encroachment and at the same time learned a great deal from their archrivals.[4] They became aware of modern ways of subduing local populations but faced major difficulties in adopting these techniques. Limited state capacity and the policy of indirect rule presented major obstacles. Nevertheless, the Turkish state has been incorporating new elements into its counterinsurgency repertoire since the nineteenth century. Organizational response figured most prominently in this undertaking. The central state clustered administrative units in innovative ways to penetrate communities and eliminate foreign intervention. By creating special regions, rescaling administrative units, and attaching them directly to the political center, the Turkish state manipulated administrative boundaries to exert control over contentious territory.

Administrative practices played an important role in the Turkish state's fight against the PKK. The state's organizational response was primarily a containment strategy that sought to isolate the insurgents in territorial terms. This approach had two important qualities. First, it was a boundary making effort that drew heavily from the state's previous experience: The Ottoman-Turkish state relied on a specialist solution each time it faced intercommunal warfare or ethnic demands. Second, it was spatial: Despite its ethnic credentials, Turkish statesmen viewed political contention in geographical terms and responded accordingly.[5]

This chapter examines the Turkish state's organizational response to armed contention. In the first two sections, we explore the creation of special administrative units to combat rebels and conclude that special rule separated the experience of these units from the rest of the country. We then turn to redistricting practices within this special region and show how these administrative arrangements aimed to increase state presence in the target territory. We end with an examination of the state's retreat from rural areas. This final section demonstrates that the central state depopulated the countryside to deprive insurgents of logistical support. However, this policy unintentionally contributed to the emergence of an ethnic agenda in urban sites that had become refuges for migrant populations.

Administrative Solutions

The idea of creating special administrative regions has a strong precedent in Ottoman-Turkish history. The late Ottoman state put troubled areas under special rule. This practice was commonly implemented in the aftermath of intercommunal warfare and represented an administrative solution negotiated between the Ottomans and the Great Powers of Europe (Düvel-i Muazzama).[6] Special rule promised local Christians some form of regional autonomy and increasingly involved Westerners as officials and advisors. This specialist framework had a conflict management agenda. Under the supervision of powerful governors, inspectorates were designed to prevent further bloodshed by solving two critical issues: information deficit and lack of accountability both of which provided opportunities for violent mobilizations. As such, inspectorates were administrative arrangements that allowed the state to closely monitor sensitive areas. Despite a unity of purpose, the Ottoman state and the Europeans had different motivations: the Ottomans viewed inspectorates as a last resort to avoid foreign intervention, whereas for European states, this was a low-cost strategy that kept imperialist competition in check.

The turning point in specialist governance was the establishment of an autonomous entity in Mount Lebanon (1864). After bloody clashes took place between Maronites and Druze, French pressure forced the Ottoman state to grant regional autonomy to Catholic Maronites.[7] Mount Lebanon (the "Mountain") was separated from Beirut and was put directly under Istanbul's jurisdiction. It was administered by a district governor who had to be an Ottoman Maronite. One year later, the Ottomans tried to avoid a similar political outcome. Vested with extraordinary powers, the military commander, Derviş Paşa, settled tribes in Kozan, a sensitive territory where Armenians lived side by side with Muslims, and provided safe passage from Anatolia to Syria.[8] Viewed in retrospect, this First Inspectorate was a preemptive counterinsurgency move. A few decades later, intercommunal tensions between Muslims and Armenians in eastern Anatolia in 1894–1896, convinced the Ottoman sultan, Abdulhamid II, to send his confidant, Ahmet Şakir Paşa, to bring peace and security to the region.[9] As the Second Inspector, the military commander was responsible for implementing reforms on behalf of Armenians, a remit that the sultan accepted grudgingly under Western pressure.[10]

At the turn of the twentieth century, Ottoman Macedonia was characterized by political violence. Nationalist groups were vying for power in this region.[11] In the wake of growing political violence, the Third Inspectorate (Umumi Rumeli Müfettişliği) was founded in 1903, and an Ottoman governor-general, Hüseyin Hilmi Paşa, was assigned to the post with extraordinary powers. In comparison to previous inspectorates, Westerners had a growing influence in the administration of the Third Inspectorate. For instance, Kosovo, a center of ethnic contention in Macedonia, was run by foreign advisors, each European power controlling a different department of state.[12] Finally, the Fourth Inspectorate was announced for eastern Anatolia (1913) by the Ottomans before World War I. Under the supervision of European advisors, the inspectorate was to implement reforms that would empower the Armenian community in provinces under its jurisdiction. Its main task was to complete the work promised by the Second Inspectorate.[13] However, World War I made this institutional framework obsolete before it went into effect and ended the experience of inspectorates in the late Ottoman period.

Like its Ottoman predecessor, Turkey's Republican administration also installed inspectorates four times and thereby created special administrative regions.[14] The First Inspectorate-General (Birinci Umumi Müfettişlik) was fully Ottoman in character. It was implemented in the aftermath of a major rebellion, and its latent purpose was to prevent foreign intervention. As bureaucratic correspondence of the era clearly demonstrates, the pro-Kurdish Şeyh Said Rebellion (1925) alarmed statesmen about the prospects of a Kurdish state that could be supported by imperialist powers and their proxies in northern Iraq and Syria.[15] At this point, the First Inspectorate was created for southeastern Anatolia (1927–1947).[16] The Republican leaders planned to halt ethnic mobilization by designating a special region where they could first pacify the community and then implement reform. Even so, the Republican elite gave an important twist to this institutional arrangement. The inspectorate was no longer the imposition of European powers on behalf of Christian minorities. Instead, it reflected the central state's vision to pacify and transform an unruly minority, the Kurds.

The Fourth Inspectorate represented the climax of the Republican experiment with special regions in the interwar era. It was created in the district of Dersim in east-central Anatolia and was then extended to several surrounding provinces (1935). In a carefully planned counterinsurgency campaign, the central state militarily defeated local leaderships in the area and then started a massive program of reform.[17] Even the name of Dersim was abandoned in favor of Tunceli, which the Turkish statesmen considered to be more in tune with the rhetoric of Republican citizenship.[18] The selection of Dersim was no coincidence. As noted earlier, the region was settled by Zaza-speaking Alevites who were internally divided by a competitive clan system but operated as a close trust network in their relations with the outside world.[19] Using this anthropological insight, the Republican leaders moved into Dersim to divide Kurdish geography from within and demonstrate the power of the Republic's "treatment methods."[20]

Late Ottoman and early Republican experiences have informed the way the Turkish state has dealt with the PKK threat since the 1980s. The state's immediate response was to set up an Emergency Governorship (OHAL Valiliği) to contain the insurgency (1987–2002).[21] Yet the OHAL's boundaries did not reflect the actual military performance of the rebel group. It was merely a geographical replica of the First Inspectorate in the Republican period. By making a path-dependent decision, the state incorporated what would become the contested area between the state and the PKK into this framework before insurgents had even exerted a powerful presence in the area. Over time, the OHAL region was extended. By 1995, several provinces in eastern Anatolia had been put under its rule. The fact that these additional units presented major challenges to the insurgent group did not factor into the state's decision. In doing so, the OHAL transformed the idea of an ethnic homeland into a visible territory, with the Turkish state effectively carving out a de facto Kurdistan.

Meanwhile, the state's ability to deny access to rebels in the rest of the country hardened boundaries. Several organizational strategies were employed to defend Zone 3. Most important, certain provinces adjacent to OHAL were given a unique administrative status. This bureaucratic irregularity gave the Emergency Governorship a vaguely defined set of rights beyond its immediate jurisdiction.[22] The same rule was also applied to provinces that were removed from the OHAL. The state put these provinces "on probation" and carefully monitored their progress. At the peak of insurgent activity in 1993, the Turkish state came up with another innovation. It appointed coordinator governors in areas where the insurgent group threatened to establish a presence. While providing oversight to counterinsurgency efforts, the main mission of coordinator governors was preemptive. They tried to block rebel activity on the Iranian border and kept a close eye on cosmopolitan cities that received recent Kurdish migrants.[23]

Special Rule

Special regions were administered with a distinct set of rules that set them apart from the rest of the country.[24] This governing strategy sought to eradicate the insurgent threat with a swift and high-powered response. It solved coordination problems, expedited the decision-making process, and punished lawbreakers without mercy. As such, specialist governance was a redress strategy to restore order.[25] There were two striking features of the Turkish experience. First, the OHAL was a security framework operated by a leadership with backgrounds similar to those of its predecessors in Ottoman-Turkish history. Second, despite the continuity in specialist governance, the OHAL's priorities were episodic. The Turkish state returned to its past practices when a particular strategy did not work.

When the emergency region was first announced in 1987, the central state knew how to govern it. A supergovernor was assigned to administer eight provinces in contentious southeastern Anatolia. As with its boundaries, the OHAL also borrowed its governing style from the First Inspectorate of the early Republican period. The supergovernor was a bureaucrat vested with extensive powers who would implement drastic measures in close cooperation with the central government. Hayri Kozakçıoğlu fit the bill. Like his predecessor in the interwar era, he was a trusted ally of Ankara, had previous experience in the region, and came from the civil bureaucracy tradition. A government decree (number 285, July 14, 1987) specified the powers of the supergovernor.[26] He was directly attached to the Ministry of the Interior, became head of all OHAL officials, and supervised security forces. He was also allowed to relocate people and bureaucrats at will. Despite extensive powers, the supergovernor model failed to produce the desired outcomes. Insurgent attacks reached an all-time high in 1991, and the small rebel group, once called "bandits" by statesmen, had transformed into a mass guerrilla force.

In the wake of these developments, another legislative effort (1990–1991) redefined the responsibilities of the supergovernor. The state's main goal was to cut the growing ties between civilians and insurgents. A new government decree (number 430, December 16, 1990) allowed the supergovernor to relocate people on a massive scale, change administrative boundaries, and ban economic boycotts and "unfit" publications.[27] More important, civilians accused of helping the insurgents faced major penalties. They could be jailed for longer terms and taken into custody on the recommendation of the Emergency Governorship. Finally, the decisions of the interior minister and supergovernor could not be challenged in court.[28] The hardening stance of the state toward noncombatants relied on historical precedent. As one parliamentarian admitted, the Turkish state replicated the Fourth Inspectorate model, which constituted the peak of Republican counterinsurgency efforts.[29] Like the first governor of Tunceli, the supergovernor now embodied the powers of both a civil bureaucrat and a military commander. Nevertheless, a greater concentration of power did not lead to better results. Within a few months of his installation, the press was complaining that the new governor, Ali Çetinkaya, was coming increasingly under the influence of security forces.[30] An insurgent attack in Istanbul on a business that he was affiliated with brought an abrupt end to his term. The state had to find new ways to address the growing insurgent threat in 1992.

At the peak of PKK insurgency, the state's solution was military pacification. The Turkish state returned to the basic pattern of Ottoman centralization: eliminate the insurgent threat on military grounds first, and then secure the area with economic initiatives. With this vision in mind, special teams were expanded, the Gendarmerie for Internal Security (İç Asayiş Jandarma Kolordu Komutanlığı) took effective control of security operations, and several military units were deployed in the area. The choice of Ünal Erkan as the new governor of the OHAL reflected the priorities of the state, which operated with security objectives and delegated leadership to the military. The government facilitated the transition by devolving powers from the supergovernor to the provincial governors. This move, which was praised in Turkey's official circles, consolidated the leadership of the military in the war against the PKK. Accordingly, special teams and gendarmerie forces acted on their own with little bureaucratic oversight.[31]

The final episode of the OHAL (1996–2002) had a different set of priorities. By 1995, it had became clear that the rebels had no chance of winning the war militarily. The number of insurgent attacks had fallen below pre-1987 figures, and the Turkish army was chasing the rebels both inside and outside the country. Once again, the new governor chosen for the emergency region signaled the transition. In his first meeting with ministers in Ankara, Necati Bilican, the new supergovernor, called for an "Economic Emergency Zone," downplaying the security threat.[32] With this new outlook, economic and social programs were planned to lift up the region. A government program was initiated to encourage the return of displaced people to their villages; district governors explored ways to boost local economies; and the supergovernor asked for positive economic discrimination for the troubled region. Yet there was limited time to undo the war's devastating consequences. The scale of internal migration was too big to manage, and efforts toward economic regeneration produced few concrete results.

When OHAL was finally dismantled in 2002, it left behind a territory with a distinct identity. Contrary to the state's expectations, and similar to the fate of the Special Military Zone (Daerah Operasi Militer, 1977–1998) in Aceh, Indonesia, special rule practices and specialist governance contributed to zone making. They cemented the differences between the special region and the rest of the country. Meanwhile, the state used other organizational tools to manage the rebellion. Redistricting was perhaps the least known but most common form.

Redistricting

The Turkish state has used redistricting policy extensively since the nineteenth century. This administrative solution was evident in Dersim, a contentious territory in the heart of Anatolia in the late Ottoman period.[33] Created as a *sancak* in the 1880s, Dersim became a province toward the end of the century and reverted back to district status with the founding of the Republic.[34] By 1935, it was a new province with a different name, administrative center, and boundaries. Although extreme, the story of Dersim was not exceptional. Since the enactment of the Ottoman Provincial Law (1864), the state had upgraded and downgraded administrative units at will, moved their centers without hesitation, and created new ones from scratch.[35] Administrative rearrangements neither reflected local sensibilities nor increased efficiency in the provision of public goods. Instead, the state used redistricting primarily as a political instrument to address security challenges.[36] The Turkish state strongly believed that this administrative tool would play a fundamental role in gaining geopolitical advantage in borderlands and containing insurgent movements in sensitive areas.[37]

In the interwar era, redistricting emerged as a policy tool for managing interstate competition on the border. Turkish statesmen sought to consolidate a nationalist geography at a time when new political boundaries did not converge with social realities in the Middle East. During his long tenure as prime minister (1923–1924, 1925–1937), İsmet İnönü promoted the creation of large administrative units to counter French influence on the Syrian border.[38] He believed that new centers of attraction (*cazibe merkezi*) would be the ultimate panacea for French-supported Kurdish-Armenian movements originating in Syria. Soon after, the Turkish state disbanded the *sancak* of Alexandretta, which it had acquired from Syria in the 1930s, and named its new province Hatay. Hatay's administrative center was moved to Antioch in an effort to weaken Syrian claims and integrate this cosmopolitan province firmly into Turkey.[39] A similar logic was at play in the Turkish Caucasus, which was under Russian rule toward the end of the nineteenth century (1878–1914). Suspicious of continued Russian influence in the region, the Turkish state elevated Artvin (Çoruh) to provincial status and then created a special region (Third Inspectorate) in the larger Black Sea area to dismantle regional economic ties.[40]

Containing insurgency through territorial control was the most cru-
cial goal of redistricting. Historically speaking, the Ottoman-Turkish
state relied on this tactic to manage and, if possible, minimize insurgent
damage. The state scaled down administrative units where it anticipated
future rebel activity. Its rationale was to deny insurgents easy victories
in administrative centers, which could delegitimize the state and undermine its presence. This was obvious in Genç province, which was quickly
captured by rebels in the Şeyh Said Rebellion. Republican leaders acted
with vengeance. They downgraded Genç to district status and banned its
high-ranking civil servants from state service.[41] The province of Hakkari,
which was open to cross-border attacks from Kurdish tribes, suffered the
same fate in the 1930s.[42] The state also attached sensitive districts to provinces that were considered to be secure and loyal. For example, it attached
Bingöl to Elazığ in 1926 and to Muş in 1929 in the aftermath of the Şeyh
Said Rebellion.[43] Elazığ in particular hosted populations that were mostly
Turkish in origin whose interests were closely aligned with those of the
central state.

The Turkish state relied on administrative redistricting as a policy
against the PKK insurgency as well. This found its most dramatic application in Şırnak. This border district experienced the highest percentage of
insurgent attacks in the 1980s.[44] Şırnak was given provincial status in 1990.
The new province was carved out of Siirt and incorporated several contentious border districts. As the supergovernor later made clear, this counterinsurgency move rested on a containment strategy and served a common
security goal: to increase the size, efficiency, and coordination of military
operations. The Şırnak bill quickly passed in the TBMM, as strong historical precedents informed legislators' votes.[45] In the interwar era, Dersim had been upgraded to a province to eliminate tribal-Zaza resistance.[46]
Guided by similar concerns, the late Ottoman state had carved out Diyar-ı
Zor province in northern Syria. This administrative unit became instrumental in controlling the tribal movements that threatened Aleppo and
disrupted long-distance trade between Anatolia and Syria for decades.[47]

Turkish leaders also strengthened administrative units to preempt insurgent expansion. They upgraded Iğdır and Ardahan to provincial status
in 1992. These cities were located on the Armenian and Iranian borders,
where the Turkish state had a tense relationship with its neighbors.[48] In
the 1990s, the PKK made an elaborate effort in these border provinces.

To transform these areas, the rebels relied on village raids to win local allies. Yet a timely counterinsurgency response prevented the insurgents from accomplishing their goals. Village raids achieved limited success in mobilizing intercommunal rivalries, and the state's diplomatic efforts weakened cross-border support for the rebel group. Early administrative upgrading that deepened state's military presence played an integral part in these efforts.

Finally, redistricting was a state policy designed to divide the target territory. Faced with rebel expansion beyond Zone 1, the state elevated Batman to provincial status in 1990. Although Batman's increasing economic clout and demographic size also factored into the decision, the underlying rationale was to put a major roadblock in the path of the insurgents. Within a few years, it became clear that local officials were secretly assisting Hezbollah, a religious insurgent group, as a way to weaken the PKK's presence in the province.[49] Seen in that light, administrative rearrangement served to mobilize preexisting identity boundaries against the rebels. This organizational tactic also had historical precedents. Located in the heart of Kurdish geography, Muş became a province in 1930. In the late Ottoman period, Muş was mostly populated by Armenians. Mass deportations during World War I enabled the new Turkish state to change the region's demography by settling Muslim-Turkish migrants from the Balkans and the Caucasus.[50] As early Republican leaders envisioned, Muş served as a buffer between different Kurdish identities in the region (the Kurdish core in Botan, Zaza-speaking groups in Dersim, and Islamist Kurds in east-central Anatolia) and denied Kurdish contention the chance of geographical unity.

As the Muş example illustrates, redistricting contributed most to counterinsurgency efforts when the central state found local allies within the new boundaries.[51] However, local support that came solely from influential families, for example, the Tatar tribe in Şırnak during the 1990s, was not sufficient to stop the PKK. Viewed from a long-term perspective, redistricting did not deliver the intended outcomes. It failed as an organizational response to geopolitical pressure. Redistricting also had limited use in containing insurgency, and gave security forces only short-term advantages. The rebels had no difficulty in shifting their operations elsewhere after new boundaries were established.[52] More critically, redistricting could not set the territory under question on a new track. Without changing socioeconomic and demographic realities on the ground, this policy utterly failed to "sterilize" sites of resistance.

Abandoning the Countryside

Another organizational response to insurgent threat was the relinquishing of control over rural areas. In the 1990s, the Turkish state began to depopulate the countryside to cut insurgents' logistical support. Thousands were forced to leave their homes; access to pastures and meadows was banned; and in some areas, such as Tunceli, food consumption was supervised by local authorities.[53] Abandoning the countryside relied on the principles of specialist governance and was implemented in the emergency region. As with special rule and redistricting practices, emptying rural units was planned as an administrative rearrangement. It aimed at reclustering territory and people to weaken the insurgency. State officials promised to create larger and more secure administrative units by combining and disbanding existing settlements. However, relocation never materialized. Internal displacement remained the main form of the state's retreat. This created a mixed outcome for the Turkish state: it helped block insurgent expansion, but the same process turned Kurdish towns into political opponents of the state.

The Ottoman-Turkish state activated the policy of forced displacement whenever it faced the threat of a major rebellion. Still, the form and the consequences of this policy changed over time. For the most part, the Ottoman state relied on an exile strategy and singled out a few community leaders for fostering social unrest. Like the Yemeni Imams, they were temporarily transferred to other parts of the empire and were assigned to state service.[54] In the interwar period, the Turkish Republic treated uncooperative community leaders as a distinct group of people with common traits. Blamed for brokering communal mobilizations, they were relocated to other parts of Turkey. Unlike the Ottoman practice, relocation efforts in the Turkish Republic involved larger numbers of people who were settled into "loyal territory," based on a master plan.[55] This was the result of a new way of thinking about contention: The Republicans put the blame squarely on social status groups (such as tribes) and held their members as well as their leaders accountable.

The most dramatic form of emptying the countryside occurred when the state feared the worst outcome: a social rebellion where the entire community could support or take part in a mass mobilization against the central state. Kurds in the 1990s and the Armenians in the late Ottoman period shared the same fate in this regard. Both communities were uprooted, and internal displacement rather than relocation defined their experience. This organizational response sought to cut the political ties between a revolutionary group and the larger community. The state response exhibited two broad patterns. First, the Turkish state increasingly relied on indiscriminate targeting to punish contenders. Second, communal uprooting was put into practice only when the state perceived a serious political threat to its survival.[56]

Internal displacement in the 1990s also had unique features. The most reliable estimates suggest that approximately one million people left their homes because of the war.[57] The state accepted responsibility for uprooting one-third of this group, which corresponded to roughly 50,000 households. Forced migration was a rural phenomenon. Close to 30 percent of all rural units in the OHAL region were depopulated.[58] Hamlets, rather than villages, were the main targets.[59] According to official statistics, security forces evacuated more than 2,500 hamlets. Forced migration meant emptying the rural unit and in some cases involved burning the village. As a recent survey confirms, abandoning the countryside became a systematic policy only after 1991, when the PKK significantly stepped up its attacks. Viewed in spatial terms, this was a policy to block insurgent expansion. More than two-thirds of the local population displaced by the state were located in the contested Zone 2.[60] Tunceli bore the brunt of this policy.[61] As we saw in chapter 3, this was the province the insurgents attempted to turn into a second Botan in the 1990s.

The Turkish state failed to handle forced migration in an orderly fashion. There was little supervision and coordination of village evacuations, as decision making was delegated to security forces operating at the local level. Even the supergovernor of the OHAL later confessed that he never authorized the relocation of villagers in the countryside.[62] Still, evacuations were swift. There was no record keeping, and, in most situations, villagers had to leave in less than a week.[63] The state promised to solve the settlement issue. Since the 1980s, several megaprojects had been announced to achieve that goal. "Central-Villages," "Village-Cities," and "Village Farms" were some of the names given to the same idea: building large and secure administrative units to settle displaced people in the countryside.[64] These projects, however, never saw the light of day. They were too costly, and, perhaps more important, the state had second thoughts about building new rural units.[65] Historically speaking, the state lacked cooperative relations with the countryside, especially in the frontier regions, and the realities of war dictated a different set of priorities. Unable and/or unwilling to relocate rural populations, the state left thousands to their own devices.

One of the dramatic consequences of state's retreat was demographic dislocation. More than 600,000 villagers were forced to go through the same experience. Seeking protection, they migrated to district centers as the closest destination. This was especially the case in the border provinces, located in Zone 1. Accordingly, all district centers recorded dramatic increases in urban population during the 1990s. For instance, the population of Silopi increased fourfold in fifteen years (1985–2000) when its surrounding areas became a fighting ground.[66] In other cases, displaced people preferred to go to provincial centers and brought the misery of war to urban settings. Diyarbakır especially attracted migrants from its northern districts, such as Lice and Silvan. Others decided to go beyond the boundaries of the OHAL and settled in large cities such as Adana and Mersin. For instance, two-thirds of Pülümür's rural population left Tunceli province altogether. Migrants created closed communities in their new environments. The slums in the Seyhan district of Adana, where population density was fifteen times higher than the provincial average, reminded them of their differences from the rest of the city's residents.[67] Clustered in ghetto neighborhoods or in urban centers with poor infrastructure, the visitors nonetheless decided to stay.[68]

Economic problems defined the experience of migrants in urban centers. They had to shoulder the cost of resettlement on their own. In fact, the state's poor record keeping made it impossible for villagers to claim compensation for their assets such as houses and agricultural land that were damaged or fell into disuse because of armed conflict.[69] Soon, large migrant households faced another problem. Most of their members lacked the skills to compete in urban labor markets. With a rural background from a frontier region, migrants had had limited contacts with state institutions and national markets in the past. For example, more than 80 percent of all rural migrants were at best elementary school graduates. Poverty became their destiny. More than half of them became unemployed; the number of homeowners declined dramatically; and, like the rest of the region's residents, they relied on government assistance (Green Cards) to cover their health costs.[70]

Meanwhile, the city transformed the migrant Kurdish household. Once they were exposed to city life, women and youth began challenging social hierarchies that favored the older male in the family. Despite the misery migration brought, the city also opened up new horizons to both groups. Individual freedoms were not the only gains, however. A new political universe was slowly emerging in urban centers during the 1990s.

Forced migration contributed to the emergence of a Kurdish political identity. As internally displaced people poured into urban centers, a nationalist leadership began to take shape. Kurdish nationalists increasingly controlled important towns, key venues for state authority in the emergency region. Meanwhile, in Zone 1, where friend-foe distinctions mattered, the Kurdish nationalist party found a mass following. Still, the impact of these provinces on Kurdish politics was limited. They neither hosted urban leaderships that promoted the nationalist cause nor had a demographic size that could make a strong case for a Kurdish nation. Elsewhere in Turkey, the groups most sympathetic to the nationalist cause were found in migrant ghettos. In the name of political ideals, these neighborhoods lent support to the insurgent organization, hoping to address their resentment of the past and alienation from the present.

The Turkish state has long viewed domestic unrest with a sense of urgency. Since the late Ottoman period, it has considered rebellion a direct threat to its survival. In response, the state reorganized territory to win the war against insurgents. Most prominently, it designated special administrative regions that were organized around a security logic. Informed by medical approaches, the political rationale was to keep the threat in a controlled environment (quarantine) and then remove it with shock therapy. The treatment was administered by a superexecutive, a high-profile bureaucrat who was vested with extensive powers. Superexecutives saved the central state from potential principal-agent issues and solved coordination problems in the implementation phase. Turkish statesmen believed that thorough treatment would erase the distinct character of the region and eventually integrate it into the rest of the country.

Negative sanctioning, however, failed to eliminate insurgency. Contrary to the intentions of the central state, this specialist response, which operated with a distinct set of institutional practices, consolidated a contentious universe and separated its experience from the rest of the country. Yet to the state's benefit, the same policy divided the Kurdish experience in spatial terms and sealed the majority of Kurds from insurgent influence. Boundary making, however, was not simply territorial. As the next chapter will demonstrate, counterinsurgency ideology also subscribed to a specialist vision in an attempt to control people. Operating with friend-foe distinctions in the emergency region, it would divide Kurdish society from within.

5

IDEOLOGY

Counterinsurgency is not a value-neutral enterprise. States develop deep-rooted ideologies about insurgencies. Framing the conflict allows the state to label the enemy and formulate a plan of action.[1] In that respect, counterinsurgency discourse works as a powerful tool that informs state action in several ways.[2] This cognitive framework, however, is neither universal nor incident specific. It relies on historical information. As slow learners with a long record, states borrow from their own experience to make sense of an insurgency. Fixed perceptions constrain the number of options and give counterinsurgency efforts a certain order. In this chapter we make two points about the way states view insurgencies and how they respond to them. First, we demonstrate that state perceptions follow a path-dependent character with strong historical lineages. Second, we suggest that, despite its short-term advantages, this unique quality makes state response rigid and inefficient in the long run.[3]

A product of a multiethnic and multireligious empire, the Turkish Republic has inherited a rich history of contentious collective action. When

Kurdish rebels made their first appearance in the 1980s, the central state had no difficulty in framing them: they were political bandits who lived in the mountains with foreign assistance. This label produced a distinct state response. The state promised top-down transformation to eliminate the basis of rebellion, yet favored a co-optation model when pressed hard by security threats. The Ottoman-Turkish elite were committed to a developmentalist agenda that would civilize the Kurds and bring peace and prosperity to these backward regions. Still, in the face of a domestic threat, they were willing to subcontract state functions to intermediaries and channel resources to local allies. The hybrid character of Turkish counterinsurgency, which selectively borrowed from each solution set, shaped an important political outcome. It sealed the divided character of Kurdish areas while neither achieving full integration nor granting regional autonomy.[4]

We start by discussing the historical origins of Turkish counterinsurgency discourse. The first two sections illustrate the rural bias of the Turkish state in locating contentious action and show that it has held outside world responsible for mustering domestic unrest in the country. We then explain how these views translated into policy. The third section explores the developmentalist logic of the Ottoman-Turkish elite that promoted centralization to remedy the problem. The final section brings to light the backup plan of the state elite, emphasizing the willingness of the central authority to bargain with traditional actors when an insurgent threat is perceived as a foreign plot.

Rural Bias

The Turkish state viewed Kurdish insurgents as primitive rebels. Belonging to the past, they were armed men from the mountains who disrupted social peace by destroying people's property and attacking state officials. They were few in numbers, lived in a state of nature, and were isolated from the community. Government officials assured the public that the troublemakers would disappear from history with no chance of return. In doing so, the state refused to acknowledge the modern origins of the insurgency.[5] In an attempt to discredit the movement, President Turgut Özal once called them "two and a half bandits."[6] In a similar fashion, the public ignored the ethnic character of the insurgent movement, viewing it solely as a brigand group. The state's bandit frame was not simply a strategy to minimize the political clout of insurgency in its early years. Its main function was preemptive. The Turkish state categorically denied the rebels the right to politically represent the Kurdish community and sent strong signals to civilians about the illegitimacy of the insurgent group.

Rural bias in the counterinsurgency narrative stemmed from the urban character of Ottoman-Turkish state formation. Urban governance defined the mental boundaries of the Turkish state and was the key indicator of the state's political performance. For instance, the late Ottoman state could not effectively tax, count, and recruit the rural populations of Anatolia in the nineteenth century, whereas it had long-lasting political bargains with urban groups.[7] This historical trend continued after the founding of the Turkish Republic in 1923. The new state was quick to discover that rural communities were unmoved by its revolutionary zeal. In the countryside, the state's bureaucratic apparatus was weak, and Republican ideals did not carry much ideological weight. State-society interactions were limited in scope, and regional realities, folk Islam, and peripheral leaderships mattered more to locals. Yakup Kadri Karaosmanoğlu, a celebrated Turkish novelist and a member of the Turkish ruling elite in the interwar era, captured this reality in *Yaban*. The novel told the story of an army officer, a disillusioned war hero, who had to come to terms with the indifference of the rural masses to the nationalist cause.[8]

The urban character of the Turkish state turned the countryside into a site of systemic threats in the eyes of government officials. Not surprisingly, counterinsurgency discourse viewed peripheral movements and tribal uprisings as major challenges to state survival.[9] This reading has historical precedents. Building on Ibn-Khaldun's ideas, Ernest Gellner showed that for centuries the political universe of Islamic societies was structured around tribal threats.[10] The Ottoman-Turkish state experienced the rural challenge in two distinct ways. First, the state had to deal with tribal unrest that opposed centralization measures. Tribal leaderships resisted the state's efforts to monopolize coercion, collect taxes, and penetrate into local communities. Roving bandits successfully repelled the late Ottoman state at the frontiers, but they were soundly defeated in the interwar era.[11] Second, the late Ottoman state encountered a different type of insurgency in the 1890s. Under the leadership of educated groups, Macedonian and

Armenian nationalists built powerful revolutionary organizations in the countryside that consolidated communal identity and mobilized peasants for uprisings against state authority.[12] Framed as political bandits in state discourse, these nationalists were not simply defending themselves against the encroachment of a central state; they were making new claims that were territorial in nature.

The state tried to solve the rural question in innovative ways. In direct contrast to the European experience, the Ottomans built a centralized army, relied on the small peasantry for political support, and rotated imperial bureaucrats to prevent the rise of powerful interests in the provinces during its classical age (1300–1600).[13] In the modern era, the central state tried to penetrate into rural communities by installing village headmen (*muhtar*), an Ottoman political invention in the modern Middle East. The founders of the Republic took one step further, sending teachers into villages and founding Village Institutes to transform the countryside.[14] The central state justified its policies with a discourse of top-down transformation. First, tribal organization, which was at the heart of rural hierarchy, was considered obsolete in the modern world. Second, local practices such as rent-seeking by local notables and landlords were criminalized.[15] In this way, the Turkish Republic deployed a progressive ideology to topple its rural rivals.

Citizenship was the final move of the Republic to eliminate peripheral actors in the countryside.[16] Top-down in nature, the Turkish citizenship model promised equality before the law, where each individual could claim to be a proud member of the nation. Irrespective of their social origins, citizens were then entitled to the same rights and were bounded by similar responsibilities.[17] This legal framework freed individuals from all sorts of communal pressures, weakening the social leverage that religious and tribal leaders enjoyed over their communities in the Ottoman period. Although it was revolutionary in content, the Turkish citizenship model had a major flaw. It left no room for the representation of collective identities. Being a Kurd, a religious *şeyh*, or a tribal leader received no recognition in the public sphere. With this strategic move, the Republican elite solved the thorny issue of communal rights and categorically denied the possibility of making political claims in the future.

This historical record informed the way the Turkish state approached the PKK. Sticking to its citizenship model, the state disputed the idea that

Kurdish insurgents were making ethnic claims.[18] The state narrative high-lighted stories of Turkish citizens of Kurdish origin who faced no ethnic discrimination, citing successful Kurdish businessmen and politicians in the public sphere.[19] Meanwhile, counterinsurgency discourse labeled in-surgents as bandits. The leadership of the PKK was presented through the lens of previous religious-tribal groups who had mobilized masses for personal gain. As in the interwar era, the state tried to persuade the rank and file that they were being misled by greedy leaders who lacked a higher goal.[20] The state narrative also alerted civilians that insurgency put their communal solidarity at risk. As public officials repeatedly claimed, rebels were in fact "Armenians," "godless heretics," and/or "communists" who threatened the Kurdish community at its core.[21]

The prerequisite for the citizenship model to work was the protection of urban areas from the insurgency. Large cities hosted millions of Kurds, and the state's political universe in Kurdish areas was limited to major towns. Accordingly, the central state was afraid of political mobilizations in urban settings. As the PKK expanded the conflict in the early 1990s, the Turkish state had a clear understanding of insurgent goals: penetration of insurgency into cities made its bandit narrative useless and undermined its community-neutral citizenship discourse. This development would open the door for group-specific rights and justify rebel claims to represent the Kurds. Subsequently, the state would be forced to recognize a Kurdish na-tion under the leadership of the insurgent organization and give in to an autonomy arrangement.[22]

With this threat in mind, the Turkish state was determined to dislodge the rebels from urban areas. At the top of the urban hierarchy, Istanbul with its cosmopolitan demographics became the state's first priority. Peri-odic arrests of PKK members confirmed this approach and earned the city the highest rank in arrest cases despite a limited rebel presence. Counter-insurgency efforts also targeted cities where Kurds had recently migrated and lived in impoverished neighborhoods. Using tactics such as infiltration and detention, police forces tried to block the PKK's community orga-nizing efforts. The state used tougher measures in OHAL towns. These were places where political competition between the state and rebels had been fierce. Security forces tried to uproot the urban branch of the PKK (ERNK), especially in border towns, and brutally crushed civilian unrest, leaving hundreds dead at protest sites.[23]

In sum, its rural bias prompted the Turkish state to secure urban settings first and label the enemy as bandits living in the mountains. However, the state narrative did not always identify the countryside as the only source of country's troubles. As the insurgent organization expanded in the early 1990s, counterinsurgency discourse elevated the sense of urgency. The state now characterized the PKK as a serious threat that had foreign connections. History once again informed this discursive shift. The PKK no longer belonged on the list of roving bandits like the Kurdish tribal opposition of the interwar era. Rather, it came to occupy a unique place in collective memory. As with Armenian and Macedonian revolutionary movements of the late Ottoman period, Kurdish insurgents were named as political bandits who aimed to destroy the territorial unity of the state with the help of foreign powers.

Blaming Foreign Sponsors

The counterinsurgency discourse of the 1990s viewed Kurdish insurgency as a foreign-sponsored terrorist activity to divide Turkey. Despite their political differences, Turkish governments consistently referred to foreign powers as the major cause of the Kurdish problem. The public shared these sentiments. Several independent surveys conducted throughout the 1990s reported that the majority of Turkish citizens considered the PKK to be a foreign-sponsored violent group.[24] This plain but effective idea missed the domestic origins of the Kurdish issue. From the vantage point of counterinsurgency, though, it served practical purposes. The state narrative tried to convince the masses that the state's political survival was at stake. This could also be read as a warning for civilian supporters of the insurgency: By presenting the rebel group as a proxy for foreign powers, the Turkish state made clear that it now considered the PKK to be a national issue and therefore a loyalty test for its citizens.[25]

The idea of foreign influence is deeply entrenched in the Turkish pysche.[26] The fact that the Ottomans lost an empire after a long struggle against colonialism and could save only Anatolia with the War of Independence (1919–1922) has shaped the way Turks view domestic disturbances.[27] The state narrative put the blame squarely on Western powers for destroying the Ottoman Empire. In particular, Europeans were accused of having provided a hospitable environment for group claims against the late Ottoman state. The propaganda efforts of Armenian revolutionaries were a case in point. Revolutionary groups located in several European cities were busy planning an armed insurrection in Ottoman territories at the turn of the twentieth century. They established political branches, became involved in arms trafficking, and built close relations with European leaders.[28] As one counterinsurgency document later explained, the Ottoman state thought that European audiences were misled by insurgent propaganda, confused the views of Ottoman-Armenian subjects with those of the Armenian revolutionaries, and turned a blind eye to the violent nature of the Armenian struggle.[29]

Another lasting legacy of the Ottoman experience was the minority issue. The state narrative pointed fingers at Europeans for meddling with the affairs of the empire through minorities. As a matter of fact, Europeans did build a special relationship with Christian members of the empire during the nineteenth century. They traded mostly through non-Muslim intermediaries, employed them at consulates as trustworthy locals, and protected their coreligionists, who were believed to be at the mercy of "despotic Ottoman rulers" and "fanatical Muslim masses."[30] Accordingly, Europeans granted citizenship to thousands of Ottoman Christian subjects, became the protector of Christian confessional identities, and sent several missionary groups to the Middle East. The modernizing Ottoman state claimed that this special relationship, which extended communal privileges at the expense of Ottoman brotherhood, was the main reason why Christian subjects of the empire were reluctant to invest in the Ottoman citizenship model. The unmixing of populations in the region with the birth of nation-states and recurrent wars brought a speedy conclusion to the minority issue: There would be no more minorities in Turkey, with the exception of Istanbul Greeks.[31]

Europeans appeared in counterinsurgency discourse with reference to their territorial claims as well. State perceptions once again had strong historical lineages. The Ottoman Empire lost one-third of its territory at the Berlin Congress (1878); the majority of the Balkan states were founded in the aftermath of Russian military victories over the Ottomans (1829 and 1877–1878); and Europeans forcefully took the Middle East from the Ottomans in World War I.[32] Perhaps more important, imperialist powers planned to partition Anatolia with the Treaty of Sevres in 1920, which would have made Istanbul a neutral zone and distributed the rest among Italy, Britain, France, and Greece. It was the surprising victory of the War of Independence that reversed this fate. Modern Turkey and Europeans continued to fight over territorial issues in the interwar era. Most notably, Turkish statesmen and the public continued to question the League of Nations decision to give Mosul province (northern Iraq) to Iraq as a result of British manipulation and international pressure.[33]

With the escalation of the conflict in the 1990s, the state narrative blamed foreign sponsors of the PKK for the ongoing violence. This was not simply a matter of name-calling. Building on historical memory, state discourse clearly differentiated the type, purpose, and actors of external assistance. As in late Ottoman times, statesmen focused their attention to Europe. Their complaints were similar. Europeans were accused of providing the insurgents with a propaganda opportunity abroad. The Turkish state referred in particular to ERNK activities that had turned the PKK into a political force in Europe and guaranteed diaspora funding to the rebel organization. The state narrative also viewed the European position on the Kurdish issue as an attempt to reinstate the minority framework. Throughout the 1990s, Europeans and Turks continued to quarrel about the status of Kurds in Turkey. Finally, the counterinsurgency discourse alerted the public about the territorial claims of Europeans. This message was clear in 1993 when President Süleyman Demirel compared granting autonomy to Kurds to the re-signing of the Treaty of Sevres.[34] With this move, the president warned citizens that a federative solution was a European scheme to divide Turkey.

The counterinsurgency discourse continued to borrow from history in order to locate the foreign sponsors of insurgency. Former Christian minorities of the Ottoman Empire were blamed for giving logistical support to the PKK. The state narrative turned old enemies of the Empire into untrustworthy neighbors of Turkey. In this view, countries such as Armenia and Greece were trying to settle old accounts through proxies such as the PKK. Minister of the Interior Mehmet Gazioğlu went as far as to claim that the rebel group was in fact an Armenian organization whose goal was to establish Armenia at the heart of the Kurdish populations.[35] The actual role of these countries as foreign sponsors, however, was less than critical if not irrelevant. Greece gave its full support to the PKK at a time when Kurdish rebels were entering a period of precipitous military decline.

Meanwhile, Armenia hosted a smaller number of rebel camps than Syria, Iran, and Iraq, which provided a variety of logistical services to the rebel group. Furthermore, contrary to the accusations of Turkish statesmen, the number of Armenian nationals in insurgent ranks was negligible. Indeed, the rebel leader Öcalan was disappointed about Armenia's reluctance to support the insurgency.[36]

The final set of foreign powers in the state narrative was Turkey's neighbors. The Turkish state accused Iraq, Iran, and Syria of allowing the insurgent group to set up rebel camps, recruit members, and organize cross-border attacks from their territories. Yet the portrayal of these countries was qualitatively different from the way Europeans and Christian minorities were depicted in counterinsurgency discourse. Europe and its domestic allies became eternal enemies of the state because they had presented a formidable challenge to Ottoman state survival and Turkish state-making efforts at a critical time. In contrast, regional states were at best political units that largely flew under the radar. Turkey and Iran had shared the same border since 1621, and Iraq and Syria had been parts of the Ottoman Empire for centuries. As such, the Turkish state relied on a well-entrenched but qualitatively different view for understanding the role and intentions of its neighbors in supporting the insurgency.

Viewed in that light, the Turkish statesmen knew exactly what Iran's position was on the PKK issue: Iran did not want the insurgents to thrive, nor did it want them to founder. When a successful counterinsurgency drive made northern Iraq a dangerous place for the rebel organization (1992–1995), Iran gave the rebel group a lifeline for a few years. Iran's rationale was straightforward: It had its own Kurdish problem but had viewed Turkey as a regional rival since the sixteenth century. Turkish statesmen subscribed to the same idea and interpreted Iran's involvement as a tactic to undermine Turkey's rising position in the region.[37] Meanwhile, the state's view on Iraq drew largely from late Ottoman realities and focused on the Kurdish leaders, Barzani and Talabani, in northern Iraq. Counterinsurgency discourse approached them as opportunistic local leaders from the Ottoman frontier regions. Their ethnic affinity with the rebels was soon forgotten as the Ottoman frontier vision began to guide Turkey's northern Iraq policy.[38] Like its Ottoman predecessor in the Arabian Peninsula, the Turkish state was aware of its limitations in northern Iraq and tried to manipulate local politics. It engaged in temporary alliances with

Barzani and Talabani to defeat the PKK. This tactic failed to produce the desired outcome. State discourse put the blame on Kurdish leaders who lacked a firm commitment to the Turkish cause.

Syria was the key country that provided assistance to the rebel organization. As briefly discussed in chapter 3, it hosted the PKK's leadership for two decades, facilitated the transition of the rebel group into a full-fledged guerrilla force, and encouraged its Kurdish citizens to join insurgent ranks. For a long time, Turkey was confounded by Syria's strong support to the insurgents. Commonsense explanations were neither deep nor satisfactory. Syria was believed to be assisting the insurgents to justify its historic claims over Hatay province or to force Turkey to a settlement over the water issue. The former referred to a territorial dispute over Alexandretta in the 1930s. The latter concerned the waters of the Euphrates River that were controlled by Turkey in the north.[39] The state narrative did not credit the territorial claims of Syria but considered the water dispute to be a practical issue that could be resolved at the negotiating table. With no historical grudges on the Turkish side, two major agreements (1987 and 1993) were signed between the two countries that guaranteed Turkey's security in return for Syrian water rights. However, this political barter did not stop Syria from supporting the rebel organization on several levels until 1998.

In sum, the Turkish state relied on historical discourses to define the identity and motivation of insurgents. While rural bias allowed the central state to depict insurgents as primitive rebels in the countryside, the narrative of foreign sponsors saw insurgency as a dirty fight in the service of foreign powers. This rigidity in the state's understanding of the PKK created two important (but inefficient) outcomes. First, counterinsurgency perceptions missed the domestic and modern origins of the issue. Rebel leaders came from the educated groups in Kurdish society and the rank and file were predominantly Kurdish citizens of Turkey. Yet, these facts did not appear as central elements in the state's analysis. Second, the Turkish state made less-than-intelligent political choices in fighting the insurgency. It gave up too easily on rural areas in the 1980s and failed to put enough pressure on Syria at a critical turning point. Instead, the Turkish state was preoccupied with the protection of urban areas and was committed to eliminating European influence on its internal affairs.

Despite their ineffectiveness, the discourses of rural bias and external assistance informed state action in important ways. The state had a clear game plan as to how to defeat an insurgency.

A Developmentalist Response

The Turkish state viewed insurgency as an unhappy ending to its rural and frontier questions. With the late Ottoman record in recent memory, Republican leaders were convinced that social unrest would eventually erupt on the frontiers, where the central state was traditionally weak and rural social organization was kept intact. The political remedy for the threat of rebellion was regional transformation and modernization of Kurdish areas. This would eliminate the structural bases of discontent and return state–society interactions to a peaceful condition. Unlike European experience in the colonies, regional transformation required channeling state resources to the frontiers.[40] This political vision fostered an integration agenda. The central state pursued a civilizing mission toward the Kurds until the 1950s and had addressed issues of underdevelopment in the region since then.[41] With a colossal task ahead of them, the Turkish elite had a deliberate scheme to implement this grand strategy.

The state's transformation agenda had a unique mode of action. It operated in stages and was implemented in a path-dependent fashion. Historically speaking, military measures pacified a community first; administrative units then attached the area to the center; and economic incentives finally confirmed the loyalty of citizens to the state. Despite the unity of purpose, the reformist plan prioritized military initiatives. This meant that certain reformist measures could be sacrificed or tailored to military logic in difficult times. Still, Turkish statesmen had high expectations for the transformation agenda. They believed that it would lift up the "East" from centuries-old "backwardness" and turn the masses into obedient Republican citizens.

Military pacification was the most important item in counterinsurgency efforts. Centralization policies undermined local leaderships and eroded their power in these communities. Historical examples abound. In the late Ottoman period, the state used military campaigns to re-Ottomanize eastern Anatolia, Iraq, and Syria. The Turkish Republic preserved the same tradition. The state defeated the Şeyh Said Rebellion and conducted more than a dozen counterinsurgency operations to subdue Kurdish dissent in the interwar era.[42] Each operation was followed by an elaborate attempt to disarm the community. Facing little pressure from abroad, Republican counterinsurgency perfected Ottoman methods and built an active interest in the post-conflict phase. Accordingly, the central state extended the boundaries of its exile strategy to include communal deportations and designated no-entry zones such as Sason in southeastern Anatolia. This was the site where the Ottoman state had crushed a powerful Armenian resistance in 1894 with the support of Kurdish tribes.[43]

The next item on the state's agenda was the installation of a bureaucratic machine in dissident areas. Local bureaucrats and military advisors advised the state to build barracks, roads, and bridges to facilitate troop movements. Historical evidence from Basra to Yemen in late Ottoman times confirms the validity of this call.[44] Soon after, communication emerged as a critical issue to bridge the information gap between the center and the local. In the late nineteenth century, the telegraph became a favorite technology of state agents. The central state then installed bureaucrats in newly created administrative units to penetrate deeper into the community. The transformation of the Druze Mountain in the 1890s and Dersim in the 1930s from hotbeds of resistance to state-ruled territories followed this trajectory.[45] Once an area was secure, the state introduced education and health services. The founders of the Republic had a greater state capacity at their disposal and personally knew the power of education in constructing identities.[46] As such, the Republican project went beyond the mere provision of public goods. As its rivals were also aware, with this strategic move the central state was trying to transform the countryside/frontiers in its own image.

Finally, public officials pursued an aggressive economic program to crown the state's efforts toward integration. Economic change would attach the common folk to the state by eliminating intermediary groups. This took several forms. The late Ottoman state waged a permanent war against racketeers from Anatolia to Palestine to uphold security and order in the countryside. A few decades later, the Turkish state worked hard to build the infrastructure that was necessary for promoting trade and agriculture. In fact, the Republican history is full of state proposals that carefully analyzed the prospects for development in backward areas.[47] The most radical of all was to solve the agrarian question by liquidating large landlordism. In this vein, a reformist statesman, Midhat Paşa, attempted—albeit unsuccessfully—to distribute tribal lands in Iraq with the introduction of the Ottoman Land Code of 1858.[48] The Republican elite also promised but later backed down from implementing land reform in the 1940s, which would have given publicly owned land to the rural poor.

The Turkish state presented the developmentalist response as the ultimate cure for the PKK problem. Military measures still took the largest share of counterinsurgency efforts. The state spent most of its energy on border protection in the 1980s. This tactic, however, had limited success because it proved impossible to seal the Iraqi border.[49] As the insurgent organization grew increasingly powerful in the countryside, the state accelerated its forced migration policy. By 1992, the Turkish state was convinced that the existing template was not winning the war against the PKK. As a result, military measures were taken to the next level. Military technology was dramatically updated; an offensive tactic was implemented; and military leadership was put in charge of the civilian bureaucracy.[50]

Military priorities shaped administrative practices as well. With the escalation of the conflict, the state found it necessary to modernize its transportation and communication networks. The governors of the OHAL fully subscribed to the center's proposal and saw this as an opportunity to solve the information problem in the region. Roads were built to reach most remote locations, especially west of Mardin province, and telephones were distributed to several villages with confirmed loyalties.[51] The state also relied on administrative redistricting to contain insurgency. It created new provinces such as Şırnak and Batman. Despite increasing pressure from the insurgents, boarding schools continued to operate in the region, and education resumed when the rebel group lost most of its fighting capabilities after 1999.

State officials shared the common belief that economic transformation would weaken the PKK and solve the Kurdish issue. Aided by theories of underdevelopment from the 1960s, this was Turkish developmentalist discourse at its best. The Turkish state tried a variety of strategies to bolster the region's economy and improve living standards. The state provided easy financing to entrepreneurs to create employment. Turkey also continued to invest in the largest infrastructure project in the Middle East, the Southeast Anatolia Project (GAP), which President Demirel praised as the shining symbol of Turkish-Kurdish brotherhood.[52] Turkish statesmen also attempted to build economic centers to lift up poor provinces. Finally, cross-border trade with northern Iraq was promoted. Bülent Ecevit, a seasoned politician with a respectable career in Turkish politics, offered the most radical view on this issue. A true Republican, he believed that economic transformation—which included land reform and state-led industrialization—would eliminate the intermediary feudal class. This would then put the region on an equal ground with the rest of the country, allowing the Republic to fulfill its egalitarian promises.[53]

The developmentalist agenda, which had its roots in a civilizing ideology and sought national integration, was never fully implemented. The Turkish state made inroads into the Kurdish community by pacifying it, setting up administrative structures, and providing public goods. But these attempts were limited at best. Despite temporary setbacks, traditional leaderships survived; exiled bureaucrats ran administrative units; and public goods remained mostly inaccessible in rural areas. With the exception of cross-border trade, the economic initiatives of the 1990s did not produce significant results, either.[54] This arrested transformation was not simply an issue of state capacity, it was also the result of the state's political choices.[55] The state backed down from its revolutionary zeal with multiparty politics in the Cold War era and reduced its reformist stand to military initiatives in the 1990s. Half measures created an important outcome: A group of individuals from Kurdistan rose to the national stage. They did not command the type of capital that traditional leaders controlled within Kurdish society, and they were unimpressed with the career plans that the Republic envisioned for them. Educated youth would challenge the state and traditional leaderships in ways that neither could foresee.

The Backup Plan: Co-optation

The Turkish state had no special reason to worry about the political prospects of Kurdish youth. They were part of the leftist university movement in the 1970s and appeared to be a few eccentric adventurers in the early 1980s. Intellectual debates and romantic ideas about armed struggle defined their political experience. Yet a successful campaign of guerrilla warfare toward the end of the 1980s changed the way the state approached the rebels. Borrowing from its past, the central state reintroduced a co-optation model to eliminate a domestic threat. The heightened sense of security was evident in state circles. Statesmen increasingly emphasized foreign sponsors of insurgent activity rather than its traditional credentials and were primarily interested in recruiting local allies instead of completing the agenda for regional transformation. The co-optation model was designed as a short-term strategy for defeating an actual insurgency. In return, it sealed the divided character of the region by making a clear distinction between friends and foes.[56]

Local allies had a unique place in Turkish counterinsurgency efforts. They emerged at a time when the state lacked the military capacity to manage threats in a contentious territory. The most important item of cooperation was security. The late Ottoman state counted on tribal support for its centralization campaigns in Iraq, and the Republican administration pacified Kurdish dissent with the help of other Kurdish tribes in the interwar period.[57] In both cases, statesmen used the competitive tribal model to their favor by recruiting local partners as militia forces. Although this mechanism was widely used, it was not institutionalized. The only exception occurred in the 1890s when the central state became convinced that its political survival was at stake. Abdulhamid II established Hamidian cavalry regiments to fight Armenian insurgents in eastern Anatolia.[58] Regiments were selected from weaker tribes and were concentrated in zones of Armenian contention. Subcontracting defense functions to private actors led to unintended consequences. As the regiments began to pursue their own interests, they solidified social divisions in the region. They built boundaries between Muslims and non-Muslims and pitted regiment tribes against other military units.

Shouldering the security mission, local allies expected material benefits. Ottoman rulers turned a blind eye to their illegal practices and provided new channels of empowerment. For example, Hamidian cavalry regiments were given free rein to collect protection fees from Armenian peasants and eliminate rival tribes. Religious entrepreneurs (*nakşibendi şeyhs*) were given tax-farms for the same reason. The Ottoman sultan thought that they could act as a barrier to Armenian and Christian missionary influences in the region.[59] In the early Republican period, tribal leaders, such as the Tatars of Şırnak, guaranteed their survival by allying with the state at a time when other tribes were being crushed by the state's centralization efforts. In the Cold War era, political parties made a deal with large landlords and tribal leaders and thereby confirmed the economic and political privileges of an intermediary group in return for national integration.

The final aspect of the co-optation model was to confer legitimacy on local allies of the state. Abdulhamid II realized the role of ideology in certifying local friends. He fortified the ranks of religious brotherhoods in eastern Anatolia via a pan-Islamic discourse.[60] This moral compatibility elevated the social status of religious entrepreneurs in the region and justified their political activity against the nation-building efforts of Armenian nationalists. Meanwhile, faced with Kurdish dissent in the interwar era, the Republic refused to promote a similar state ideology. A decisive military victory seemed more feasible than the co-optation model. The insurgent threat was weaker than the Armenian movement of the 1890s, and the international context favored the nation-state. Furthermore, the Turkish state was not in a position to develop such an ideology in the 1930s. The Republican elite had already kick-started a full-fledged nation-building agenda, which left no room for subnational or supranational identities.

The co-optation model informed the way the state had responded to the PKK threat since the 1980s. The rebels' growing military presence convinced the Turkish state that this experience was different from the Kurdish unrest of the past. The state narrative viewed the PKK as a group of political bandits with foreign assistance that should be eliminated by recruiting local allies and implementing long-term development policies. The state hoped that recruiting coethnics would solve key problems of counterinsurgency. First, it would demonstrate that the PKK was not in a position to speak in the name of the Kurds. Second, local allies would be instrumental in providing security and consolidating state-allied interests in Kurdish society.

The Turkish state started to recruit Kurds as village guards as early as 1985. Like the self-defense organizations (*rondas*) that were founded to oppose the Shining Path in Peru, village guards were responsible for policing their villages, patrolling roads and highways, and helping security forces chase insurgents.[61] Their numbers expanded dramatically over time, reaching 100,000 by 2000. Although it was part of the state's institutional framework, the village guard position was a temporary one. Most often, recruitment of village guards was based on tribal allegiances.[62] With their several thousand members, influential tribes such as the Jirki, Alan, and Izdinan joined the fight against the PKK. Over time, village guards became entrenched in the social fabric of Kurdish society. Like their Ottoman counterparts, they became involved in practices that went beyond their designated mission. They organized small-scale attacks on villages suspected of rebel sympathies, punished rival tribes, and engaged in illegal activities such as arms smuggling, the drug trade, and racketeering.[63]

Sharing the security burden, village guards looked for official compensation in return. Unemployment ran high in Kurdish society, and a worsening security situation brought economic activity to a halt in the region during the 1990s. In this economic setting, the position of village guard became one of the few options for making a living in Kurdish society. Tribal leaders also had a stake in the process. As brokers of the village guard deal, they collected fees from tribe members and reaffirmed tribal hierarchies in the community. As a result, the central state paid a huge bill to sustain these alliances. Meanwhile, there were additional economic rewards for local friends. As trusted locals, heads of larger tribes were invited to provide select logistical services, especially in infrastructure projects. Being on good terms with the state brought political opportunities as well. For the first time in Republican history, allied tribe leaders were invited to the capital to meet with Prime Minister Tansu Çiller in 1993.[64] Major political parties found it beneficial to do business with state's local allies. Not surprisingly, then, it was the members of the Tatar tribe who represented every political party in Şırnak province in 1993.[65]

In its fight against the PKK insurgency, the Turkish state had a hard time appealing to local allies with an ideology. The counterinsurgency narrative adhered to Republican discourse throughout the conflict and delivered only low-key Islamic messages to the Kurdish masses. Friends of the state provided security in return for material gains but lacked a cultural framework that justified their relationship with the capital. In this regard, the political messages of the Welfare Party (RP) were well received in the region.[66] The RP appealed to the masses with an Islamic identity and became a serious competitor of the Kurdish nationalist party after 1994. The relationship between local allies and the central state, however, came to fruition later. After 2002, the Justice and Development Party (AKP) governments cultivated a non-Turkish identity for the center and expanded economic opportunities for Islamic entrepreneurs in the region. As a result, the Turkish co-optation model was perfected at the turn of the twenty-first century. As in the Abdulhamidian period, eastern Anatolia was now controlled by two rival political networks, each representing a different type of (specialist) solution to the ethnic issue.

The Turkish state's half-hearted developmentalism was a path-dependent response to the Kurdish threat. It emerged from the state's cyclical counterinsurgency ideology (transform or co-opt). The state tried regional transformation in peaceful times and reverted back to the co-optation model when there was a security threat. As local forces from Kurdish areas threatened the state, the Turkish counterinsurgency responded with its own specialism. Certified localism created allies in Kurdish society and challenged insurgent demands. Meanwhile, the transformation agenda lost its momentum as it moved up the ladder of difficulty beyond security measures. Partial success contributed to an inefficient outcome. It divided Kurdish areas without granting local autonomy or achieving full integration. Kurdish society became divided from within, and the special region's difference from the rest of the country was acknowledged.

6

STRATEGY

States rely on different tactics to defeat their enemies. While China locks down restive areas to weaken Tibetan dissent, the United States flies drones to track down Taliban insurgents in Afghanistan. In urban areas of Iraq, night raids were conducted to find suspects during the U.S. occupation. In the countryside of Guatemala, the state used death squads and resorted to mass killings to destroy guerrilla armies (1966–1982).[1] During the 1990s, the Russian army shelled villages indiscriminately to suppress Chechen resistance.[2] At the beginning of the Syrian civil war, snipers deliberately targeted masses to disperse antigovernment protests. These examples reveal two fundamental facts about state strategies. First, counterinsurgency methods can be qualitatively different across cases, and, second, they show variation across time and space.[3]

One of the most consistent findings in the counterinsurgency writings has been the futility of indiscriminate violence and conventional tactics of attrition.[4] Instead, classifying and controlling populated areas through censuses, protected zones, and self-defense militias are argued to be more effective in turning the tide for the counterinsurgent. Yet these measures have not been available to states in all times. Colonial incumbents, for example, found out that as international norms and values evolved against their enterprise, it became increasingly difficult to base colonial rule on ambitious policing and favorable minority groups.[5]

The origins of counterinsurgency practices are however less well known. There seems to be a multidimensional transmission of experience across counterinsurgency campaigns that aim to pacify dissident groups and their communities. For instance, Laleh Khalili has demonstrated that Israeli counterinsurgency closely mimicked the British colonial practices in Palestine.[6] British tactics in the Malayan insurgency were advanced by officers who had served in Iraq, Burma, and Palestine.[7] U.S. military governors who established special rule in the Philippines at the turn of the twentieth century learned from their previous experience in Native American territories. Like their Spanish predecessors, they treated Muslim minorities differently and became fascinated with the Anglo-Saxon colonial record in Africa.[8]

The key feature of Turkish counterinsurgency was its spatial character. Long-term choices of the state have informed this vision. As we saw in chapter 4, the Turkish state viewed the ethnic question as a security issue and approached it from a geographical perspective. This idea led to the creation of an emergency region (the OHAL) to contain rebel activity. Meanwhile, chapter 5 showed that the Turkish state has had an urban character. Its political project, economic mindset, and cultural identity have been designed to convince urban groups. When faced with insurgent threat, the state gave the highest priority to defending towns and cities. These historically constituted logics defined the state's response to armed contention and in turn shaped distinct counterinsurgency zones in the Turkish civil war (see figure 6.1).

The Battle Zone encompassed most of the OHAL region. The state was determined to roll back insurgents and defeat them through military encounters. Depopulating the countryside further ensured success on the battlefield. The Transition Zone included major Kurdish towns under OHAL jurisdiction. In this L-shaped strip, the state and insurgents competed fiercely for political legitimacy. Security forces employed mixed repertoires, military encounters and political arrests, to stop mass mobilizations. The state viewed the rest of the country as a no-entry zone for insurgents (Zone 3), and used arrests systematically to hinder the formation

Figure 6.1. Zones of counterinsurgency

of rebel niches. Accordingly, selective violence was instrumental in preventing rebels from disseminating propaganda in large cities (see table 6.1).

This chapter discusses Turkish counterinsurgency efforts, using a dataset that includes 5,576 counterinsurgency operations (1984–2008). It also uses an exhaustive list of civilian unrest in Kurdish urban centers involving 846 incidents (1989–2008). We start by examining the state's military record in the Battle Zone. The first two sections demonstrate that the key to the Turkish army's success was using space better than the insurgents. The third section then tells the story of the Transition Zone. It shows how mixed repertoires thwarted a popular revolt in the 1990s, yet consolidated a long-lasting ethnic opposition against the state. The final section traces counterinsurgency efforts outside the boundaries of the OHAL. It concludes that selective political arrests in Zone 3 limited the participation of Kurds in the ethnic project and closed off central political markets to the rebel group.

TABLE 6.1. Counterinsurgency repertoires

Zone	Repertoires	Objective	Outcomes
Battle	Military encounter	Eliminate insurgents	Military success
Transition	Military encounter and arrest	Curb popular support	Political failure
Zone 3	Arrest	Cut ties to civilians	Military and political success

Locating Insurgents

The Turkish state viewed the Battle Zone as the main theater of military operations. Subsequently, military encounters emerged as the primary counterinsurgency repertoire in this zone. Military encounters were armed interactions with insurgents that were initiated by security forces. Almost 90 percent of these interactions occurred in the Battle Zone. The saliency of military encounters in this particular area can be demonstrated in comparative terms as well. For every political arrest, security forces engaged in five military encounters in the Battle Zone. This ratio was ten times higher than the record of military encounters in Zone 3 (0.5 military encounters per arrest) and compared favorably to the experience of the Transition Zone (2 military encounters per arrest).

Armed interactions were rural phenomena. In line with the urban priorities of the state, only 5 percent of military encounters occurred in towns and cities. The scene of military operations in the countryside was the village. The village is the smallest unit in Turkish administrative hierarchy and represents the actual limits of state sovereignty. Close to half of all military encounters happened in its this realm. In the 1990s, security forces began to terminate the ties between villages and insurgents, pushing the latter toward a "no-man's land." Between 1993 and 1999, these clashes with insurgents amounted to three-fifths of rural operations.[9] The Gabar, Herakol, and Tendürek Mountains, in particular, became scenes of intense encounters: In 1994 alone, security forces conducted no fewer than 254 deadly operations in these difficult geographical spots. The same year, the Turkish army reoccupied the strategically located Cudi Mountain and reclaimed the Dedeören military post, which had been abandoned to insurgents since 1989.[10]

Armed encounters were instrumental in depleting insurgent ranks. The PKK lost 70 percent of its manpower—approximately 12,000 militants—in intense encounters that took place in the Battle Zone. Other methods proved ineffective. First, few rebels were captured on the battlefield. Second, the total number of rebel suspects in arrest cases was merely 7 percent of PKK's overall fatalities. Third, similar to arrests, defections cost the PKK no more than a thousand members.[11] Afraid of being called "traitors" in the mountains, rebels surrendered to the state in small groups, mostly from the rebel camps in northern Iraq. Fourth, several legislative attempts by Turkish governments to lure members from the rebel organization also failed.[12] The legislation typically attracted those who were already in prison. Finally, as the small number of unaccounted rebel deaths makes it clear, internal dissent and ecological factors played marginal roles in depopulating the rebel group.[13]

The turning point for military success was the Nevrouz of 1992, when the rebel group tried, albeit unsuccessfully, to incite popular revolts. Prime Minister Süleyman Demirel's comment on the incident signaled the new direction of counterinsurgency efforts: "The PKK started a war, and the only option left for the state was to leave the region or guarantee its survival."[14] During the 1980s, the rebel group enjoyed a psychological advantage over the security forces. This fact changed after 1993. Security forces kept the number of insurgent attacks to a minimum and stepped up military operations. The Turkish military also improved its operational record. While insurgent fatalities averaged 2.5 per operation before the 1990s, they climbed to 6.2 in the 1992–1999 period.[15] The increasing intensity and improved performance of operations resulted in dramatic insurgent losses: 88 percent of all insurgent deaths in armed encounters took place in this period.

Military success was driven by new leadership. As James Fearon had predicted, a political clique emerged at the peak of the conflict.[16] This group embraced military goals and expedited the decision-making process by connecting the military, state bureaucrats, and government officials.[17] When Tansu Çiller became the prime minister in 1993, several bureaucratic posts went to those who would later become Çiller loyalists.[18] The tenure of Doğan Güreş, who was then the chief of Turkey's General Staff, was extended despite legal obstacles and opposition from the president.

Güreş viewed the PKK as the biggest threat to Turkey and stepped up military operations to unprecedented levels.[19] Meanwhile, Mehmet Ağar became the head of the police forces. He expanded the special teams whose task was to curb popular support for the rebel organization in cities. Another important figure was Hasan Kundakçı. An expert on psychological warfare, Kundakçı would play an important role in cross-border operations.[20] Finally, with a police force background, Ünal Erkan became the new governor of the OHAL and accepted the leadership of security forces in managing the war.

The new leadership reorganized security forces at several levels. Most important, the army acquired a central place in the war against the PKK. This found its best expression in a new institution, the Gendarmerie for Internal Security, whose mission was to coordinate counterinsurgency operations.[21] Intelligence colllection was monopolized by the Turkish General Staff. Around the same time, the Turkish army became leaner and more mobile in the OHAL region. By November 1993, only 12 percent of the army consisted of mechanized forces. Instead, more than half of all ground troops were in commando and gendarmerie units.[22] Police forces underwent a similar transformation. Tripling in less than three years, special teams reached 7,000 members by 1996.[23] As such, political leadership successfully restructured the Turkish security forces without privatizing security or creating an autonomous group within the state.[24]

Finally, security forces acquired superior military technology in the 1990s. In the early years, locating the rebels had been particularly difficult. There was not a single operation that resulted in ten or more insurgent deaths in the first four years of the conflict.[25] The first step in the army's technological makeover was its leasing of Puma helicopters from France. The real change, however, came in 1992, when the United States donated twenty-two helicopters to Turkey as part of its military aid.[26] Over time, the Turkish forces gained more experience in operating Sikorsky and Super-Cobra helicopters in combat situations and incorporated fighter jets (such as the F-104 and F-5) into their operations. Airpower perfected the Turkish army's military encounter template.[27] In a typical four-stage operation, military jets would bombard the targeted area first, helicopters would attack rebel hideouts from lower ranges, special teams would then launch an offensive against the rebel group, and finally ground troops would be deployed to keep the insurgents in the encircled area.

Sweep and Strike

A new tactic sealed counterinsurgency success in the 1990s. Security forces operated within a medium-coverage and medium-depth framework that increased the geographical range and intensity of counterinsurgency operations. Formulated in network terms, covering more districts and revisiting the same ones cut the distance between security forces and insurgents.[28] The end result was a dramatic rise in counterinsurgency performance (see table 6.2). Security forces used a special approach to reach this efficient outcome. They first swept the rebels toward certain spots by increasing geographical coverage and then struck repeatedly at those locations.[29] The "sweep and strike" approach forced the rebels into a defensive position where they were eliminated in large numbers.

The sweep tactic was in effect in the early 1990s. Army strategists referred to this vision as area control, which entailed engaging rebels over a larger area. The gendarmerie commander of Şemdinli Erdal Sarızeybek shared the new vision with his soldiers: "If you don't want to die, you will walk hours and days."[30] Accordingly, district coverage in counterinsurgency operations, which represents the number of districts with at least one military encounter in a year, expanded dramatically. District coverage was four times larger in 1991–1994 than it was in the 1984–1990 and 2000–2008 periods.[31] A rapid increase in coverage coupled with rising intensity of military operations translated into improved performance. The

TABLE 6.2. Three dimensions of military encounters, 1984–2008

Period	Coverage	Depth	Performance
1984–1990	Low (0.21)	Low (0.22)	Low (0.09)
1991–1994	High (0.82)	Medium (0.47)	Medium (0.31)
1995–1999	Medium (0.57)	Medium (0.44)	High (0.62)
2000–2008	Low (0.18)	Low (0.10)	Low (0.16)

Note: All three variables have been rescaled between 0 and 1 to facilitate comparison. Parenthetical numbers are calculated as follows. Coverage is the average of the total number of districts where at least one military encounter took place. Depth is the ratio of the total number of military encounters to the number of districts where at least one military encounter took place. Performance is the ratio of the total number of insurgents killed in a military encounter to the total number of military encounters. For all three variables, yearly values have been averaged to create period values. Broadly speaking, the most efficient scenario for counterinsurgency operations seems to be low coverage and high depth. The least efficient one is low coverage and low depth.

TABLE 6.3. Comparing security and insurgent casualties, 1984–2008

Period	Security deaths (military encounters)	Security deaths (insurgent attacks)	Insurgent deaths (military encounters)
1984–1990	1.79	2.38	2.17
1991–1994	1.73	3.25	4.4
1995–1999	3.74	3.51	7.5
2000–2008	1.82	1.97	3

Note: Figures represent average casualty numbers per military encounter or insurgent attack. Security deaths in insurgent attacks do not include village guard casualties.

rebel group was losing on average 4.4 militants in each armed encounter, twice the figure for the 1984–1990 period (see table 6.3). As the military acquired momentum, almost 7,000 insurgents were killed in this period (1991–1994). Half of these deaths occured in 1994. This was the year counterinsurgency efforts took a new direction. Rebel sanctuaries would be the next target of military operations.

As the army dislodged rebels from several districts, the PKK took refugee in sanctuaries. A brief General Staff announcement in 1995 confirmed that major hostilities were over in most of the OHAL region.[32] Subsequently, four major sanctuaries emerged as the site of armed encounters in the 1998–1999 period.[33] The Turkish army implemented a two-step plan for eliminating the rebel presence in these spots. First, the army conducted "trimming operations" to narrow down the radius of insurgent activity from 1995 to 1997. Second, the army struck hard against a few select districts. Districts known as rebel sanctuaries became the main sites of PKK losses. According to our calculations, 59 percent of fatalities, roughly 10,000 militants, occurred on these four fronts.

The first sanctuary consisted of six districts on the Iraqi border. This was where the Turkish army inflicted the heaviest casualties on the rebel group. The rebels were pushed in an eastward direction. Security forces swept Cizre and Silopi in 1992–1994, trimmed the rebel presence in Uludere and Çukurca in 1995–1997, and finally concentrated their efforts in Yüksekova and Şemdinli districts in 1998–1999. Variations in the annual shares of armed interactions in these districts strongly confirm this trend.[34] Located at the intersection of the Iranian, Iraqi, and Turkish borders, Yüksekova in particular became the scene of heavy fighting, where the PKK lost the highest number of its members per operation (an average of 11.2 per military encounter).

The second sanctuary was the Şırnak corridor. Its rough terrain, proximity to the Iraqi border, and hospitable populations made it a perfect refuge. After trimming the insurgent presence in Eruh, security forces isolated Şırnak. Subsequently, Şırnak became the major scene of military encounters in 1998–1999.[35] In an operation to honor fallen lieutenant Mehmet Işıkal, the army searched strategic mountains in the area, including Cudi, Kato, and Herakol. The operation received air support from F-16 fighter jets and Cobra helicopters. In eight days of intense encounters, no fewer than eighty-six insurgents were eliminated.[36] The final blow to the rebel group was the destruction of Botan Headquarters in the Tuşumiya Valley of Cudi Mountain. Unable to withstand these massive operations, the insurgents tried to flee but were caught in the security net.[37]

The other two rebel bases were located deep in the OHAL region and carried a strong potential to spread violence into surroundings areas. The first one was the Lice, Kulp, and Genç Triangle, which was nestled at the intersection of several provinces. The Triangle was a physical sanctuary because of its thick forests and mountain ranges. Security forces planned to encircle the heart of the insurgency to block the diffusion of violence. The counterinsurgency record was mixed: Although it was able to trim the presence of insurgents in Hani and Mutki, there was stiff resistance in Lice and Sason. Next, as was the case in Şırnak, Turkish forces struck the heart of the insurgency, the Kulp and Genç districts.[38] In the largest military operation ever conducted against the PKK inside Turkey, Operation Murat targeted Sağgöze in Genç district in April 1998. This was the area where security forces had destroyed the rebel camps of Musa Anter and Şehit Rıza two years earlier.[39] The operation was conducted by twenty-four generals and included 40,000 soldiers and 3,000 village guards. Targeting the Şenyayla group of the PKK, the operation lasted more than two weeks and resulted in major casualties on the rebel side.[40]

The final sanctuary was the northern districts of Tunceli. This province appeared late on the counterinsurgency map when rebels made a last-ditch effort to sustain the armed conflict. Given Tunceli's political past and physical sanctuary status, this seemed to be a wise choice for the PKK.[41] The heightened threat led security forces to double their operations between 1992 and 1998–1999. The objective was to block the diffusion of the conflict into other districts of the province. Security forces periodically conducted large-scale operations across the northern districts. Thousands of soldiers searched insurgent hideouts such as Kutuderesi and Aliboğazı in December 1994, March 1995, September 1995, and May 1996.[42] In the Pülümür district, which featured large caves and hidden valleys cut by mountain ranges, rebels sustained heavy losses despite their geographical advantage. In the Kinzir Forest in Hozat, Operation Dawn, which was supported by mechanized divisions and airpower, killed forty-five insurgents in September 1996.[43]

Two distinct military moves facilitated the sweep-and-strike tactic. The first was cross-border operations into northern Iraq that targeted rebel camps. Early operations were retaliatory moves that failed to deliver long-term results. They were responses to major insurgent attacks on military posts on the border and served to calm the public. This changed, however, in the 1990s, when a series of incursions into northern Iraq disrupted insurgent plans and aided the new counterinsurgency tactic inside Turkey. The Last Strike Operation (1992) slowed down insurgent expansion at a critical time.[44] When the Turkish army crossed the border with 15,000 ground troops for its largest operation up to that point, the PKK waged a frontline defense to stop the mobile armored attack.[45] As the rebel leader Öcalan later lamented, this was a bad miscalculation.[46] Aided by airpower, the Last Strike Operation lasted three weeks and destroyed 40 percent of the rebel group, especially in the Hakurk, Haftanin, and Zap camps. As a result, the PKK learned the capabilities of the Turkish army and lost the military momentum in Turkey.

The next phase of cross-border operations put the insurgents on the defensive. With one exception, all major cross-border operations took place in the 1994–2000 period.[47] Each had a code name, involved a large ground force, and resulted in major casualties. When the Turkish army left northern Iraq in 1992, they trusted regional Kurdish leaders to keep the region free of rebel presence. This scenario, however, did not materialize. The 1995–1997 operations took place in this political context. The Turkish army engaged in one massive operation each year and organized several small-scale operations. The goal was to prevent insurgents from regrouping inside Turkey. These cross-border operations were conducted during the time when the Turkish army had forced the PKK to take shelter in sanctuaries. Periodic operations gave the rebels no time to retrain

their members and destroyed the coordination between camps and guerrilla units.

While cross-border operations assisted the strike phase, cutting PKK's
civilian ties in the countryside guaranteed the success of sweep operations.
Rural support was key to insurgent survival in the OHAL region. Civilians
gathered valuable information as guides, served rebels' recruitment needs,
and provided shelter. As early as 1985, the security forces were encountering local guides during military operations.[48] Meanwhile, the PKK's
shelters were widespread in rural areas and contained similar items: an
abundance of food, medical supplies, winter clothing, and a wide range of
weapons.[49] Throughout the 1990s, the rebel arsenal in the shelters continued to increase in size and included new items such as long-range rifles,
RPGs, and mines. The other novelty in the shelter system was the reliance
on intermediaries who brought food in bulk quantities and sustained rebel
supply lines.[50]

Security forces failed to locate civilian supporters of the insurgency in
the countryside. Political arrests were limited compared to their counterparts in cities. This observation dovetailed with the broader experience
of the Battle Zone, where arrests neither reached critical numbers nor
became politically significant.[51] Security forces tried other options. They
blamed local state representatives (village headmen) or, as was the case in
the Kılavuz village of Dargeçit, rounded up villagers temporarily for providing logistical support to the insurgents.[52] When none of these tactics
worked, depopulating rural areas became the ultimate solution. The state
expedited village evacuations and installed village guards to put an end
to its information starvation in the countryside.[53] As it had in the interwar era, the central state held the geographical unit (village) and social ties
(family/kinship) responsible for insurgency.[54]

Rebels were unable to protect peasants. The only exception was in the
border districts of Hakkari and Şırnak, where they convinced villagers
to migrate to northern Iraq and live in refugee camps with the help of
international aid.[55] In other cases, such as in Tunceli, rebels' threats to ex-
propriate property failed to keep villagers on their land. Peasant mobilizations against state repression did not work either. Four thousand peasants
from forty-eight villages tried to enter the district center in Digor (Kars
province) in August 1993 to celebrate the anniversary of the PKK's first
successful guerrilla attacks. They were violently blocked by security forces.

Special teams fired on the crowd, killing sixteen civilians and injuring hundreds.[56] A survey of civilian deaths in counterinsurgency operations gives us a glimpse of the violent crackdown on peasant mobilizations, especially in the early 1990s.[57]

Despite its brutal nature, the Digor massacre showed what was missing in rural mobilizations in the Battle Zone. They were few, were isolated from one another, and happened at a time when civilian unrest in the Transition Zone was about to end. Unaware of this fact, villagers from Malazgirt paid the price with their lives. In 1992 and 1993, when hundreds tried to enter the district center, they faced the bullets of security forces.[58] Still, protest events were hard to come by in the countryside, and no support from the public emerged after such violent rural encounters. The main problem was the absence of political brokerage. Most critically, religious entrepreneurs, who transcended local boundaries and coordinated collective action in eastern Anatolia, had already been eliminated by the Republican administration in the interwar era.

In sum, counterinsurgency successfully defeated the PKK in the Battle Zone. This was made possible by a unique military tactic, the sweep and strike. Sweep operations pushed the rebels into sanctuaries, and strike operations eliminated them in these hot spots. Meanwhile, the Transition Zone posed new challenges to the state. These contested sites possessed the necessary political resources to forge a new identity. The state would be trapped in a long-running political struggle with the masses rallied around new political mediums and nationalist ideas.

Curbing Civilian Unrest

The Transition Zone consisted of eighteen districts, covering one-fifth of the OHAL's administrative space. An L-shaped strip, it fitted nicely into the pre-1990 boundaries of Diyarbakır and Mardin provinces.[59] Its head in the north and its tail in the east were connected to major insurgent sanctuaries, the Lice-Kulp-Genç Triangle and the Şırnak corridor. The Transition Zone represented key sites in Kurdish geography that were centers of economy, politics, and culture. It was also the junction point of oppositional Kurdish identities.[60] As such, it held the key to political leadership in the OHAL and could expand the ethnic project beyond its boundaries.

The state employed mixed tactics in the Transition Zone. The counterinsurgency objective was to defeat insurgents in armed encounters and win the political struggle in towns by curbing popular mobilizations. In this respect, the competition between the state and the PKK took place in both urban and rural settings. Arrests became a commonly employed repression tool in the Transition Zone. The significance of arrests in these towns can be demonstrated with a simple comparison: Although arrests accounted for 35 percent of counterinsurgency operations in the Transition Zone, almost half of all arrests within OHAL boundaries took place here.

The growing political threat in the Transition Zone soon turned civilians into militants in state discourse. The chief of Turkey's General Staff, Necip Torumtay, signaled the new direction in 1989 when he announced that supporters of the rebel group should be treated as enemies. One year later, military courts subscribed to the same vision.[61] In October 1993, the National Security Council (MGK) outlined a new list of counterinsurgency measures to punish those who distributed rebel propaganda and provided material support for the rebels. In this political climate, mass arrests became the standard approach to discourage civilians from supporting the PKK. Unable or unwilling to locate insurgents in urban centers, the state rounded up a large number of noncombatants along with a few suspected rebels. Although arrests in the Transition Zone were more selective than the village evacuations in rural areas, they operated in a gray area blurring the lines between civilians and combatants.[62]

The first wave of mass arrests took place in the Transition Zone (1987–1989). When arrests increased more than fourfold in the late 1980s, 40 percent of all cases were reported in the Transition Zone. Cizre, Nusaybin, and the city centers of Diyarbakır and Mardin were focal points.[63] Civilians, including local politicians, were taken into custody in these operations.[64] Suspects were accused of organizing shop closures, which the security forces interpreted as a symbolic act of support for the rebel cause. The administrative universe of arrests confirmed the centrality of the Transition Zone in these operations. In contrast to provincial centers and large cities, a large chunk of arrests took place in districts in the 1985–1992 period. Most of these districts were the administrative seats of border towns in the Transition Zone.[65]

The early target of arrests in the Transition Zone was the urban organization of the rebel group, the committees. Soon after the war began, the

PKK set up political branches in towns and cities. Under the leadership of the ERNK (and later KCK), urban committees had a unique mission: to assume governmental functions. Still, the more urgent goal of the committees in the early 1990s was to politicize the masses and mobilize them for mass revolts. The rebel group's choice of area was the Transition Zone. From 1987 to 1989, security forces engaged in a pitched battle with the rebel group, especially in the border districts of Mardin and the city center of Diyarbakır. With the exception of Istanbul, all cases of political arrest targeting urban committees were reported here. For instance, the Cizre committee was revealed by security forces as early as July 1988, only to be disbanded again in August 1988 and September 1989.[66] Safe houses, which were widespread in the Transition Zone, further indicated rebel power in these towns.[67]

Over time, mass arrests increasingly targeted civilians. One such pattern emerged in the aftermath of urban raids: special teams would lock down towns, fire indiscriminately, and make arrests on a large scale. In most situations, the typical number of detainees was over thirty, suggesting the arbitrariness of these operations. In one particular instance in February 1994, security forces responded to an urban raid by detaining more than 200 civilians in İdil district in a manhunt that continued until dawn.[68] Arbitrary arrests were common. In the 30-month period from April 1991 to February 1994, such arrests were reported in at least twenty districts. As the site of several politically active towns, the Transition Zone was hit the hardest. In November 1993, several shops and houses were destroyed in Lice (Diyarbakır) after a rebel sniper killed an army general, Bahtiyar Aydın, in the town.[69] Arrests were widespread and were even carried out in towns with limited insurgent activity such as Kızıltepe in Mardin.

For state officials, the more pressing concern in the Transition Zone was civilian unrest (*Serhildan*). Triggered by an early wave of arrests, two-thirds of mass mobilizations were reported inside the boundaries of the Transition Zone. The timing of civilian unrest was also critical. It came to life between 1989 and 1993 when the PKK was at its military peak.[70] In that respect, civilian unrest had the potential to translate into popular revolts. Protesters expressed their disapproval of repressive measures and demonstrated in support of the rebel cause. Typical repertoires were rallies, shop closings, demonstrations, and gatherings at insurgent funerals. Protestors questioned detentions with no evidence, blamed the state for disappeared individuals, and demanded treatment with dignity for deceased militants. A key aspect of civilian unrest was its networked character. An act of protest in one town easily diffused to others in the Transition Zone.[71] For example, when police action at an insurgent funeral resulted in hundreds of detentions in Nusaybin in March 1990, there were massive protests in Cizre.[72] The Cizre incidents left five civilians dead and eight wounded. It was now the turn of Kızıltepe and Derik residents to respond to the call and protest against the police brutality in Cizre.[73]

Security forces were adamant about stopping political mobilization at all costs. They feared that the Transition Zone would become a home for popular uprisings and serve as a political catalyst for mass mobilizations elsewhere. Brokerage function of the Transition Zone could become instrumental in legitimizing armed struggle and politicizing Kurdish identity. This reading of political unrest led to indiscriminate violence against civilian targets. Political arrests, which were conducted with no apparent connection to the rebel group, reached an unprecedented scale in the Transition Zone. In the critical period of 1990–1993, almost half of such arrests nationwide took place here.[74] Nusaybin, Cizre, and the Diyarbakır city center ranked highest on the list.

State violence against civilians mostly occurred at mass events. Celebrations with ethnic significance and rebel funerals particularly attracted state attention. During the Nevrouz celebrations of 1992, thirty-three people were killed and hundreds were wounded in Cizre, Nusaybin, Yüksekova, and Şırnak. The funeral of a high-profile Kurdish nationalist politician, Vedat Aydın, had a similar violent ending. Aydın was the head of the Diyarbakır branch of the HEP when he was found dead in 1991 after his forced disappearance. His funeral led to several clashes in the city that left seven civilians dead and sixty injured. Security forces detained more than 400 people and arrested fifty on that occasion.[75] The state's use of force in similar public events resulted in 134 civilian deaths and left more than 1,000 wounded. Civilian casualties reached a peak in the 1989–1993 period and were disproportionately (two-thirds) clustered in the Transition Zone.

In addition to mass arrests, the Turkish state promoted rebel rivalry in the Transition Zone. This was where Kurdish oppositional identities met. Fomenting rivalry was a tactic to slow down insurgent expansion by mobilizing rival identities. Accordingly, the state turned a blind eye to the violent competition between the PKK and its Islamic-oriented rival, Hezbollah.[76] In Batman, local officials were instrumental in promoting Hezbollah as a means of preventing nationalists from monopolizing Kurdish political space. Extrajudicial executions became widespread. These incidents happened at a critical time and at a critical place. Politically motivated murders picked up in 1991 and reached an all-time high in 1993, overlapping with the wave of civilian unrest. The location of killings was also no coincidence. More than half of the 2,000 unsolved cases took place in Diyarbakır, Mardin, and Batman, all located in the Transition Zone.[77] The political competition between the two groups led to major outcomes.[78] The rebels missed the opportunity to mobilize the masses for revolt, and the Kurdish nationalist project failed to dominate rival identities. As a bulwark, Kurdish Islam hindered expansion of unrest toward the north and west and kept the nationalists in competition mode in the Transition Zone.

In sum, counterinsurgency efforts focused on repressing politically networked towns in the Transition Zone. With its distinct identity, this was where mass arrests and civilian unrest were concentrated. Unsolved political murders were also clustered in particular districts inside the Transition Zone. Mixed tactics of counterinsurgency succeeded in destroying the insurgents' military capacity but created a political problem. Three-way competition among the state, the PKK, and Hezbollah hardened identities and gave a strong boost to the Kurdish nationalist project. As such, Cizre and Diyarbakır became insurgency's key political centers. The long-term impact of counterinsurgency measures however was neither escalatory nor deterrent.[79] It gave way to a third outcome, in which Kurdish rebels and the Turkish state had to settle for the second-best option. This was resource partitioning, where forces of integration competed with centrifugal forces over the OHAL region and its identity.

The No-Entry Zone

Outside the OHAL framework, the Turkish state had a different vision. This was where large cities were located, and millions of Kurds lived in social peace. The loosening of OHAL boundaries could enable the insurgents to spread the war to the rest of the country. Similarly, rebel propaganda in large cities could bring Kurdish majorities under the PKK's influence. The birth of an overarching Kurdish political identity that transcended space would mean the demise of the Republican project and its community-neutral discourse. To avoid such an outcome, the Turkish state relied on another path-dependent response: social distancing. Every effort was made to block rebels from establishing a presence in Zone 3 and prevent the Kurdish nationalist project from reaching out to civilians in large cities.

This preemptive logic brought political arrests to the forefront of counterinsurgency efforts. Like the armed encounters that took place in the Battle Zone, arrests across the country emerged as the principal repertoire of security operations from Istanbul to Adana. Half of all political arrests targeting the rebel group were made in Zone 3. A comparison of tactics across zones registers the same point. Broadly speaking, there were two arrests for every military encounter in Zone 3. In other zones, the ratio of arrests to military encounters favored the latter, albeit at different rates. Meanwhile, the share of Zone 3 in the universe of armed encounters was insignificant: not surprisingly, only a small number of military encounters occurred there. These incidents corresponded to 12 percent of armed encounters in counterinsurgency operations and mostly took place in provinces adjacent to the OHAL.[80]

Political arrests were urban operations. The counterinsurgency objective was to maintain political order and social peace by denying entry to the rebels. Throughout the conflict, more than 80 percent of all cases were reported in towns and cities. With a two-thirds share, urban arrests were heavily concentrated in Zone 3. Unlike the Transition Zone, where districts carried the burden of these arrests, large cities with metropolitan municipalities stood out in Zone 3. Istanbul, Izmir, Adana, and Mersin emerged as main arrest sites. Istanbul alone accounted for 28 percent of the reported cases in the country in 1995.[81]

The majority of arrests in Zone 3 were made in the 1990s. In fact, Zone 3 was the home to more than half of all incidents in the 1992–1996 period. Arrest patterns closely followed the "sweep and strike" framework. First, rising intensity and broad coverage guaranteed the success of sweeping arrest operations across the country in 1992 and 1993.[82] Second, playing a role similar to that of sanctuaries in military operations, large cities emerged as special targets. Accordingly, the share of arrests in four large cities climbed from one-fourth in 1992 to half of all reported cases in 1995. This trend was also evident in the decreasing district coverage of arrest incidents that peaked in 1993 with ninety-three districts and then settled around thirty districts in the second half of the 1990s.

Arrests targeted the urban organization of the rebel group. While civilian support in rural areas assisted the insurgents in the Battle Zone, urban committees aimed at mobilizing the masses in the Transition Zone. In Zone 3, they had a different goal. Their mission was to extract material resources and create isolated rebel niches. As detention stories attest, the rebel group collected money from its own community, punished informants, and tried to transform the socially excluded migrants around its agenda. In the early 1990s, security forces used periodic arrests in an attempt to cut the PKK's access to community resources. This was especially the case in Adana and Istanbul. For instance, in June 1992, nine people were captured in Adana; they were collecting money for the ERNK, organizing neighborhood committees, and helping the recruitment drive.[83] Four months later, another twenty-six people who occupied key spots in the local branches of the PKK were detained in Istanbul. They were accused of producing fake ID cards, possessing a party seal, and, most important, collecting money.[84]

As the conflict escalated, urban committees increasingly took on a violent function. By 1991, it was clear that urban committees had a dual structure that consisted of a political wing and a military wing. The rebel group and its supporters were vandalizing banks and organizing high-profile attacks against security forces. As the rebels were forced into a defensive position on the battlefield, urban committees underwent a dramatic restructuring around 1994. The urban priorities of the PKK now revolved around a new specialist group, the bombing squad.[85] The bombing squad usually consisted of operatives who were unfamiliar to security forces and had received technical training abroad. They targeted transportation networks of large cities and public events, which was especially evident in Istanbul. The insurgent group switched to suicide bombing in the 1996–1999 period, attacking state officials. After 2000, when the PKK had accumulated enough experience with using explosives (such as C-4, A-4, and TNT), it turned its attention to shopping malls and public squares. Its main targets were now civilians.

The pattern of political arrests reflected the shifting modes of the PKK's urban structure. In the early 1990s, security forces were chasing the military wing of urban committees. In one successful operation, the police captured PKK operatives in the Dağlıoğlu, Barbaros, and Gülbahçe neighborhoods, key spots of insurgent action in Adana.[86] After 1994, suspects had a different profile. A bombing squad was apprehended in Istanbul for planting a bomb in the Tuzla train station in February 1994 that killed several military cadets and left others wounded.[87] From 1996 to 1999, suicide bombers, who primarily targeted public celebrations, were spotted in several cities such as Sivas, Adana, and Antalya. After 2000, small insurgent networks that were responsible for carrying, hiding, and planting explosives in large cities were on the state's radar. In 2005, a police raid on an urban safe house in Alibeyköy, a poor neighboorhood of Istanbul, led to the capture of several insurgents with explosives. Based on a security lead from this operation, another insurgent was apprehended at the main bus terminal of Istanbul. He was there to receive a cargo of C-4 plastic explosives hidden in cheese boxes.[88]

Counterinsurgency operations against the PKK's urban committees were successful. As we noted earlier, they were made possible by the increasing intensity and decreasing geographical coverage of security operations. Ironically, the success of arrests was also facilitated by the change in the internal structure of these committees. A narrow approach that increasingly centered on indiscriminate violence halted the PKK's political efforts and cut its emerging ties with civilians. Security forces were able to isolate insurgents in cities. New patterns strongly confirm this observation: The insurgent-noncombatant ratio increased in favor of the former, and arrest size declined dramatically in the second half of the 1990s. All these developments enhanced the preemptive capabilities of security forces.

Arrests in Zone 3 were selective and carefully singled out the urban branch of the rebel organization. The state continued its traditional policy of observing a clear distinction between the "bandits" in the OHAL region and millions of Kurds in large cities. This approach saved the state from having to engage with an ethnic question and kept intercommunal relations relatively peaceful. Nevertheless, counterinsurgency operations profiled specific groups in the Kurdish universe. One such group was educated youth. Universities were seen as fertile ground for the rebel group to find new recruits and spread their ideology. As early as August 1991, security forces were predicting that at least 180 students had left school to join the rebel ranks.[89] Perhaps more important, through these arrests the state was able to silence public figures such as journalists, union leaders, and members of the Kurdish nationalist party before rebel propaganda reached its central political markets.

Security forces also put ghetto neighborhoods under close watch. This was especially visible in Adana and Mersin, where the rebel organization had penetrated deeply into the Kurdish community. The PKK worked hard to create closed networks in certain neighborhoods, such as Dağlıoğlu and Gülbahçe in Adana, reaching out to recent migrants who were living in poverty and isolation. In these spots, the rebel group successfully exploited community resources. Organizational penetration was instrumental. For instance, in Mersin, the PKK's urban branches organized neighborhood committees, controlled certain mosques, and reached out to women.[90] Still, the rebel group could not replicate the same success in every large city. It was able to bring about mass mobilizations in urban sites where social boundaries were strengthened as a result of armed conflict and/or residential segregation was rigid. These social patterns can be observed in Mersin, Adana, and Izmir. In other metropolitan cities that lacked these features, the polarization scenario did not materialize. The Kurdish majorities in Gaziantep and the significant Kurdish presence in Ankara could not be transformed into heavily politicized and closed ethnic communities.

A few armed encounters took place in Zone 3 as security forces tried to block insurgent expansion. Close to half of these military encounters were in provinces adjacent to the OHAL region.[91] The underlying rationale for containing the rebel group inside OHAL boundaries was political. An insurgent presence in adjacent provinces could easily fuel intercommunal tensions and lead to boundary making between confessional groups. After insurgent attacks on two Sunni areas (Yavi and Çiçekli) in Erzurum, thousands of residents were mobilized.[92] They protested the political parties and the rebel group, and vandalized houses and shops in a Kurdish neighborhood. This incident was an early warning to state officials that communal tensions between Sunnis and Alevites could turn into open conflict, especially in Erzurum, Erzincan, and Sivas. Counterinsurgency efforts were concentrated in these provinces to preempt such symbolic attacks.[93]

Security operations in Zone 3 led to two major outcomes, both of which favored the Turkish state. First, selective violence brought political success. Urban arrests carefully avoided boundary making along ethnic lines. Ghetto-type areas in large cities were the only exception. As such, the rebels' nationalist call was successfully silenced. The meager performance of the Kurdish nationalist party in the largest Kurdish city, Istanbul, validates this point (albeit indirectly).[94] Second, despite a temporary military presence, the rebels could not penetrate into Zone 3. Armed encounters in provinces adjacent to the OHAL halted the PKK's expansion efforts and firmly held OHAL boundaries.

The state's successful counterinsurgency campaign crushed the PKK's dream of a free Kurdistan. Increasing control over territory reduced the insurgency's military presence in the OHAL region, effectively limiting it to a few sanctuaries. The sweep-and-strike tactic, which was helped by forced migration and cross-border operations, made this efficient military outcome possible. Yet the state's specialist responses to the insurgent threat, informed by long experience with rebellions, were less suited to achieving control over people. Administrative practices consolidated a contentious region, the OHAL, whereas the co-optation model that involved making bargains with loyal coethnics could only go so far in winning local friends.

Counterinsurgency tactics that blurred the lines between civilians and combatants further underwrote political failure. In Zone 3, selective targeting was possible: With little civilian support, the PKK operatives were isolated and became easy targets for the state. In the Battle Zone, indiscriminate targeting emerged as the only option. The rural bias of the Turkish state caused information starvation in the countryside, making it impossible to locate the PKK's civilian supporters. In the Transition Zone, local support shielded insurgents and led to a similar identification problem. With widespread political arrests and a harsh response to civilian unrest, the state unwittingly contributed to the PKK's group-making project. In the end, neither the state nor the PKK was successful in consolidating the Transition Zone. Their violent competition for legitimacy sustained the contested character of the Transition Zone and confirmed major divisions in Kurdish society.

CONCLUSION

In this book we have examined the distribution of violence and its political origins in the Turkish civil war. We argued that the Kurds and Kurdish areas followed different political trajectories, and that civil war sides kept the Kurdish universe divided. The Turkish state responded to ethnic contention with a spatial confinement strategy (special regions) and tried to win civilian loyalties by recruiting local allies (co-optation). The insurgency failed to bridge these divisions. It was unable to consolidate an ethnic homeland and mobilize its community around a political agenda. As a result, neither national integration nor Kurdish independence materialized.

We have emphasized ecology in order to understand war dynamics and have borrowed from historical institutionalism to make sense of combatant choices. Civil wars are primarily shaped by the earlier interactions of each side with resources: territory and people. These interactions seek to create compliance and are sustained over time through institutional mechanisms. Civil war violence—its occurrence and intensity—varies spatially and temporally in ways that are shaped by these earlier interactions. Strong path dependencies may have an unintended outcome: They can create deadlocks and block negotiated settlements. We unveiled the preferences that both sides made in the Turkish civil war and explained why each side pursued policies that might seem inefficient to an outside observer.

Forging Identities

We use the Kurdish insurgency to raise new questions about civil wars.[1] Most critically, we highlight the role of brokers, entrepreneurs that link two previously unconnected social sites, in organizing collective action in support of the insurgency. Brokerage is instrumental in forging common fronts out of local cleavages. While the presence of brokers solves the thorny issues of mass mobilization and legitimacy, the absence of such entrepreneurs means limited civilian support to the rebel cause. In that respect, brokers play a critical role in generating compliance. These "frame-bridgers" can be found only in certain political spaces: It requires a unique type of social capital to bridge the differences among individuals, groups, and regions. The PKK example is instructive. As an intermediary, the Transition Zone legitimated the military struggle with nationalist messages and set an example for the rest of the country with its collective action agenda. However, civilian unrest was hard to come by in other Kurdish areas. The problem was the absence of political brokers in these sites.

Forms of claim-making are an unrecognized aspect of civil war contention.[2] Operating in this uncharted territory, we found that violent and nonviolent repertoires had important features. First, they were zone specific, closely following the combatants' interaction with resources. This quality became an advantage on the home front, the zone under control. The Turkish state relied on arrests to root out insurgent niches, and Kurdish rebels used village raids to transform the target community. Second, coercive strategies became highly diversified in the contested zone. Both sides employed multiple tactics to hurt their opponents and win people's allegiance. Such creativity with repertoires of violence seems to be unique to the contested zone. Third, combatants adopted nonviolent strategies in the midst of civil war violence. These contentious performances intend to mobilize civilians around their agendas. As such, political loyalties and military contestation presented different challenges and opportunities for combatants.

Civil war violence is also episodic. We have underlined the fact that combatants' targets changed over the course of the conflict. Once rebels learn to be a closed group of practitioners, they turn first on rival groups. Next is the community, which they seek to transform through violence and other means. Finally, the state emerges on the horizon as a political target—only if the rebel group has been resourceful enough to survive in early stages. In their struggle with the state, rebels calibrate their political demands to their military performance. An insurgent group will pursue independence, autonomy, or some other form of power-sharing arrangement, depending on the extent to which it can challenge the state.

Shifting political demands suggest a skeptical view about the argument that minorities have well-defined preexisting rights that are denied by power holders, and that separatist insurgencies simply seek to secure those rights. Drawing from this framework, researchers have tried to explain why the Kurds rebelled in a variety of contexts and have highlighted their exclusion from political processes.[3] These accounts present several intellectual challenges: They view ethnic identity as a fixed category and downplay the role of violence in the evolution of Kurdish demands. Conflict processes are complex and defy clear positioning of individuals along ethnic lines, which remained another issue in the grievance explanation.

The last point also raises questions about the firmness of collective identities in civil wars.[4] Insurgencies do not necessarily fight for identities that already exist. Instead, they spend most of their time building new ones. In that respect, civil wars can be viewed as incomplete group-making projects. As several rebel groups have found out over the years, the construction of an ethnic/revolutionary political community has its limits. For example, the PKK was unable to transform areas where the Kurds identify themselves primarily in religious and confessional terms. In eastern Anatolia, where modern identities have been an outcome of the religious competition between Muslims and Christians and between Sunnis and Alevites since the 1890s, the ethnic project was unable to find significant support despite the overwhelming presence of coethnics in the region.

States can pose credible challenges to identity-making projects as well. States can build selective partnerships with the community that rebels claim to represent. They can subcontract coercion, share political power, channel economic resources, and emphasize the cultural bonds between the common folk and the center. Once war begins, the activation of boundaries by both sides gradually shapes friend-foe distinctions in the community. In extreme cases, the state can help activate an insurgent group that claims to represent a rival local identity. We have shown how the civil war in Turkey created not only the secular and nationalist PKK but also a fierce Islamic rival, Hezbollah, in contested sites. Eventually rebels are forced to realize that the master identity they claim to represent has multiple forms and operates with divided loyalties.

The malleability of identities illustrates the uneven distribution of ethnic loyalties in a civil war environment. In the Turkish case, an ethnic party emerged in the contested zone with civilian unrest. Why the contested zone? This zone has represented an exceptional place where path dependencies on both sides have run into trouble. This is where compliance with state and insurgent projects existed side by side and eventually led to resource partitioning. While rebels were unable to consolidate their fundamental niche (Kurdistan), the state failed to quell political resistance despite a successful military campaign. Unique political outcomes appeared at the interstices of popular unrest and ineffective state repression. The rise of an ethnic party has corresponded to a new episode in the civil war in which two competing factions are continuously constrained by their earlier experience.[5]

Path-Dependent Origins

Few studies in civil war research have systematically based their causal explanations on the early experiences of combatants. Jeremy Weinstein's *Inside Rebellion* builds a path-dependent link between natural resources and the organization of insurgencies. Weinstein argues that the social or economic resources insurgencies have at their disposal in the beginning of the war will shape rebel leaders' strategies and explain patterns of civil war violence:

> The model linking resources and group structures to patterns of violence implies substantial path dependence. . . . It explores key instances of combat success and failure in each conflict, highlighting the ways in which groups

sought to hold their organizations together by reinforcing rather than re-forming internal structures and practices established in the earliest stages of the conflict.[6]

In *Rebel Rulers*, Zachariah Mampilly argues that the social and historical conditions that precede the conflict are important for understanding the variation among different rebel governance systems. Mampilly suggests that the mode of state penetration (habituation and co-optation) into the community and the territory claimed by rebels is a key explanation of this variation:

> Only through an understanding of the preconflict state-society relationship can we grasp the modalities that produce diverse insurgent governance efforts across cases, as various civilian populations, politically habituated in differing ways, make distinct demands. . . . Examining the history of the penetration of the state into society is one method for distinguishing between the types of civilian demands.[7]

Together, these studies suggest that a causal link should be drawn between the early experiences of states and dissident groups and the civil war processes we observe today. Recognizing path dependency in decision making takes into account the possibility that organizations adopt existing mental frames to make sense of their environments and reproduce strategies already known to them.[8] This perspective is a valuable addition to rational choice frameworks, as it shows that state-society interactions evolve over a long period of time and close off certain paths of action while opening others to decision makers.

Following this insight, we have examined the long-term choices Kurdish rebels and the Turkish state made throughout the conflict. These preferences operated as positive feedback mechanisms that allowed each side to build a stable yet rigid relationship with resources. In the Turkish case, we underlined organizational policies and ideological discourses that shaped territorial control and civilian support during the war. This approach required a deep understanding of history. We tracked down the historical lineages of combatants' political choices over a century that configured present-day violence and shaped its distribution.

In this respect, the empirical evidence in *Zones of Rebellion* supports a basic claim: Spatial and temporal variation in violence is a function of combatants' relations with resources. We have demonstrated that zone making closely follows earlier choices. As war zones gradually come into being, each with a different threshold of compliance, violence begins to vary. Subsequently, the type, target, and method of violence take different forms across civil war space. Violence toward civilians is selective on the home court and is indiscriminate on the opponent's territory. Civil war sides diversify their tactics in contested sites.

Room for Contingency

Path dependence is a shortcut strategy for solving distributional conflicts. Political actors keep lines of inclusion and exclusion intact by preserving past policies. This does not, however, mean that paths go unchallenged. There is always an undercurrent that aims to dismantle the existing formation.[9] This challenge typically originates from spaces and groups who are excluded by existing arrangements.[10] This is what happened in Turkey when ethnic entrepreneurs started a guerrilla war in the least integrated part of the country. Ironically, such challengers can also be constrained in their effort to secure full compliance from the same resource base because of their own path-dependent policies. If neither side can successfully eliminate the other, the end result is a long and intractable conflict.

Historical institutionalist accounts are usually criticized for not allowing enough room for change. It is therefore important to identify contingencies or windows of opportunity where actors have a realistic chance to adopt new policies.[11] We have observed that this moment arises at the peak of military success, when the winner needs to redefine its relationship with resources.[12] This rare opportunity for policy change presents itself only occasionally. In a civil war context, when the window of opportunity opens, the state needs to follow a practical and consistent line of reform, whereas rebels need to switch from a military to a political agenda.

In the Turkish civil war, two critical turning points, both of them decisive military outcomes, emerged as contingencies. In 1993, the PKK had the upper hand on the battlefield and its military superiority coincided with its ability to mobilize civilians in border towns. The PKK, however, failed to transform civil resistance into an organized political movement (1991–1993). It refused to compromise guerrilla struggle in favor of an inclusive political strategy. Instead, the rebels spent their energies on a military struggle that they had no chance of winning decisively. As a consequence, they neither secured the allegiance of the majority of Kurds nor understood the revolutionary potential of civilian unrest in the early 1990s.

Meanwhile, in 1999, Öcalan was captured in Kenya, and the PKK retreated to northern Iraq. Despite this window of opportunity, the Turkish state maintained its longstanding policies in the region. In power since 2002, the Islamist government continued to rely on friend-foe distinctions and worked with local (Islamic and rural) allies. The state has failed to revive its developmentalist ideology and has ignored earlier promises of equal citizenship. As a result, civilian loyalties and territorial control remained divided in Kurdish society and thereby sustained the conflict in the long run.

Enduring peace is hard to come by in civil wars. This is especially the case when a resilient insurgency faces a strong state in autonomy-seeking ethnic wars. Because the state has already divided the resources, rebels have a hard time in consolidating them. Path-dependent policies seal resource partitioning and turn bargaining into an ineffective tool. The tools of the peacekeeping community, such as mediation and third-party intervention, often carry little weight because these conflicts are mostly immune to foreign pressure. This reality has been a prominent feature of civil wars in Turkey, Russia, and China, where these states have been dealing with restive communities at their frontiers for over a century.

This examination of the PKK and the Turkish state has made a number of key observations to advance the general study of civil wars. First, it is important to understand the interactions of civil war sides with resources: territory and people. Without grasping these patterns, the interactive evolution of a civil war cannot be adequately captured. Second, civil war violence has path-dependent origins. Patterns of violence follow the long-term interactions that each party has cultivated with resources. In that respect, measuring subnational patterns can yield rewarding insights about variations in violence across time and space. Third, identical solutions will hardly work across all civil wars. To remedy the problem, more comparative and qualitative work on civil wars is required. Finally, we call for an account of civil wars that identifies long-term processes that block lasting peace. Conflicts have deeper causes than actors are willing to acknowledge.

Appendix

This appendix explains the procedures we followed to create the datasets employed in the strategy chapters. It lists the administrative units that make up each zone and describes the datasets that quantified violence. To put this methodological effort into context, it is worth remembering the book's major finding: there has been a strong affinity between zones and the nature of violence in the Turkish civil war. Based on this observation, we concluded that the state and the insurgency are resource-dependent organizations and that the distribution of violence closely reflects their ties with territory and people. This appendix introduces the universe of violence and explains our rationale for classifying civil war events. We start with the composition of zones. Next, we turn to the sources we used to create the datasets. The remaining sections identify critical variables in the data that diversified violence across time and space.

Zones

Zones register the unequal access of civil war sides to resources. *Zones will emerge gradually over time as a consequence of each side's prior record with the target territory and the target group.* Most important, the military performance of combatants varies across space. In the Turkish case, the major division was between the emergency region (the OHAL) and the rest of the country. The state was hegemonic outside the OHAL framework. We called this area Zone 3. As a security-driven territorial arrangement, the OHAL put several provinces under its rule (1987–2002). Its longevity also hardened boundaries. We classified the OHAL in ways that reflect the record of combatants. The stronghold of the PKK insurgency was the border area. To capture this subnational pattern, we carved out Zone 1, which includes all the districts on the border with Syria and Iraq and those adjacent to them. The rest of the OHAL was open to contestation. We named this area Zone 2. This was where insurgents had dreams of expansion, and rivalries between the PKK and its opponents, including the state, unfolded in the 1990s.

Since the Turkish state viewed the OHAL region differently, a new classification was necessary (box 1). This classification needed to reflect the

---

Box 1: Zones

- **The OHAL region**: 12 provinces

Batman, Bingöl, Bitlis, Diyarbakır, Elazığ, Hakkari, Mardin, Muş, Siirt, Şırnak, Tunceli, Van

- **Zone 3**: All the provinces outside the OHAL region

Zones of Rebellion:

- **Zone 1**: 30 districts within the OHAL region

  Hakkari: Hakkari-Central District, Çukurca, Şemdinli, Yüksekova; **Mardin**: Mardin-Central District, Dargeçit, Derik, Kızıltepe, Mazıdağı, Midyat, Nusaybin, Ömerli, Yeşilli; **Siirt**: Eruh, Pervari; **Batman**: Gercüş;

Şırnak: Şırnak-Central District, Beytüşşebap, Cizre, Güçlükonak, İdil, Silopi, Uludere; **Van:** Van-Central District, Başkale, Çaldıran, Gürpınar, Muradiye, Özalp, Saray.

- **Zone 2:** The rest of the OHAL region (74 districts)

Zones of Counterinsurgency:

- **Transition Zone:** 18 districts within the OHAL region

    Batman: Batman-Central District; **Diyarbakır:** Diyarbakır-Central District, Bismil, Hani, Hazro, Kulp, Lice, Silvan; **Mardin:** Mardin-Central District; Dargeçit, Derik, Kızıltepe, Mazıdağı, Midyat, Nusaybin; **Şırnak:** Cizre, İdil, Silopi

- **Battle Zone:** The rest of the OHAL region (86 districts)

---

priorities of the state and its counterinsurgency record. The Transition Zone contains places where the Turkish state faced a major political challenge. Representing less than one-fifth of all districts in the OHAL, the Transition Zone was the center of Kurdish contentious politics. This was where civilian unrest was concentrated, an ethnic platform took root, and the Turkish state resorted to mass arrests to curb popular mobilizations. The state approached the rest of the OHAL as a battlefield. Counterinsurgency typically employed military encounters to eliminate insurgents. It was military efficiency rather than political competition that defined the state's experience in the Battle Zone. As chapter 6 vividly demonstrated, the Turkish state was successful in containing the insurgency on military grounds. However, it was unable to quell political opposition in the Transition Zone, which created long-term consequences for the state.

Datasets

Several datasets have been employed to capture variation of violence in the Turkish civil war. We created these datasets after months of archival work in Turkey, relying on multiple sources to build an extensive and reliable empirical base. The presence of various media outlets in Turkey and the insistence of Abdullah Öcalan on using print media to propagate his views opened up a wealth of information on the topic. Several attempts were made to minimize potential biases. First, we crosschecked information from multiple sources before recording an incident. Two newspapers that circulate widely in Turkey, *Milliyet* and *Hürriyet*, formed the backbone of our inquiry. Other Turkish dailies such as *Radikal, Cumhuriyet, Tercüman, Güneş* and *Türkiye* were consulted for shorter periods to add new information or cross-check the accuracy of existing entries. We also tracked *Ayın Tarihi*, a press review produced by the Office of the Prime Minister. *Ayın Tarihi* reported daily events collected from Turkish news outlets. It also included information distributed by the Anatolian News Agency (Anadolu Ajansı). The end result of this effort was a large collection of newspaper articles.

Relying primarily on news reports introduces certain biases. There is a recent scholarship in sociology and political science about using newspaper reports in understanding protest action. This literature identifies selection and description biases in newspaper reporting (which events are reported and under what terms) but concludes that there is no better source for providing us with information about the universe of contentious collective action.[1] Major studies that code violence and protest data similarly use newspaper reports in their analyses.[2]

A closer look at newspaper reporting suggests that such bias may have been episodic in the Turkish case. An important issue here is the source of information provided by newspaper reports. In the mid-1990s, the Emergency Governorship supplied most of the information for the press. The figures were typically given as aggregate numbers, which made it difficult to track the outcome, location, and exact date of individual incidents. Confirming the narrative of the incident from an alternative source often proved impossible. Under the heavy-handed rule of Emergency Governorship, journalists were denied access to the OHAL region. In addition, the early 1990s was the expansion period of the PKK. There were too many incidents spread out over a wide area and newspapers could not fully account for them all.

To our surprise, the situation was different in the 1980s. Newspapers reported incidents by relying on local affiliates who could travel to the incident scene without the permission of OHAL officials. The PKK's frequent use of village raids during this period further facilitated the reporting process. Unlike the counterinsurgency campaigns, an insurgent attack typically took place within a short window and was therefore easy to track. Civilian casualties attracted more media attention to village raids. Thus, the coverage and reliability of our data were better for the 1980s than for the 1990s. After 1999, newspapers once again began to report incidents in some detail. They relied on local journalists, the number of incidents declined, and local access provided detailed information about the victims.

In addition to news outlets, we used several sources to crosscheck and add new information. Ümit Özdağ's book *Pusu ve Katliamların Kronolojisi* (A Chronology of Ambush and Massacres), published by Kripto Press in 2009, claims to rely on official intelligence documents and includes a detailed list of 383 insurgent attacks. In addition, Osman Pamukoğlu, a retired general who was on active duty in Hakkari in the 1990s, produced a list of security forces who died in combat. In the appendix of his book, *Unutulanlar Dışında Yeni bir Şey Yok* (Nothing New Other Than Those Forgotten), Pamukoğlu lists the names of 623 security personnel who died in the 1984–1995 period while fighting in and around Hakkari province. The list also specifies the location and date of these incidents. We also used the government website on veterans and martyrs (www.sehitlervegaziler. gov.tr), which contains information on the deaths of 680 state officials from 1984 to 2008. The Turkish General Staff's website has been providing instant updates on insurgent casualties since 2007.

The rebel publication *Serxwebun* was a critical source for our insurgency dataset. We extracted narratives from this source about individuals who were listed as collaborationists and were punished for their alliance with the state. The fact that the PKK printed victims' names showed the reach of its information networks and the ability of the organization to selectively target civilians. This strategy was designed to discourage locals and militants from defecting to the state side. Accordingly, *Serxwebun* proved invaluable for tracking civilian casualties in the 1980s. In this period, the PKK primarily targeted coethnics in the OHAL region. The rebels used village raids creatively to ensure community transformation. The journal provided the names of 223 individuals the rebel group killed from 1984 to 1987. The journal was helpful on another front as well. It was instrumental in cross-checking data on insurgent casualties. The journal listed the names of guerrillas who died in combat, providing information on their background as well as the location and date of the fatal incident.

We coded incidents with a cautious eye. Unreliable incidents were not included in our datasets. We were able to eliminate more than 100 incidents for which there was contested reporting. Another procedure that we followed was to code a variable as missing if there was simply not enough information. For example, in several instances where we were not sure about the intended target of the insurgent attack, the entries for the target variable are left blank. We calculated the distribution of discriminate and indiscriminate violence based on in-depth reports that linked combatants to their targets. We adopted a similar coding rule regarding extrajudicial killings (*faili meçhuller*). An extensive list in preparation was not used in the book because it was incomplete and needed crosschecking. Instead, we based our analysis on a commission report prepared by the TBMM. Throughout the text, we also refrained from using examples for which there was conflicting information.

Finally, we took the time to sort out counterinsurgency accidents and unaccounted-for rebel deaths, coding them in separate datasets. The former typically involved instances where security personnel had an accident as they were dispatched to a combat operation. The latter involved rebel fatalities (typically found buried or deserted) with no direct evidence of how and when the individual died. Both types of incidents were excluded from our insurgency and counterinsurgency datasets. Accidents left 598 security casualties outside the confines of our main datasets. Four hundred forty-eight rebel deaths discovered in eighty-two separate occasions were similarly excluded from our data and were recorded separately.

This research effort led to unequaled datasets on civil war violence that cover a 24-year period (1984–2008) and all violent events across Turkey. They provide comprehensive micro-level evidence, and contain information on roughly 10,000 incidents. We organized these incidents into separate datasets. The first dataset includes incidents initiated by the insurgency, while the second one groups counterinsurgency operations. These data document more than 80 percent of insurgent, security force, and civilian casualties. Village guard casualties were underreported in the sources that we consulted and account for most of our missing observations under the category of security losses. Likewise, the figures on injured individuals are incomplete. Accordingly, we have not presented any analysis in the book that includes data on injuries and village guard casualties. In addition, we closely followed civilian unrest at Kurdish urban centers for almost two decades (1989–2008) to detail the relationship between military conflict and political mobilization.

We unpacked the incidents from several angles by coding their exact date, method, target, and outcome. This prevented the datasets from being a mere compilation of casualty numbers. Knowing an incident inside out proved invaluable in constructing rich narratives. Perhaps, most critically, we were able to show how agency, identity, and history were integral parts of waging violence. Figuring out the resource-dependent character of tactics and methods was the first step toward identifying the political origins of violence that reflected the ties between combatants and resources.

Dataset on Insurgency

Our first dataset was a compilation of violent incidents initiated by the rebel group. An incident was defined as rebel activity if it inflicts physical harm upon people and/or property. We gathered information on 4,299 insurgent attacks that took place over a 24-year period (1984–2008). We coded the date and location of each incident. While the dataset contains information on the exact day and hamlet of the incident, we frequently aggregated the data to year and district in our empirical analyses. The outcome of an incident was also coded with detailed categories. Fatalities and injuries were recorded in separate variables for insurgents, security forces, village guards, and civilians. Hostages taken from each group as well as insurgents captured by security forces during an incident were also reported as separate variables. In addition, we provided a narrative of each incident. Accordingly, a description variable is added to the dataset to present additional evidence, cite sources, and mention any reporting discrepancies about the incident.

One of the key variables of the insurgency dataset is the *method* variable. By method, we mean the tactic employed by the rebel group for waging violence. We followed certain protocols in order to get the most accurate picture of the PKK's methods. First, method and target were coded separately even though there was a strong affinity between the two. Second, instead of settling for broad categories, we identified several violent methods previously unknown to civil war researchers. Third, in our analysis we refrained from treating methods as mutually exclusive categories and instead, took into account the fact that insurgents frequently employed multiple tactics in a single incident. As a result, our dataset registered fourteen rebel methods that range from village raids to suicide bombings (box 2).

Box 2: Rebel Methods

- Raid, village
- Raid, district
- Raid, province
- Raid, other
- Armed assault
- Ambush
- Mines

- Hostage taking
- Sabotage
- Roadblocks
- Assassination
- Extortion
- Bombing
- Suicide Bombing

The other key variable is the *target* of the insurgent attack. We clustered targets on two critical levels. First, we identified three broad categories: civilians, security agents, and service providers. Although part of the civilian universe, the third group consisted of state agents and economic actors who connected the region to nationwide networks. This classification scheme was also consistent with insurgent ideology that considered service providers to be "foreign elements" in Kurdish areas. Second, we disaggregated each of these three categories (box 3). For instance, civilian targets included relatives of local collaborators, whereas service providers involved civil servants and teachers.

The rich data on targets led to critical observations. A micropolitical analysis of violence in the Kurdish insurgency illustrates that two sets of targets were chosen in line with the ideological reading of a free Kurdistan. Security targets involved military personnel and village guards in rural areas, and police forces in urban settings. Yet, civilian targets of the PKK were too nuanced to fit the definition of what scholars have referred to as civilian victimization. Frequent attacks on village guards, recruited by the state from Kurdish tribes, and members of their extended families illustrate that selection of targets transcended simple civilian-military distinctions.

Box 3: Rebel Targets

Civilians	Security Agents	Service Providers
• Village administrators	• Military	• Educational targets
• Relatives of local collaborators	• Police	• Economic targets
• Demobilized ex-militants	• Village guards	• Workers
• Shepherds		• Communication/ Transportation targets
• Youth		• Press
• Tribes and traditional actors		• Politicians
• Other and unidentified collaborators		• Civil servants
• Civilian targets (indiscriminate, OHAL)		• Religious workers
• Civilian targets (indiscriminate, rest of Turkey)		

Local allies of the state also included village headmen (*muhtar*) and their family members which figured prominently as PKK targets. Traditional actors such as tribal members became victims of violence largely in connection with their employment as village guards.

The second category of civilian victims was service providers. They were viewed as carrying out a colonizing mission delegated by the state. Civil servants, religious and health workers, and teachers; national political parties and the press; and, communication and transportation networks promoted loyalty to the state and threatened to assimilate Kurdish people. In that respect, indiscriminate violence remained a less frequently observed phenomenon, whereas collaborationists and agents of the state were relentlessly targeted by the PKK.

The technology of violence involved a wide range of methods that were calibrated to each target category. Characteristics of the target were closely linked to the choice of method. Village raids opened a window of opportunity to simultaneously eliminate multiple targets in the countryside, and resulted in the highest casualties per incident. While mostly inconsequential, urban raids (district and province) aimed to show off force in settings where the state had a strong institutional presence. Assassinations targeted collaborationists as well as rival groups and took place in urban areas. Roadblocks halted transportation and attempted to close the region to the rest of Turkey, while keeping locals trapped in the cycle of violence.

Dataset on Counterinsurgency

The second dataset consists of 5,576 counterinsurgency operations in the same time frame (1984–2008). Operations were coded as incidents when they met one of two criteria: the operation resulted in political arrests or involved a deadly military encounter between combatants. Our coding rules excluded certain types of incidents that were systematically under-represented in our sources. In this respect, the dataset did not include village evacuations/burnings. Our decision was driven by the fact that only aggregate numbers were available, and a variety of sources reported highly discrepant figures for this category. For example, estimates of the number of displaced people during the conflict years ranged from 300,000 to 3,000,000. Instead, we took up this theme in the "Abandoning the Countryside" section of chapter 4, and discussed historical lineages and contemporary outcomes of this state policy.

Similarly, we could easily have counted abuses against civilians by village guards as counterinsurgency incidents. Village guards were local allies of the state and were armed by the security forces. We raised this issue in chapter 5 based on the report prepared by the Diyarbakır branch of the Human Rights Association (IHD). However, the few documents available on the matter were not sufficient to come up with reliable numbers. Sparse reporting on coercive practices was at the heart of the problem. When we conducted fieldwork in the area, we learned from villagers in Mardin that such violations were numerous and could take many forms, ranging from simple threats to forcing villagers to sign checks. Locals rarely reported these incidents. Instead, they relied mostly on local strongmen, village heads or elders, to resolve their disputes with village guards.

To ensure compatibility, the counterinsurgency dataset included the variables introduced in the previous section. There were also new variables. Most important, arrests, one of the two main counterinsurgency methods, were reported as a separate variable. The co-evolution of *armed encounters* and *arrests* unveiled the distinctly patterned character of state response to insurgent threat.[3] The coding of arrests followed a nuanced reading, excluding cases where insurgents were captured on the battlefield or surrendered on their own. In this way, the dataset reflects the magnitude of political repression more accurately, and provides multiple ways to measure the depletion of insurgent ranks. The other new variable in the dataset was *cross-border operations*. Their separate coding saved us from measurement errors for domestic operations and demonstrated the episodic character of Turkish state's military strategy.

Turkish counterinsurgency efforts followed different trajectories across space. This property allowed us to measure territorial control in meaningful ways. Our starting point was to classify operations as urban or rural. Incidents that took place below the district level were considered as rural and those above as urban. Each incident was then placed in an *administrative unit* (box 4). For an urban operation, we identified metropolitan cities, provincial centers, and district centers as separate units. This disaggregation effort revealed strong patterns. It showed how the intensity and format of counterinsurgency tactics changed according to administrative hierarchy and that state's priorities shifted substantially during the civil

---

Box 4: Administrative Units

Rural Administration:
- Hamlet (*mezra*)
- Village
- Subdistrict (*belde*)
- Township (*bucak*)

Urban Administration:
- District center
- Central district of a province (*merkez ilçe*)
- Metropolitan municipality (*büyükşehir belediyesi*)

Box 5: Topography of Rural Areas

- Mountain
- Hill or cliff
- Border
- Valley
- Meadow
- Forest
- River or stream

- Strait
- Highway, bridge, or pass
- Rural
- Other

---

war. *Topography* was another dimension of space that we incorporated into the analysis. For operations conducted in rural areas, we collected detailed information about the exact location of the incidents. Several geographical categories including mountainous areas were employed in our coding scheme (box 5). Viewed together with the time dimension, topography variable aptly demonstrated the changing fortunes of the state in the war. As the Turkish state switched to an offensive mode, it became apparent from the dataset that operations increasingly took place in areas further away from rural administrative units.

As in the previous dataset, *target* is a key variable of the counterinsurgency data. This variable nicely illustrated that the Turkish state had multiple targets throughout the conflict. We classified targets according to their relation to the rebel group, while keeping the rural/urban dimension intact (box 6). The main target of counterinsurgency efforts was the insurgent in the countryside. Security forces engaged this group through armed encounters predominantly in the Battle Zone. Locating civilian support for the insurgents in the countryside however proved difficult. Low arrest numbers recorded this failure and signaled the acceleration of forced migration policy because of the state's information deficit in rural areas. Meanwhile, identifying the insurgent was the main problem in urban settings. Insurgents and their civilian supporters were detained as a group when their role and past record remained unclear. Mostly targeting the PKK's urban committees, counterinsurgency operated in the gray area, unable or reluctant to discriminate between combatants and noncombatants. The final category of targets is civilians.

Box 6: Counterinsurgency Targets

- Insurgents in rural areas
- Insurgents and their support units in urban areas
- Support units in rural areas
- Civilians
- Support units, location not known

Civilians represented a group of politically active individuals who participated in civilian resistance. Mass arrests targeted this group, particularly in the Transition Zone, where popular mobilizations shook the region in the early 1990s.

Patterns of Civilian Unrest

In addition to insurgency and counterinsurgency datasets, we constructed an exhaustive list of incidents of civilian unrest in Kurdish urban centers. The list included 846 incidents that spanned two decades (1989–2008). In these acts of resistance, civilians protested harsh state measures and/or showed their support for insurgency. Demonstrations, insurgent funerals, and shop closings were the most commonly adopted forms of resistance. Civilian unrest offered a unique opportunity to explore the relationship between armed conflict and political mobilization. It unpacked the role of brokerage in civil wars and showed how a group of networked towns and individuals could make a difference in the course of a civil war. The date, location, and repertoires of resistance also provided important clues to understanding the role of civilian unrest in civil wars.

The list classified the incidents at several levels. This dataset coded the date, location, and repertoire of the incident. It also traced the number of participants, the intensity of the state's response, and the specific motivations for each act of resistance. This empirically rich account led to major observations. First, civilian unrest emerged when the insurgency gained momentum and the state employed arrests systematically for the first time to contain the rebel group. Second, acts of resistance were concentrated in the Transition Zone, which hosted several politically active towns. Third,

civilian unrest evolved into a nationalist platform in the 1990s and became the source of the state's political troubles in the long run. Finally, the
changing intensity of the state's response, measured as civilian casualties,
demonstrated the shift in the priorities of the state over the course of the
conflict. Political repression was most brutal when mass mobilizations had
the potential to succeed in the early 1990s. When this dynamic was lost, the
state turned its attention to large cities and rural areas.

NOTES

Introduction

1. Raşit Kısacık, *Minareden Kandil'e PKK* (Istanbul: Ozan, 2012), 198–211. Mahsun Korkmaz died in a clash with security forces in March 1986. The incident took place somewhere between Gabar (Küpeli) mountain and the Seslice village of Şırnak and also led to the death of three other rebels along with Korkmaz. For more information on the first rebel attacks, see chapter 3, note 5.

2. This was the tenth time the insurgents had raided the Taraklı hamlet in the remote village of Dereler, which was part of the Şırnak district at the time. In the raid, which took place on May 7, 1988, the insurgents killed fifteen people, taking four hostage. "Yine PKK: 2 Günde 26 Ölü," *Milliyet*, May 10, 1988.

3. Leyla Kaplan, who was originally from Kızıltepe, Mardin, was detained as a rebel sympathizer in 1992. As the second suicide bomber of the rebel group, she detonated herself at the gate to a riot police (Çevik Kuvvet) compound in Adana. The incident killed four people and injured eighteen, including civilians and police officers. One month before the incident, she wrote a letter to a PKK operative in Adana and told him that she was leaving the organization. The minister of the interior shared the handwritten letter with the press. For its full content, see "Teröristin İntihar Eylemi," *Milliyet*, October 26, 1996.

4. Mesut Taner Genç was an inexperienced bureaucrat. Before coming to Beytüşşebap, he spent a few years in the United Kingdom on a scholarship from the Ministry of the Interior and served in Kayseri and Sivas. During his tenure in Beytüşşebap (1993–1995), the new governor

worked hard to win the allegiance of several tribes that were coming under the influence of the rebel group. Genç later moved up in the administrative hiearchy and became the lieutenant governor of Ankara. Mesut Taner Genç, *Ateş Hattında:Beytüşşebap Kaymakamının PKK ile Mücadele Günlüğü* (Istanbul: Kaknüs, 2010).

5. The People's Labor Party (HEP) was the first pro-Kurdish nationalist party to be represented in the Turkish Grand National Assembly (TBMM). It was founded by seven representatives who left the Social Democratic People's Party (SHP) in 1990 because of disagreements over the Kurdish issue. One year later, in the 1991 election, the HEP returned to the Assembly on the SHP ticket, winning twenty-two seats.

6. Population ecologists draw attention to a symbiotic relationship between competing actors. They refer to resource partitioning as a situation where two organizations coexist in the same environment. Glenn R. Carroll, "Concentration and Specialization: Dynamics of Niche Width in Populations of Organizations," *American Journal of Sociology* 90, no. 6 (1985): 1262–1283; Glenn R. Carroll and Anand Swaminathan, "Why the Microbrewery Movement? Organizational Dynamics of Resource Partitioning in the U.S. Brewing Industry," *American Journal of Sociology* 106, no. 3 (2000): 715–762.

7. Andreas Wimmer, *Ethnic Boundary Making: Institutions, Power, Networks* (Oxford: Oxford University Press, 2012).

8. The term *resources* has predominantly been used to refer to lootable resources, weapons, and cash in civil war research. Natural resources can be regarded as a means rather than an end for rebel groups that have gone beyond mere looting and theft and aim to establish some form of governance. Our approach emphasizes territory and civilians as the two main resources that combatants ultimately want to control.

9. On territorial control, see Stathis N. Kalyvas, *The Logic of Violence in Civil War* (New York: Cambridge University Press, 2006), chapters 7–8. His analysis departs from ours in an important way. Kalyvas views zones of control as symmetric formations that mirror the distribution of power between combatants. We argue that zones are not mutually exclusive entities; instead they reflect each side's long-term record with resources (territory and people).

10. Michael T. Hannan, László Pólos, and Glenn R. Carroll, *Logics of Organization Theory: Audiences, Codes, and Ecologies* (Princeton, N.J.: Princeton University Press, 2007).

11. Both observations have informed cutting-edge scholarship on the behavior of firms, race riots, and protest organizations. See Susan Olzak, *The Dynamics of Ethnic Competition and Conflict* (Stanford, Calif.: Stanford University Press, 1992); and Sarah A. Soule and Brayden G. King, "Competition and Resource Partitioning in Three Social Movement Industries," *American Journal of Sociology* 113, no. 6 (2008): 1568–1610.

12. The centrality of intracommunity dynamics in civil wars is discussed in Rogers Brubaker and David D. Laitin, "Ethnic and Nationalist Violence," *Annual Review of Sociology* 24 (1998): 423–452.

13. A conceptual discussion on thresholds of rebellion is available in Roger D. Petersen, *Resistance and Rebellion* (New York: Cambridge University Press, 2001). On the same issue, see also Timur Kuran, *Private Truths, Public Lies: The Social Consequences of Preference Falsification* (Cambridge, Mass.: Harvard University Press, 1995).

14. Since the founding of the HEP in 1990, Kurdish nationalist parties have shared the same vision. They demand ethnic representation and ask for a power-sharing arrangement for the region. During this period, a succession of new parties emerged under the same leadership. The goal was to bypass the decision of the Constitutional Court that banned pro-Kurdish parties as separatist organizations. Accordingly, between 1993 and 2013, the HEP had four successors: the Democracy Party (DEP), the People's Democracy Party (HADEP), the Democratic Society Party (DTP), and, most recently, the Peace and Democracy Party (BDP).

15. Jacques Bertrand, *Nationalism and Ethnic Conflict in Indonesia* (New York: Cambridge University Press, 2004).

16. On path dependency, see James Mahoney, "Comparative-Historical Methodology," *Annual Review of Sociology* 30 (2004): 81–101; and Paul Pierson, "Increasing Returns, Path Dependence, and the Study of Politics," *American Political Science Review* 94, no. 2 (2000): 251–267.

17. Paul Pierson, "Public Policies as Institutions," in *Rethinking Political Institutions: The Art of the State*, ed. Ian Shapiro, Stephen Skowronek, and Daniel Galvin (New York: New York University Press, 2007), 114–131; Sven Steinmo, "What Is Historical Institutionalism?," in *Approaches and Methodologies in the Social Sciences*, ed. Donatella Della Porta and Michael Keating (Cambridge, UK: Cambridge University Press, 2008), 118–138.

18. See Ira Katznelson and Barry R. Weingast, "Intersections between Historical and Rational Choice Institutionalism," in *Preferences and Situations-Points of Intersection between Historical and Rational Choice Institutionalism*, ed. Ira Katznelson and Barry R. Weingast (New York: Russell Sage Foundation, 2005), 1–24; Kathleen Thelen, "Historical Institutionalism in Comparative Politics," *Annual Review of Political Science* 2 (1999): 369–404.

19. We use process tracing, a commonly adopted technique in case studies, to demonstrate the path-dependent sequence of events. See Alexander L. George and Andrew Bennett, *Case Studies and Theory Development in the Social Sciences* (Cambridge, Mass.: MIT Press, 2005), 213.

20. Matthew N. Davies, *Indonesia's War over Aceh: Last Stand on Mecca's Porch* (London: Routledge, 2006), chapter 2.

21. Cook, Hardin, and Levi suggest that lesser access to alternatives would increase individuals' trust toward and dependence on groups and organizations. For a relational understanding of trust, see Karen S. Cook, Russell Hardin, and Margaret Levi, *Cooperation without Trust* (New York: Russell Sage Foundation, 2005), 15.

22. The principal-agent problem refers to a situation where the delegation of authority to the agent can allow the latter to pursue its own interests. This is because the principal often lacks the technology and other means to overcome its information deficit. Administrative hierarchies are commonly prone to this conflict. See Edgar Kiser, "Comparing Varieties of Agency Theory in Economics, Political Science and Sociology: an Illustration from State Policy Implementation," *Sociological Theory* 17, no. 2 (1999): 146–170.

23. Faced with similar challenges at the height of their power, the Shining Path of Peru and the Communist Party of the Philippines also had to choose between decentralization and authoritarian rule. In both cases, organizational inefficiency failed the objective of securing large territories.

24. For similarities with the Indonesian case, see Edward Aspinall, *Islam and Nation: Separatist Rebellion in Aceh, Indonesia* (Stanford, Calif.: Stanford University Press, 2009), chapter 7.

25. Alevites preach an Anatolian version of Shi'ite Islam. They have millions of Turkish and Kurdish followers and are mostly concentrated in east-central Anatolia. Zazas, who are also known as Dimli and Kirmanc groups, speak a different dialect and have a distinct path of historical development within the Kurdish community. For an authoritative account, see Malsimanıj, *Kırd, Kırmanc, Dımıli veya Zaza Kürtleri* (Istanbul: Deng, 1996). See chapters 1 through 4 for more on both groups.

26. Steve J. Stern, ed., *Shining and Other Paths* (Durham, N.C.: Duke University Press, 1998), Part 2.

27. For historical origins of this ideological position, see Cem Emrence, *Remapping the Ottoman Middle East* (London: I. B. Tauris, 2012), chapter 4.

28. International Crisis Group, "Colombia's Elusive Quest for Peace," ICG Latin America Report no. 1, International Crisis Group, Washington, D.C., 2001.

29. On the latter point, see James D. Fearon, "Why Do Some Civil Wars Last So Much Longer than Others?" *Journal of Peace Research* 41, no. 3 (2004): 275–301.

1. Organization

1. For an authoritative account of the Turkish left, see Aclan Sayılgan, *Türkiye'de Sol Hareketler*, vol. 2 (Istanbul: Doğu Kütüphanesi, 2009), 455–531. On the making of an organizational field, see Paul J. DiMaggio and Walter W. Powell, "The Iron Cage Revisited: Institutional Isomorphism and Collective Rationality in Organizational Fields," *American Sociological Review* 48, no. 2 (1983): 147–160.

2. For the role of regulators, see Martin Ruef, "The Emergence of Organizational Forms: A Community Ecology Approach," *American Journal of Sociology* 106, no. 3 (2000): 658–714.

3. On protest cycles, see Sydney Tarrow, *Power in Movement: Social Movements, Collective Action and Politics* (Cambridge, UK: Cambridge University Press, 1994). Recently, the study of protest cycles has benefited from ecology approaches; see Debra C. Minkoff, "The Sequencing of Social Movements," *American Sociological Review* 62, no. 5 (1997): 779–799; and Susan Olzak and S. C. Noah Uhrig, "The Ecology of Tactical Overlap," *American Sociological Review* 66, no. 5 (2001): 694–717.

4. An exhaustive treatment of the TIP is available in Turhan Salman, *TİP Parlamento'da*, 5 vols. (Istanbul: Türkiye Sosyal Tarih Araştırma Vakfı, 2004–2005).

5. In a documentary account, Aykol demonstrates that the number of leftist political organizations founded in Turkey jumped from twenty-two in 1960–1971 to fifty in 1971–1980. Hüseyin Aykol, *Türkiye'de Sol Örgütler (Bölüne Bölüne Büyümek)* (Ankara: Phoenix Yayınevi, 2010), 29–58. The proliferation of leftist groups seems to have been a general pattern during the 1970s. A high-ranking M-19 militant, who was a student at Universidad Nacional de Colombia in that decade, remembers the fragmented character of leftist student politics in Colombia: "It was a time of intense sectarianism. Each political group declared itself the possessor of the absolute truth. . . . Everything was summed up in initials; every set of initials was an abbreviation, and every abbreviation was a different political group that did not get along with others." Maria Eugenia Vasquez Perdomo, *My Life as a Colombian Revolutionary*, trans. Lorena Terando (Philadelphia, Pa.: Temple University Press, 2005), 37–38.

6. On the DDKO's origins and goals, see Tarık Ziya Ekinci, *Türkiye İşçi Partisi ve Kürt Aydınlanması* (Istanbul: Cem Yayınevi, 2004), 269–317; and M. Emin Bozarslan, *Doğu'nun Sorunları* (1966; repr., Istanbul: Avesta, 2002), 191–228. For publications of the DDKO that raised issues about Kurdish areas and socialism in Turkey, see *Devrimci Doğu Kültür Ocakları Dava Dosyası* (Ankara: Kalite Matbaası, 1975), 479–630.

7. Carrying capacity refers to the maximum number of organizations that can be sustained in a certain organizational form. Using military court records and the testimony of informants, a Diyarbakır-based journalist, Kısacık, surveyed major ethnic organizations that operated in the region. For Kawa's leadership, its rivalry with the PKK, and tragic end, see Raşit Kısacık, *Kawa: Denge Kawa, Red Kawa, PSŞK* (Istanbul: Ozan, 2010), esp. 61–71, 150, 190–210. On Rızgari's vision and its fragmentation, see Raşit Kısacık, *Rızgari ve Ala Rızgari* (Istanbul: Ozan, 2010), 57–67, 109–154.

8. Hamit Bozarslan, "Kurds and the Turkish State," in *The Cambridge History of Turkey*, vol. 4, ed. Reşat Kasaba (Cambridge: Cambridge University Press, 2008), 345–346.

9. Baki Karer, *PKK Nedir, Ne Değildir?* (Stockholm: n.p., 1999), 55–57.

10. For the liability of newness problem, see John Freeman, Glenn R. Carroll, and Michael T. Hannan, "The Liability of Newness: Age Dependence in Organizational Death Rates," *American Sociological Review* 48, no. 5 (1983): 692–710. For an illustration, see Michael T. Hannan and John Freeman, "The Ecology of Organizational Mortality: American Labor Unions, 1836–1985," *American Journal of Sociology* 94, no. 1 (1988): 25–52. For the PKK evidence, see Abdullah Öcalan, *PKK'da Gelişme Sorunları ve Görevlerimiz* (Köln: Weşanên Serxwebûn, 1994), 163.

11. On niche shift as a response to competitive crowding, see Stanislav D. Dobrev, Tai-Young Kim, and Michael T. Hannan, "Dynamics of Niche Width and Resource Partitioning," *American Journal of Sociology* 106, no. 5 (2001): 1299–1337.

12. On the high-level meetings that formalized the PKK's presence in the region and established a division of labor in the organization in the 1977–1980 period, see the documentation in Raşit Kısacık, *Minareden Kandil'e PKK* (Istanbul: Ozan, 2012), 29–77.

13. The importance of organizational identity is explored in James N. Baron, "Employing Identities in Organizational Ecology," *Industrial and Corporate Change* 13, no. 1 (2004): 3–32.

14. Eric Jan Zürcher, *Turkey: a Modern History*, Third Edition (London: I.B. Tauris, 2004), 316.

15. Kenan Evren, chief of Turkey's General Staff at the time, discusses the influence of the PKK in the province of Şanlıurfa and its surrounding districts. Kenan Evren, *Kenan Evren'in Anıları*, vol. 1 (Istanbul: Milliyet Yayınları, 1990), 280–281.

16. On collective action as an asset, see Elaine Romanelli, "The Evolution of New Organizational Forms," *Annual Review of Sociology* 17 (1991): 79–103. As Bruinessen rightly pointed out, "The PKK succeeded in drawing many of the youth of the region away from other political organizations." Martin van Bruinessen, "Between Guerrilla War and Political Murder: The Workers' Party of Kurdistan," *Middle East Report* 153 (1988): 40–46.

17. These were Kurdistan National Liberationists (KUK) in Mardin, the People's Salvation (Halkın Kurtuluşu) in Tunceli, Tekoşin and Strekasor in Gaziantep, and the Turkish Kurdistan Socialist Party (TKSP, Özgürlük Yolu) and the Revolutionary Democratic Culture Association (DDKD) in Diyarbakır.

18. Mehmet Celal Bucak was the head of the powerful Bucak tribe and a member of the TBMM. The PKK attacked him in the Kırbaşı village of Hilvan on July 30, 1979; the goal was to announce PKK's founding with a spectacular event. The animosity between the Bucak tribe and the PKK has continued since then. In 2011, the PKK proposed a fresh start. "Karayılan'dan Bucak Aşiretine Tehdit," *Radikal*, June 4, 2011.

19. Court cases in the military tribunal of Diyarbakır, which were held from April 1979 to July 1987, confirm the significance of the PKK threat. "Sıkıyönetimden Geriye 94 İdam Kaldı," *Milliyet*, July 19, 1987.

20. For the classic argument, see John W. Meyer and Brian Rowan, "Institutionalized Organizations: Formal Structure as Myth and Ceremony," *American Journal of Sociology* 83, no. 2 (1977): 340–363.

21. Aliza Marcus, *Blood and Belief: The PKK and the Kurdish Fight for Independence* (New York: New York University Press, 2007), 58.

22. First, Mazlum Doğan lit himself on fire on Nevrouz Day (Kurdish new year), March 21. Four others followed in May. A few months later, Mehmet Hayri Durmuş, Kemal Pir, Ali Çiçek, and Akif Yılmaz died during a hunger strike. There was widespread torture in the Diyarbakır prison that was integrated into the daily routines of prisoners. For a personal testimony, see Bayram Bozyel, *Diyarbakır 5 No. Lu* (Istanbul: İletişim, 2013), 85–200.

23. Doğu Ergil, "Suicide Terrorism in Turkey," *Civil Wars* 3, no. 1 (2000): 42.

24. For the importance of "cryptic messages" in transforming victim status into a political identity, see Vamık Volkan, *Blood Lines: From Ethnic Pride to Ethnic Terrorism* (New York: Farrar, Straus and Giroux, 1997), 156–167. The Peruvian example was strikingly similar. For the millenarian tone of the Shining Path's leader, Abimael Guzman, see Gustavo Gorriti, *The Shining Path*, trans. Robin Kirk (Chapel Hill, N.C.: University of North Carolina Press, 1999), 21–36, 105–106.

25. Hannan and Freeman call these "segregating mechanisms"; see Michael T. Hannan and John Freeman, "Where Do Organizational Forms Come From?" *Sociological Forum* 1, no. 1 (1986): 50–72.

26. On Çetin Güngör's (code name Semir) story, see Marcus, *Blood and Belief*, 89–96.

27. Öcalan made it clear on several occasions that he was opposed to those who rejected armed struggle, promoted Europe-centered politics, and practiced warlordism. See Abdullah Öcalan,

PKK IV: Kongresine Sunulan Politik Rapor (Istanbul: Aydınlar Matbaası, 1993), 108–114; and Abdullah Öcalan, *PKK V. Kongresine Sunulan Politik Rapor* (Istanbul: Güneş Ülkesi Yayıncılık, 1995), 163–166.

28. İsmet G. İmset, *The PKK: A Report on Separatist Violence in Turkey, 1973–1992* (Ankara: Turkish Daily News, 1992), 83. For example, Duran Kalkan (code name Abbas) was detained and Ali Ömürcan (code name Terzi Cemal) was arrested after the Third Party Congress (1986). Both were military commanders in the first successful guerrilla attacks of 1984.

29. Şemdin Sakık, *İmralı'da Bir Tiran: Abdullah Öcalan* (Istanbul: Togan, 2012), 319–320, 324–332. İbrahim Güçlü, a longtime Kurdish activist, compiled a list of people the PKK had executed. He presented the list to the Human Rights Commission of the Turkish Parliament. See TBMM İnsan Haklarını İnceleme Komisyonu, "Terör ve Şiddet Olayları Kapsamında Yaşam Hakkı İhlallerini İnceleme Raporu," unpublished report, Ankara, 2013, 67–70.

30. Philip Selznick, "An Approach to a Theory of Bureaucracy," *American Sociological Review* 8, no. 1 (1943): 47–54.

31. Selim M. Çürükkaya, *Beyrut Günlüğü: Apo'nun Ayetleri* (Istanbul: Doz Yayınları, 2005), 36.

32. Arthur L. Stinchcombe, "Social Structure and Social Organizations," in *Handbook of Organizations*, ed. James G. March (New York: Rand McNally, 1965), esp. 149.

33. Ahmet Cem Ersever, *Kürtler, PKK ve Abdulah Öcalan* (Ankara: Ocak Yayınları, 1998), 123.

34. Ümit Özdağ, *Türkiye'de Düşük Yoğunluklu Çatışma ve PKK* (Ankara: Üçok Yayıncılık, 2005), 51–52.

35. A PKK military commander confirms the trend; see Nevzat Çiftçi, *Girdap: PKK'da Yaşanmayan Yıllar* (Istanbul: Turan Yayıncılık, 1998), 58.

36. After spending twenty-five days in the mountains with rebels, Gürsel had a similar impression. The majority of rebels were villagers who were poor, uneducated, and young. See Kadri Gürsel, *Dağdakiler* (Istanbul: Metis Yayınları, 1996), 59–60. On the Colombian case, see Juanita Leon, *Country of Bullets: Chronicles of War*, trans. Guillermo Bleichmar (Albuquerque: University of New Mexico Press, 2009), 80–88.

37. Miller McPherson, "An Ecology of Affiliation," *American Sociological Review* 48, no. 4 (1983): 519–532.

38. Burhan Semiz, *Çıkmaz Sokak: PKK Dağ Kadrosunun Metodolojisi ve Sosyolojisi* (Ankara: Lalezar Kitabevi, 2007), 139–154.

39. As will be discussed in chapters 3 and 6, village raids, hostage-taking, and civilian unrest were concentrated in Botan. Gould underlines the importance of informal social ties and spatial proximity on collective action; see Roger V. Gould, *Insurgent Identities: Class, Community and Protest in Paris from 1848 to the Commune* (Chicago: University of Chicago Press, 1995), 114, 118, 205–206.

40. Alkan conducted open-ended interviews with former female militants to explore women's incentives for joining the organization. See Necati Alkan, *PKK'da Semboller, Aktörler, Kadınlar* (Istanbul: Karakutu, 2012). Similarly, Martinez, who traced the motivations of certain groups involved in the Algerian civil war, showed how the conflict became a vehicle of change for those in the suburbs of Algiers. Luis Martinez, *The Algerian Civil War, 1990–1998*, trans. Jonathan Derrick (New York: Columbia University Press, 2000).

41. Michael Radu, "The Rise and Fall of the PKK," in *Dangerous Neighborhood: Contemporary Issues in Turkey's Foreign Relations*, ed. Michael S. Radu (New Brunswick, N.J.: Transaction Publishers, 2003), 143–164; and *PKK Terrorism* (Ankara: Ministry of Foreign Affairs, 1998), 19–29. However, the PKK's record compares poorly with those of Colombian and Peruvian insurgent groups. For the account of a former gendarmerie commander of Şemdinli that highlights

the symbiotic ties between the PKK and smuggling interests along the Iranian border, see Erdal Sarızeybek, *Şemdinli'de Sınırı Aşmak* (Istanbul: Pozitif Yayınları, 2011), 29–30, 33, 94–97, 106–108, 182–186.

42. For example, when it became public that the villagers of Yeşilyurt (Cizre) had been subjected to gross human rights violations, PKK sympathizers occupied the Turkish Airlines building in Copenhagen and the Yapı Kredi Bank in Hamburg. "Dışkı Yedirme Eylemi," *Milliyet*, February 3, 1989.

43. Aliza Marcus, "City in the War Zone," *Middle East Report* 189 (1994): 16–19.

44. On the ERNK and its several tasks, see Abdullah Öcalan, *Kürdistan Yurtseverliği ve Ulusal Kurtuluş Cephesi* (Köln: Weşanen Serxwebûn, 1992), esp. 59–60, 65–68, and 125–142.

45. The ERNK had five branches in Germany and six branches in the rest of Europe. European branches reported to their counterparts in Germany, and the German branches reported to the rebel leader in Damascus. No administrative position was allowed in the European ERNK that would consolidate power in the hands of a single individual. Other important ERNK branches in Russia, the Middle East, and the Marmara region of Turkey also reported directly to the rebel leader. For administrative hierarchy in the ERNK, see Ali Nihat Özcan, *PKK (Kürdistan İşçi Partisi) Tarihi, İdeolojisi ve Yöntemi* (Ankara: ASAM, 1999), 288–317.

46. On the evolution of youth and women's organizations, see Mutlu Akkurt, *PKK Terör Örgütünün Gençlik Yapılanması* (Istanbul: IQ Kültür Yayıncılık, 2010), 79–88; and Alkan, *PKK'da Semboller, Aktörler, Kadınlar*, 121–131.

47. Stathis Kalyvas and Laia Balcells, "International System and Technologies of Rebellion: How the End of the Cold War Shaped Internal Conflict," *American Political Science Review* 104, no. 3 (2010): 415–429.

48. From 1984 to 1987, the military wing of the PKK, the Kurdistan Salvation Union (HRK), and from 1987 on, the Kurdistan People's Salvation Army (ARGK) were responsible for challenging the state through irregular warfare. In the late 1980s, groups of seven to nine lightly armed guerrillas (*manga*) would cross the border by foot to mount attacks, then retreat immediately to external PKK bases in Syria, northern Iraq, and Iran. These hit-and-run tactics were so efficient that few members of the organization could be captured by security forces in the early years of the conflict. By the early 1990s, the size of attack units had grown to twenty-seven guerrillas (*takım*) following successful recruitment and increasing guerrilla control of rural areas. More control of rural areas meant that the largest units (*tabur*), which consisted of 270 to 300 guerrillas, could attack military checkpoints on the border. After the PKK's military success declined, it reverted to using the smaller units that had been responsible for its initial success.

49. Öcalan, *PKK V. Kongresine Sunulan Politik Rapor*, 33.

50. Ibid., 157.

51. Öcalan, *PKK'da Gelişme Sorunları ve Görevlerimiz*, 181–249.

52. Kalyvas and Kocher recognize that "the optimal size of rebel organizations is smaller than otherwise assumed." Stathis N. Kalyvas and Matthew Adam Kocher, "How 'Free' Is Free Riding in Civil Wars?" *World Politics* 59, no. 2 (2007): 212.

53. Öcalan, *PKK IV: Kongresine Sunulan Politik Rapor*, 82. Öcalan's fascination with the education of party members reveals his Republican, modernist origins. On education in PKK rebel camps, see Ali Kemal Özcan, *Turkey's Kurds: A Theoretical Analysis of the PKK and Abdullah Öcalan* (London: Routledge, 2006), 165–180.

54. White observed the same point during his visit to the rebel camp in Bekaa in 1992. For PKK's "new person project," see Paul White, *Primitive Rebels or Revolutionary Modernizers-The Kurdish National Movement in Turkey* (London: Zed Books, 2000), 136–142.

55. The PKK divided Kurdistan into several provinces, one of which was Botan. See chapter 3 for a detailed discussion.

56. On bureaucratic insurgency, see Mayer N. Zald and Michael A. Berger, "Social Movements in Organizations: Coup d'Etat, Insurgency, and Mass Movements," *American Journal of Sociology* 83, no. 4 (1978): 823–861.

57. On several occasions, Sakık accused Öcalan of establishing one-man rule and destroying PKK's organizational efficiency. See "Sakık: Apo Korkağın Biri," *Hürriyet*, April 16, 1998; and Şemdin Sakık, *Apo* (Ankara: Şark Yayınları, 2005), 132–166. Nevzat Çiftçi and Selim Çürükkaya, the influential commanders of Tunceli and Diyarbakır, agreed with many of Sakık's criticisms.

58. For the new bylaws of the PKK, see Özcan, *PKK (Kürdistan İşçi Partisi) Tarihi, İdeolojisi ve Yöntemi*, 408–416.

59. Abdullah Öcalan, *Kürdistan'da Halk Kahramanlığı* (Köln: Weşanên Serxwebûn, 1994), 253.

60. "Istanbul'da Terör Saldırısı," *Hürriyet*, July 27, 2008. The PKK has not disclosed its ties with the TAK. Its concerns about public legitimacy seem to be the main factor. However, there is evidence that links the two. First, the TAK swore allegiance to Öcalan, it relied on the PKK's expertise about explosives, and its captured members were trained in PKK camps. Second, our evidence suggests that the timing of two organizations' attacks in large cities were mutually exclusive, and the targets and strategies of TAK attacks were almost identical to those of the PKK in 1998–1999. Third, the PKK has a rich history of setting up new units when an old unit was unsuccessful (for example, HRK to ARGK to People's Defense Forces [HPG]) and/or there is a new purpose. Also, note that Metropole Revenge Teams (MİT) served a similar purpose in the second half of the 1990s and disappeared from the scene with the TAK. For the testimony of arrested TAK members, see "Bombacı TAK da PKK'nın Uzantısı," *Milliyet*, July 22, 2005; "Antalya Bombacısının Talimatı Dr. Bahoz'dan," *Milliyet*, October 11, 2011; "PKK'lı Teröristin İlginç Bağlantıları," *Milliyet*, November 19, 2011; and "Bomba'nın Şeytanı PKK'da," *Milliyet*, August 27, 2012. Human Rights Watch also suggests a link between the TAK and the PKK; see Human Rights Watch, *World Report 2012* (New York: Human Rights Watch, 2012), 503.

61. On the DHKP-C, see Bilal Sevinc, "Participation in Terrorist Organizations: an Analysis of Left-Wing DHKP-C and Religiously Motivated Turkish Hezbollah Terrorist Organizations" (PhD diss., Michigan State University, 2008).

62. For Öcalan's statement in court, see Abdullah Öcalan, *Declaration on the Democratic Solution to the Kurdish Question* (London: Mesopotamian Publishers, 1999).

63. Abdullah Öcalan, *Politik Rapor: Dönüşüm Süreci Üzerine Perspektifler* (Istanbul: Mem Yayınları, 2000).

64. PKK, *Dönüşüm Süreci ve Görevlerimiz (PKK 7. Olağanüstü Kongre'sine MK Raporu)* (Köln: Serxwebûn, 2000), 150–161.

65. Osman Öcalan later left the organization. In an exclusive interview in 2009, he discussed the new direction he had proposed for the rebel group at the time. Öcalan claimed that politics should replace military struggle and that the rebels needed to win the friendship of the European Union and the United States. See the interview in "Artık Dağdan İnme Zamanı," *Milliyet*, May 2, 2009.

66. Abdullah Öcalan, *Demokratik Devrimde Halk Serhildanları* (Köln: Weşanên Serxwebûn, 2002), 278.

67. Ceren Belge, "State Building and the Limits of Legibility: Kinship Networks and Kurdish Resistance in Turkey," *International Journal of Middle East Studies* 43, no. 1 (2011): 95–114.

68. A survey conducted by the firm A&G confirmed this perspective in 2009. While 70 percent of respondents supported the use of nonmilitary measures to solve the Kurdish issue, only 20 percent supported the idea of a general amnesty for the rebels. For details, see "Güneydoğu'da Yeni Açılıma Evet, Dağdaki Affa Hayır," *Milliyet*, July 5, 2009.

69. Mahsum Şafak, ed., *PKK VI. Ulusal Konferans Raporu* (Istanbul: Mem Yayınları, 2002), 106–119, 171–202.

70. Öcalan, *Politik Rapor: Dönüşüm Süreci Üzerine Perspektifler*, 147.

71. Güneş Murat Tezcür, "When Democratization Radicalizes: The Kurdish Nationalist Movement in Turkey," *Journal of Peace Research* 47, no. 6 (2010): 775–789.

2. Ideology

1. Jack A. Goldstone, "Comparative Historical Analysis and Knowledge Accumulation in the Study of Revolutions," in *Comparative Historical Analysis in the Social Sciences*, ed. James Mahoney and Dietrich Rueschemeyer (Cambridge, UK: Cambridge University Press, 2003), 41–90.

2. John L. Campbell, "Institutional Analysis and the Role of Ideas in Political Economy," *Theory and Society* 27 (1998): 377–409.

3. Francesca Poletta and James M. Jasper, "Collective Identity and Social Movements," *Annual Review of Sociology* 27 (2001): 283–305; Robert C. Lieberman, "Ideas, Institutions and Political Order: Explaining Political Change," *American Political Science Review* 96, no. 4 (2002): 697–712.

4. PKK, *Kürdistan Devrimi'nin Yolu* (n.p.: 1978), 229.

5. Martin van Bruinessen, "Kurdish Paths to Nation," in *The Kurds: Nationalism and Politics*, ed. Faleh A. Jabar and Hosham Dawod (London: Saqi, 2006), 21–48.

6. Article 3 of the Pact of Mutual Cooperation between Iraq and Turkey required the contracting parties to refrain from interfering in each other's internal affairs. Royal Institute of International Affairs, *The Baghdad Pact: Origins and Political Setting* (London: Royal Institute of International Affairs, 1956), Appendix II.

7. Abdullah Öcalan, *Kürdistan'da İşbirlikçilik ve İhanet* (Istanbul: Zagros Yayınları, 1993), 268–313, 351.

8. Abdullah Öcalan, *19.Yüzyıldan Günümüze Kürdistan Gerçeği ve PKK Hareketi* (Köln: Weşanen Serxwebûn, 1994). For a similar approach that focuses on economic life, see Kemal Burkay, *Kürdistan'ın Sömürgeleştirilmesi ve Kürt Ulusal Hareketleri* 2nd Printing (Cologne: Özgürlük Yolu, 1986), 113–123.

9. For a classic account, see İsmail Beşikçi, *Doğu Anadolu'nun Düzeni: Sosyo-Ekonomik ve Etnik Temeller*, exp. ed., vol. 1 (Ankara: Yurt Kitap-Yayın, 1992), 133–168; İsmail Beşikçi, *Doğu Anadolu'nun Düzeni: Sosyo-Ekonomik ve Etnik Temeller*, exp. ed., vol. 2 (Ankara: Yurt Kitap-Yayın, 1992), 448–453, 519–528.

10. Abdullah Öcalan, *PKK'da Gelişme Sorunları ve Görevlerimiz* (Köln: Weşanên Serxwebûn, 1994), 49–139.

11. Abdullah Öcalan, *Kürdistan'da İşbirlikçilik ve İhanet*, 327.

12. Öcalan criticized Kurdish leaders in northern Iraq for relying on outside support, working as agents of imperialism, and blocking the PKK revolution in Turkey through their alliances with the Turkish state. See Abdullah Öcalan, *Güney Kürdistan'da Egemenlik Mücadelesi ve Devrimci Demokratik Tutum* (Istanbul: Çetin, 2003), 9–20, 69, 79–91, 131–138; and Abdullah Öcalan, *Ortadoğu'nun Çehresini Değiştireceğiz* (Köln: Weşanen Serxwebûn, 1994), 228–229, 270–273, 313–328.

13. Interview with Abdullah Öcalan. See "Talabani, Ateşkes Önerdi," *Milliyet*, October 6, 1991.

14. Despite a brief moment of cooperation in 1993, the Kurdistan Socialist Party (PSK, formerly TKSP) viewed the PKK as a violent and sectarian organization that was controlled by intelligence services and regional powers. On the PSK's ideology and differences with the PKK, see Kemal Burkay, *Sorular ve Cevaplarla PSK Ne Diyor? Ne İstiyor?* (Stockholm: Roja Nû Yayınları, 2003), 20–31, 102–109; and Kemal Burkay, *Devrimcilik mi, Terörizm mi? PKK Üzerine* (n.p.: Özgürlük Yolu Yayınları, 1983).

15. Abdullah Öcalan, *PKK IV. Kongresi'ne Sunulan Politik Rapor* (Istanbul: Aydınlar Matbaası, 1993), 63.

16. Semiz concluded that the rebel group viewed religion as a "Trojan Horse" and paid lip service to Islam only for pragmatic purposes. Burhan Semiz, *PKK ve KCK'nın Din Stratejisi* (Istanbul: Karakutu Yayınları, 2013), 108–118, 151–156, 185–196.

17. Hakan Özoğlu, *Kurdish Notables and the Ottoman State: Evolving Identities, Competing Loyalties, and Shifting Boundaries* (Albany: State University of New York Press, 2004), 87–120.

18. For a historical analysis that examines confessional differences in the Kurdish community as a result of power struggles and boundary making efforts, see Erdal Gezik, *Alevi Kürtler: Dinsel, Etnik ve Politik Sorunlar Bağlamında* (Ankara: Kalan, 2000), 68–79. On Alevite opposition to the Şeyh Said Rebellion, see M. Şerif Fırat, *Doğu İlleri ve Varto Tarihi* (Istanbul: Şaka Matbaası, 1948), 123–149. On Kurdish-Alevite rituals and social organization in Dersim and Erzincan, see Ali Kemali Aksüt, *Erzincan Tarihi: Coğrafi, İçtimai, Etnografi, İdari, İhsai Tetkikat Tecrübesi* (Istanbul: Resimli Ay Matbaası, 1932), 187–208.

19. Paul White, *Primitive Rebels or Revolutionary Modernizers? The Kurdish National Movement in Turkey* (London: Zed Books, 2000), 48.

20. Hüseyin Aygün was kidnapped by PKK members in the Ovacık district of Tunceli on August 12, 2012. The rebel group criticized him for emphasizing the distinct place of Zazas in the Kurdish community. In an interview, Aygün later accused the PKK of not tolerating alternative viewpoints in Tunceli. See "Hüseyin Aygün Gerçeği," *Özgür Gündem*, August 18, 2012; and "Sabah PKK'lı Genci Uyandırdım," *Radikal*, August 16, 2012.

21. For the origins of underdevelopment in eastern Anatolia, see Mutlu, who emphasizes tribal hierarchy, lack of land reform, and increasing population pressure on pastures. Server Mutlu, *Doğu Sorununun Kökenleri* (Istanbul: Ötüken, 2002). For a critical perspective on Turkish-Kurdish encounters outside the OHAL region, see Murat Ergin, "The Racialization of Kurdish Identity in Turkey," *Ethnic and Racial Studies* 37, no. 2 (2014): 322–341.

22. Aspinall observed a similar phenomenon in Indonesia. Acehnese rebels ignored religion in their ideology because religion had failed as a political program in previous revolts and allowed the state to win civilian loyalties with its Islamic content. Edward Aspinall, *Islam and Nation: Separatist Rebellion in Aceh, Indonesia* (Stanford, Calif.: Stanford University Press, 2009), 48, 218.

23. The first cease-fire the PKK announced in 1993 attempted to translate military victory into a political outcome. For details, see "PKK's Ocalan Explains Peace Overtures," Foreign Broadcast Information System-Western Europe-93-053 (hereafter FBIS-WEU), March 22, 1993, 41; "PKK, PSK Leaders Issue Statement Following Meeting," FBIS-WEU-93-058, March 29, 1993, 60. For the PKK's position on the 1993 cease-fire, see Kadir Konuk, *PKK'nın İlan Ettiği Ateşkes ve Yankıları* (Istanbul: Zagros, 1993).

24. David Romano, *The Kurdish Nationalist Movement: Opportunity, Mobilization and Identity* (Cambridge: Cambridge University Press, 2006), 144–168. The GAM pursued a similar strategy in Indonesia; see Kirsten E. Schulze, "The Free Aceh Movement (GAM): Anatomy of a Separatist Organization," Policy Studies no. 2, East-West Center, Washington, D.C., 2004, 51–54.

25. On insurgent incentives to attract NGO support, see Clifford Bob, *The Marketing of Rebellion: Insurgents, Media, and International Activism* (Cambridge: Cambridge University Press, 2005).

26. Four international conferences were held from 1989 to 1995. These conferences recommended putting more international pressure on Turkey and defended the Kurds' right to choose between autonomy and independence. The Kurdish Institute of Paris, a host and sponsor of these meetings, published some of this material. International Paris Conference, *The Kurds: Human Rights and Cultural Identity* (Paris: Institut Kurde de Paris, 1992), esp. 25, 53–60; *International Inter-Parliamentary Consultation on the Kurds* (Paris: Institut Kurde de Paris, 1992).

27. *Ayın Tarihi*, February 12, 1992.

28. *Ayın Tarihi*, March 23, 1993.

29. For the role transnational activism can play in safeguarding and promoting human rights regimes, see Margaret E. Keck and Kathryn Sikkink, *Activists beyond Borders: Advocacy Networks in International Politics* (Ithaca, N.Y.: Cornell University Press, 1998), chapter 3.

30. Socialist/Green parties actively raised Turkey's Kurdish question in the European Parliament, established ties with the ERNK in Europe, and were directly involved in efforts to grant asylum to Öcalan.

31. "Belçika Kürt Sorununa Taktı," *Milliyet*, May 27, 1992. The Belgian Senate was referring to the Treaty of Sevres (1920), which concluded World War I between the Ottoman Empire and the Entente Powers. The treaty promised the creation of an independent Kurdish state in eastern Anatolia. However, the Turkish War of Independence blocked its implementation. The Treaty of Sevres was later replaced by the Treaty of Lausanne (1923), which confirmed the sovereignty of the Turkish Republic over Anatolia.

32. "DEP'liler, Mitterrand'a Sığınmak İstedi," *Milliyet*, March 11, 1994.

33. For a translated summary of the letter, see "Madam'dan Çiller'e Kürt Mektubu," *Milliyet*, July 21, 1994.

34. Remzi Kartal was one of the five members of the DEP who fled to Europe. He later joined the ERNK, the European wing of the PKK. He recommended that Congress establish a bureau in the region through the Organization of Security and Cooperation in Europe (OSCE). Kartal also asked for constitutional change in Turkey and refused to recognize the PKK as a terrorist organization. Another DEP member, Ali Yiğit, was also present in these meetings. "DEP'lilerden PKK Savunması," *Cumhuriyet*, July 24, 1994; "Washington'la En Krizli Dönem," *Cumhuriyet*, December 24, 1994.

35. In his letter to President Clinton, Öcalan claimed that the Kurds were subject to genocidal policies similar to those the Armenians and Greeks had suffered in the past and that the United States should lead the way to a peaceful solution. For the original letter, see "İşte Apo'nun Mektubu," *Milliyet*, October 25, 1995.

36. On European perceptions, see Hamid Akın Ünver, "Defining Turkey's Kurdish Question: Discourse in the US Congress, the European Parliament and the Turkish National Grand Assembly, 1990–1999" (PhD diss., University of Essex, 2009), chapter 3.

37. "Avrupa'dan 5 Şart," *Milliyet*, July 1, 1994.

38. "Italy Ending House Arrest of Rebel Chief of Kurds," *New York Times*, December 17, 1998. Solving the "Eastern Question" through international conferences has been a favorite policy tool of European states since the Berlin Conference (1878). For historical precedents, see M. S. Anderson, *The Eastern Question, 1774–1923: A Study in International Relations* (London: Macmillan, 1966).

39. Aliza Marcus, *Blood and Belief: The PKK and the Kurdish Fight for Independence* (New York: New York University Press, 2007), 236. For a different view, see Henri J. Barkey and Graham E. Fuller, *Turkey's Kurdish Question* (Lanham, Md.: Rowman and Littlefield, 1998), 34–39.

40. On the PKK's activities in Greece, see *Greece and PKK Terrorism* (Ankara: Ministry of Foreign Affairs, 1999).

41. The photographs from this meeting appeared in the Turkish press in "Çirkin İttifak," *Milliyet*, July 1, 1995.

42. "Russia: Turkey Questions Official Support for PKK," Foreign Broadcast Information System-former Soviet Union-96-101, May 23, 1996, 16; "Turkey Protests pro-Kurdish Remarks in Russian Parliament's Meeting," *Turkish Daily News*, May 23, 1996. For a comparative analysis that shows how Turkish-Russian relations were shaped by the Kurdish and Chechen questions in the 1990s, see Robert Olson, "Turkish and Russian Foreign Policies, 1991–1997: The Kurdish and Chechnya Questions," *Journal of Muslim Minority Affairs* 18, no. 2 (1998): 209–227.

43. The PKK struck twice in Europe, in June and November of 1993. Each wave of violence resulted in human casualties and material damage. In 1994, after the rebel organization was banned, several clashes took place between PKK supporters and the German police. The German secret service visited Öcalan in Lebanon in 1995 to convince him to stop the violence. Even though it was not allowed to operate in Germany, the PKK made a show of force on Nevrouz Day in 1996. The German police detained more than 1,000 demonstrators, and the German

government asked for help from the European Union. Öcalan expressed his regret about the incident later that year. Finally, Germany announced in 1997 that it considered the PKK a criminal, not a terrorist, organization. For a detailed survey of European press reports on the 1993 ban, see *Dış Basında Terör Örgütü PKK'nın Almanya'da Yasaklanması (24–30 Kasım 1993)* (Turkey: T. C. Başbakanlık, Basın-Yayın ve Enformasyon Genel Müdürlüğü, 1993); *Dış Basında Terör Örgütü PKK'nın Yasaklanması (1–15 Aralık 1993)* (Turkey: T. C. Başbakanlık, Basın-Yayın ve Enformasyon Genel Müdürlüğü, 1993).

44. Savas Kalenderidis, a Greek intelligence officer, traveled from Greece to Kenya as Öcalan's security detail. See Savas Kalenderidis, *Öcalan'ın Teslimi*, trans. Savas Kalenderidis (Istanbul: Pencere Yayınları, 2011), 189–302.

45. Abdullah Öcalan, *Declaration on the Democratic Solution to the Kurdish Question* (London: Mesopotamian Publishers, 1999).

46. In his several appeals to the European Court of Human Rights, Öcalan argued that solving the Kurdish issue would democratize the Middle East and establish democratic modernity in the region. Abdullah Ocalan, *Prison Writings: The Roots of Civilization* (London: Pluto Press, 2007), 288–297; Abdullah Öcalan, *Demokratik Uygarlık Manifestosu*, 3 vols. (Istanbul: Aram Yayınları, 2009).

47. For the best formulation, see Abdullah Öcalan, *12 Eylül Faşizmi ve PKK Direnişi* (Ankara: Yurt Kitap Yayın, 1992). On the "army-nation" thesis, see his interview with Doğu Perinçek in 1989; Doğu Perinçek, *Abdullah Öcalan ile Görüşme* (Istanbul: Kaynak Yayınları, 1990), 51, 58, 122–124, 133–136.

48. Öcalan blamed rogue elements for the escalation of violence in the 1990s. He argued that the Turkish state was controlled by a special interest group from 1993 to 1996. Similarly, in a supplemental brief for his court defense, Öcalan referred to power struggles inside the PKK during the same period. Abdullah Öcalan, *Barış Umudu* (Istanbul: Çetin, 2005), 46, 57–61, 63, 72; Abdullah Öcalan, *Kürt Sorununda Çözüm ve Çözümsüzlük İkilemi* (Istanbul: Mem Yayınları, 1999), 13, 21–26.

49. Turkey has been increasing its economic and political influence in northern Iraq. The PKK has suggested that solving the Kurdish issue is the key for Turkey's success in the region. See PKK, *Dönüşüm Süreci ve Görevlerimiz: PKK 7. Olağanüstü Kongre'sine MK Raporu* (n.p.: Serxwebûn, 2000), 37–38.

50. For the record of the Kurdish nationalist party, see Nicole F. Watts, *Activists in Office: Kurdish Politics and Protest in Turkey* (Seattle: University of Washington Press, 2010).

51. Abdullah Öcalan, *Politik Rapor: Dönüşüm Süreci Üzerine Perspektifler* (Istanbul: Mem Yayınları, 2000), 114.

52. On Turkish-Kurdish partnerships at critical moments in history, see Öcalan's interview with Mihri Belli in Abdullah Öcalan, *Kürt-Türk İlişkileri Üzerine Barış ve Demokrasi Konuşmaları 1988–1999* (Istanbul: Aram Yayınları, 1999), 125–141.

53. Michael Bishku, "The Resurgence of Kurdish Nationalism in Northern Kurdistan–Turkey from the 1970s to Present," in *The Evolution of Kurdish Nationalism*, ed. Mohammad M. A. Ahmed and Michael Gunter (Costa Mesa, Calif.: Mazda Publishers, 2006), 78–97.

54. Rebel demands changed according to military performance. It is interesting to note that cultural rights were not at the top of PKK's agenda during the expansion period. On the contrary, Öcalan argued in 1989 that the Kurdish language was "the last item to save" and that his political project was not about "giving freedom to Kurdish." A decade later, the rebel leader had a different perspective on the issue and based his defense in court on cultural rights. For these positions, see Perinçek, *Abdullah Öcalan ile Görüşme*, 30–31, 86–87; and Öcalan, *Barış Umudu*, 79.

55. The project rests on the idea of self-governance of Kurds. It was aired in several meetings of the Democratic Society Congress (DTK), an umbrella organization under the influence of Kurdish nationalists. For these proposals, see Demokratik Toplum Kongresi, *Kürt Sorununun Çözümü için Demokratik Özerklik* (Istanbul: Aram, 2012), 52–70, 122–124.

56. For an earlier formulation of the KCK's mission in the ERNK's foundational text, see Abdullah Öcalan, *Kürdistan Yurtseverliği ve Ulusal Kurtuluş Cephesi* (Köln: Weşanen Serxwebûn, 1992), 48. In April 2009, mass arrests targeted the KCK. The defense claimed that the main objective of the Justice and Development Party (AKP) government was to prevent Kurds from establishing self-government. Fatma Aktaş, *Demokratik Siyaset ve Demokratik Toplum Savunması: KCK Savunmaları* (Istanbul: Aram, 2012), 22, 25–28, 43–44.

57. For the PKK's organizational attempts to set a propaganda line, see Mahsum Şafak, ed., *PKK VI. Ulusal Konferans Raporu* (Istanbul: Mem Yayınları, 2002).

3. Strategy

1. Niche theory suggests that organizations differ from one another in terms of their scope, strategy, and identity. There are two types of organizations, generalists and specialists, each with a different relation to its environment. See Pamela A. Popielarz and Zachary P. Neal, "The Niche as a Theoretical Tool," *Annual Review of Sociology* 33 (2007): 65–84.

2. The fundamental niche refers to the "abstract dimensions of the resource space within which a population is observed." The realized niche is a subset of the fundamental niche, where an organization is capable of sustaining itself. See Glenn R. Carroll, "Concentration and Specialization: Dynamics of Niche Width in Populations of Organizations," *American Journal of Sociology* 90, no. 6 (1985): 1262–1283.

3. For a full description of variables, coding rules, and data sources, please see the Appendix.

4. Insurgents were locals from the area who had a keen understanding of state and rebellion and used this to their advantage. The PKK's success contrasts starkly with the early experience of the Sandinista National Liberation Front (FSLN) in Nicaragua. The first guerrilla campaign of the FSLN in the 1960s ended in failure. As one group member pointed out years later, the major problem was that they had no knowledge of the terrain and the people. With no prior connections to the villagers, they were seen as "truly alien beings." See Matilde Zimmermann, *Sandinista: Carlos Fonseca and the Nicaraguan Revolution* (Durham, N.C.: Duke University Press, 2000), 81. Not surprisingly, two robust findings about civil war onset are the presence of rough terrain and the superior local knowledge of insurgents. See James D. Fearon and David D. Laitin, "Ethnicity, Insurgency, and Civil War," *American Political Science Review* 9, no. 1 (2003): 75–90.

5. In simultaneous attacks on military targets in Eruh and Şemdinli districts, the rebel group killed two soldiers and wounded eleven on August 15, 1984. Three civilians were also injured. The rebels stole guns and tried to rob a bank in Şemdinli. With these attacks, the PKK announced the beginning of its guerrilla campaign. For the first reports, see "Ayrılıkçılar, İki Jandarma Karakolu ile bir Subay Gazinosuna Saldırdı," *Milliyet*, August 18, 1984; and "Ayrılıkçı Grupların Saldırısı: 1 Er Şehit," *Cumhuriyet*, August 18, 1984.

6. Cudi Mountain provided easy access to several mountain ranges in the region: Cabar Mountain in the province of Siirt, Alandaş Mountain in the Pervari district of Siirt, Celo Mountain in the Çatak district of Van, Balkaya Mountain in the province of Hakkari, and Cilo Mountain in the Şemdinli district of Hakkari. See an interview with the OHAL governor in "PKK'nın Hedefi Şemdinli idi," *Milliyet*, August 20, 1989.

7. The PKK referred back to the experience of the Botan Emirate in the first half of the nineteenth century. Bedirhan Bey of Botan played an instrumental role in terminating other Kurdish emirates. He defeated his regional rivals (Nurullah Bey of Hakkari and Şeref Bey of Bitlis) and waged a military campaign against Nestorians. It was only after Bedirhan's territorial expansion that the Ottoman state put an end to the rule of Kurdish emirates. On Kurdish emirates, see Wadie Jwaideh, *Kurdish Nationalist Movement: Its Origins and Development* (Syracuse, N.Y.: Syracuse University Press, 2006).

8. In 1989, Öcalan claimed that the PKK had a platoon in Botan with more than 2,000 fighters. Doğu Perinçek, *Abdullah Öcalan ile Görüşme* (Istanbul: Kaynak Yayınları, 1990), 44.

9. To remedy the problem, the Turkish state upgraded the Şırnak district to provincial status in 1990.

10. The pattern disappeared in the 1990s and the share of these districts dropped to less than 5 percent.

11. External bases facilitated insurgent success in several cases. See Idean Salehyan, *Rebels without Borders: Transnational Insurgencies in World Politics* (Ithaca, N.Y.: Cornell University Press, 2009). On Syria's incentives for assisting the PKK, see Robert Olson, "Turkey-Syria Relations since the Gulf War: Kurds and Water," *Middle East Policy* 5, no. 2 (1997): 168–193.

12. The public goods character of safe havens for insurgent groups can also be observed in the Mindanao Island, Philippines. A stronghold of Muslim and communist insurgencies, the island had attracted jihadis and independent fighters from South Asia and the Middle East who set up military training camps and recruited from domestic groups since the 1990s. International Crisis Group, "The Philippines: Counter-Insurgency vs. Counter-Terrorism in Mindanao," Asia Report no. 152, May 14, 2008, Washington, D.C.

13. For detailed information on the Mahsun Korkmaz Academy, see "Bekaa'daki Kamp," *Milliyet*, April 15, 1992.

14. Ümit Özdağ, *Türkiye'de Düşük Yoğunluklu Çatışma ve PKK* (Ankara: Üçok Yayıncılık, 2005), 33.

15. "İşte PKK Kampları," *Milliyet*, March 25, 1987.

16. Approximately two-thirds of all PKK attacks in the 1984–1990 period were border-related incidents. Therefore, districts on the border and those adjacent to them were almost three times more likely than others to experience an insurgent attack in this period.

17. Michael M. Gunter, *The Kurds and the Future of Turkey* (New York: St. Martin's Press, 1997), 38.

18. See "PKK'da "Devletçik" Hesabı," *Milliyet*, November 16, 1991.

19. There was intense fighting from August 18 to August 20, 1992. Security forces responded to the Şırnak raid disproportionately; the entire city was in ruins. More than 15,000 people left the area and at least 443 people were detained. Prime Minister Demirel claimed that the rebel group was trying to attract reprisals from the state. Meanwhile, President Turgut Özal acknowledged the social origins of the PKK. The August 23 issue of *Ayın Tarihi* and the August 19–23 issues of *Milliyet* provide detailed coverage of the incident.

20. No other method of violence accounted for more than one-sixth of incidents in any given year in the same period. For other PKK tactics, see the Appendix.

21. "İlk Hedef Telefon," *Milliyet*, August 4, 1987. The insurgents responded to the call by cutting telephone lines and collecting wireless radios from village headmen.

22. Jason Lyall, "Are Coethnics More Effective Counterinsurgents? Evidence from the Second Chechen War," *American Political Science Review* 104, no. 1 (2010): 1–20.

23. Abdurrahim Çelik was a park ranger. He was accused of providing information to the security forces about the whereabouts of insurgents. The tip led to the death of twenty insurgents, the largest PKK loss in a single operation until then. In the Bahminin hamlet, forty people lived in five houses. After the operation, other families also left and sought refuge in nearby areas. "Kalaşnikof'a Karşı Av Tüfeği," *Cumhuriyet*, May 10, 1988; "PKK'dan Henüz İz Yok," *Cumhuriyet*, May 12, 1988. For a detailed account of the counterinsurgency operation, see chapter 6, note 25.

24. Twenty-six civilians were killed and several others were wounded in the incident. "Soykırım, İşte Bu," *Milliyet*, June 22, 1987. A few weeks later, another incident had a deep impact on the Turkish public: Prime Minister Özal and his wife were photographed as they grieved in front of the slain villagers. "Yine Katliam, Yine PKK," *Cumhuriyet*, July 10, 1987.

25. While the government insisted that the suspects were insurgents, the opposition parties questioned the explanation of the government and sent several teams to investigate the incident. Perhaps more important, the villagers took possession of the dead bodies and more than 1,000 people gathered in front of the governor's building in Silopi in protest of the government. This public reaction was the first of its kind and triggered a wave of civilian unrest that intensified in the early 1990s. A few months later, the village headmen, Hacı Aydınlık, and his relatives were killed in downtown Silopi when rebels attacked his house with rockets and automatic rifles. For a chronology of the Derebaşı incident, see "6 Ölü PKK'lı Değil Köylü," *Milliyet*, September 19, 1989; "Silopi'de Olaylı Cenaze," *Milliyet*, September 20, 1989; "Aksu: Köylü Değil Terörist," *Milliyet*, September 21, 1989; and "Silopi'de PKK Katliamı," *Milliyet*, February 28, 1990.

26. On the mixed record of village guards, see the official report of the Turkish parliamentary commission on the topic. TBMM, *Faili Meçhul Cinayetleri Araştırma Komisyonu Raporu (Taslak)* (Ankara: Sosyalist Birlik Partisi Yayınları, 1995), 99–105.

27. The incident took place in the Akdemir hamlet of Şemdinli, which is fifteen to twenty minutes away from the Iraqi border. When insurgents raided the hamlet, they accused the villagers of collaborating with the state. They burned down the houses and fired on villagers. Unexpectedly, village guards responded for the first time, killing four militants. Five civilians were also killed and two others were wounded during the clashes. See "Koruculardan İlk Darbe," *Milliyet*, July 23, 1987.

28. In January 1992, 2,241 village guards resigned and 4,752 were dismissed from service. *Ayın Tarihi*, January 8, 1992. For a detailed discussion, see Ismet G. Imset, *The PKK: A Report on Separatist Violence in Turkey, 1973–1992* (Ankara: Turkish Daily News, 1992), 105–117.

29. "PKK Bacadan Bomba Attı: 2'si Çocuk 5 Ölü," *Milliyet*, April 11, 1990.

30. The rebels also took three civilians with them: Fikret Kaya (23), Feyzi Durgun (27), and Şeref Koç (21). "Korucular Silah Bırakıyor," *Milliyet*, August 10, 1989.

31. The announcement was made by the ERNK Botan Council in March 1992. This was days before Nevrouz, when the PKK had called for a mass revolt. *Ayın Tarihi*, March 17, 1992; *Ayın Tarihi*, March 20, 1992.

32. Relying on information from local affiliates, *Milliyet* printed the names of civilians who were kidnapped in multiple village raids that were conducted in May and June. For details, see "PKK 13 Kişiyi Kaçırdı," *Milliyet*, May 2, 1987; "PKK 5 Kişiyi Kaçırdı," *Milliyet*, June 3, 1987; "Bölücüler 26 İşçiyi Kaçırdı," *Milliyet*, June 4, 1987; "Eşkiya 3 Eri Öldürdü," *Milliyet*, June 5, 1987; and "PKK, 4 Kişiyi Daha Kaçırdı," *Milliyet*, June 9, 1987.

33. Of the ninety-nine reported abduction cases, ninety-four of them occurred during a village raid. Half of these incidents took place in five districts in the Botan area (Şırnak, Şemdinli, Eruh, Uludere, and Çatak).

34. The PKK held peaceful meetings with village headmen in 1984 to form a network of villages that sympathized with its cause.

35. Kemal Kirişçi and Gareth M. Winrow, *The Kurdish Question and Turkey* (London: Frank Cass, 1997), 162–166. Barzani and Talabani continued to fight with each other in 1995–1996, after the regional Kurdish Parliament was established in northern Iraq. Two major issues were the distribution of customs revenues and the proper response to the autonomy schemes the Iraqi government was proposing.

36. The names of these camps were Mirnezir, Ahmet Kesip, Sabri Şahin, Zive, Siyah Çeşme, Galani, Mirömer, Dusivar, Geykan, Kartal Deresi, Bari-Betkar, Urumiye, Rajan, Cerni, Kavanak, Novi, Gülistan, Serkem, Kecele, Seledüken, and Binnas. For more information, see "İran Toprağında 22 PKK Kampı," *Milliyet*, June 11, 1992.

37. Empirical trends confirm the distinct character of Zone 1. Civil servants were mostly targeted in the districts where the PKK successfully cultivated civilian loyalties and could easily identify state officials, as in Cizre and Yüksekova.

38. The elder Öcalan claimed that the PKK had 10,000 militants in the mountains and 20,000 members (*milis*) in urban areas. "Mumcu'yu Biz Öldürmedik," *Milliyet*, January 30, 1993.

39. "Doğu Ekspresine PKK Baskını," *Milliyet*, September 9, 1992; "Tezkereci Erlere PKK Saldırdı," *Cumhuriyet*, September 9, 1992.

40. The rebels also abducted a policeman and three soldiers. See "PKK Saldırıyor," *Cumhuriyet*, June 9, 1993; and "PKK Okul Yaktı, Adam Kaçırdı," *Milliyet*, June 10, 1993.

41. The rebel organization was collecting 1,000 German marks from bus companies for each bus that they operated in the region. Meanwhile, bus companies in Istanbul halted their operations after Nevrouz in 1992. See "Gözaltındaki İşadamları Serbest," *Milliyet*, August 6, 1996; and "Topkapı'da Olağanüstü Hal," *Milliyet*, March 27, 1992.

42. *Ayın Tarihi*, September 4, 1991.

43. For a sample of incidents, see "TPAO'ya PKK Baskını," *Milliyet*, June 22, 1993; and "33 PKK'lı Öldürüldü," *Milliyet*, September 12, 1992. The pipeline was attacked in 1986, 1987, 1994, 1997 and 1998; see "BOTAŞ'a PKK Saldırısı," *Milliyet*, January 25, 1994; and "BOTAŞ Boru Hattına Bomba," *Milliyet*, July 4, 1994.

44. For example, in September 1992, the rebels burned 15,000 bales of tobacco in Kulp. "SHP İlçe Başkanı Öldürüldü," *Milliyet*, September 21, 1992.

45. Osman Pamukoğlu, *Unutulanlar Dışında Yeni bir Şey Yok* (Istanbul: İnkılap, 2004), 53. The insurgents raided the same chicken farm again in June 1998 and killed 10,000 chickens this time. "Hakkari'de 32 PKK'lı Ölü," *Hürriyet*, July 1, 1998.

46. One of the most efficient rebel organizations in this regard is the Ejercito de Liberacion Nacional (ELN) of Colombia. With its ties to trade unions, the ELN successfully acted as a protection racket and collected fees from oil, gas, and coal industries in the Magdalena Medio region in the 1980s. Similarly, the communist insurgency in the Philippines (CPP) has established close ties with miners in the Compostela Valley and turned the region into a major source of funding for its operations. This is not, however, a universal pattern. In contrast to the ELN and the CPP, the GAM in Indonesia failed to extract revenue from gas and oil industries in Aceh.

47. "Yüksekova Göç Ediyor," *Milliyet*, August 21, 1993. For earlier attacks on oil companies in Lice and Kozluk, see "Petrol Tankları Kundaklandı," *Cumhuriyet*, September 1, 1992; and "9 PKK'lı Öldürüldü," *Milliyet*, October 5, 1992.

48. Excerpts from the testimony of Ergün Karadağ (code name Arteş), who was the head of the Diyarbakır ERNK at the time. See "Gözaltındaki İşadamları Serbest," *Milliyet*, August 6, 1996. For a similar story from Tunceli, see "Başkandan Fidye," *Milliyet*, October 4, 1993.

49. The Bitlis branch of the TEKEL reportedly gave bribes to the rebels. "PKK'nın Parası Haraçtan," *Milliyet*, October 1, 1993. Meanwhile, the factory of Best, a nationally known private tobacco company, was also attacked. "PKK, Trene ve Çukurca'ya Saldırdı," *Cumhuriyet*, August 27, 1992.

50. The ERNK made this public statement on the PKK's fifteenth anniversary. See "PKK'ya Bingöl'de de Darbe," *Milliyet*, December 2, 1993.

51. "Öğretmenlerin Zor Kararı," *Milliyet*, August 21, 1994.

52. At the peak of its success, the PKK decided to eliminate political competition and suppress a free press in the region. All national parties were closed, journalists were barred from entering the region, and Turkish newspapers were not allowed to circulate. "PKK'dan Basına Tehdit," *Milliyet*, October 17, 1993; "PKK'dan Meclis'e Tehdit," *Milliyet*, October 22, 1993; "PKK'dan Memura Yasak Bildirisi," *Milliyet*, October 25, 1993.

53. A locally based reporter, Ferit Demir, broke the Tunceli story. The rebels kidnapped and tried Veli Yeşil, a private contractor and the head of the True Path Party (DYP), in a "people's court." He was found guilty but his life was saved after a second trial. Yeşil was forced to sign a letter of resignation from his party and pay a fine of 33,000 German marks. Ironically, the influential PKK commander of Tunceli, Müslüm Durgun (code name Dr. Baran), was a godfather

(*kirve*) at Yeşil's son's circumcision ceremony. The *kirve* is a highly respected social institution in the region that bonds families together. *Kirve* ties allowed Yeşil to pay the fine in installments. See "Başkandan Fidye," *Milliyet*, October 4, 1993; and "PKK'ya Fidye Verdi," *Milliyet*, October 4, 1993.

54. Kohl and Litt underline the political nature of violence and warn revolutionary leaders to adjust the intensity of military struggle and timing of tactical choices to political outcomes. See James Kohl and John Litt, *Urban Guerrilla Warfare in Latin America* (Cambridge, Mass.: MIT Press, 1974), 25. The Shining Path in Peru faced increasing challenges as it expanded from Ayacucho department to Huancavelico, Junin, and Pasco, see Nelson Manrique, "The War for the Central Sierra," in *Shining and Other Paths*, ed. Steve J. Stern (Durham, N.C.: Duke University Press, 1998), 193–223.

55. Thirty-three intellectuals and artists were killed in the Sivas massacre in July 1992. A religious mob set fire to a hotel to disrupt a peaceful meeting that had been organized by an important Alevite organization, Pir Sultan Abdal Derneği. See Lütfi Kaleli, *Sivas Katliamı ve Şeriat* (Istanbul: Alev Yayınevi, 1994).

56. In an incident known as the Başbağlar massacre, the PKK raided Başbağlar village in the Kemaliye district in July 1993 and destroyed the whole village, killing thirty-two civilians and burning fifty-seven houses. The rebels gathered men at the village center and killed them outside the village. See "Erzincan'da Kanlı Baskın 28 Ölü," *Cumhuriyet*, July 7, 1993; and "Kemaliye'de Vahşet," *Milliyet*, July 7, 1993.

57. Abdullah Öcalan, *Demokratik Devrimde Halk Serhildanları* (Köln: Weşanên Serxwebûn, 2002), 311–329.

58. Hatay was part of the Aleppo province in the late Ottoman Empire. The French colonization of Syria created the autonomous *sancak* of Alexandretta out of the former province of Aleppo after World War I. The *sancak* voted to reunite with Turkey after a plebiscite in 1939. For a rich account of the unification process, see Philip S. Khoury, *Syria and the French Mandate: The Politics of Arab Nationalism, 1920–1945* (Princeton, N.J.: Princeton University Press, 1987).

59. On the TDP's Black Sea enterprise and its collaboration with the PKK, see "PKK'ya Karadeniz Tokadı," *Hürriyet*, May 7, 1998; "Hain Pusuda TIKKO Kuşkusu," *Sabah*, December 8, 2009; and "TDP'li Tutsaklar Açlık Grevine Başladı," *Özgür Gündem*, October 24, 2012.

60. Dev-Sol organized multiple attacks against security forces, especially in May 1992. For a sample of incidents, see "Dev-Sol, PKK ve TIKKO İşbirliği," *Milliyet*, March 11, 1990; and "Dev-Sol'da Yeni Yüzler," *Milliyet*, May 2, 1992.

61. Another reason for the PKK's switch to indiscriminate violence was losing the option of cooperation with other insurgent groups. Dev-Sol split into two groups in 1994 and then was further weakened by the Istanbul police.

62. The majority of these migrants settled in the Akdeniz and Toroslar districts of Mersin and in the Seyhan district of Adana.

63. On rebel rivalry, see Claire Metelits, *Inside Insurgency* (New York: New York University Press, 2010).

64. The TDKP accused the PKK of representing the interests of the Kurdish bourgeoisie and accepting reformist/parliamentarian solutions. For an interview with a high-ranking TDKP official, see Ali Eldeniz, *TDKP Röportajı* (Istanbul: Evrensel Basın Yayın, 1993), 78–89, 149–180. The other revolutionary group operating in the region was the TKP-ML/TIKKO, which had a long tradition of guerrilla struggle and was predominantly an Alevite organization. For power struggles inside the organization in the early 1990s, see *Fırtınalar İçinde Bıçak Sırtında*, vol. 2 (Istanbul: Umut Yayıncılık, 2000), 35–45. For its post-1997 record in the countryside, see *Rüzgar Bizden Yana Esiyor* (Istanbul: Umut Yayıncılık, 2001).

65. "Askeri Konvoya Pusu: 5 Şehit," *Milliyet*, October 12, 1993. For the clash, see "PKK, TDKP'li 6 Kişiyi Öldürdü," *Cumhuriyet*, October 11, 1993. A previous clash between the TDKP

and the PKK in September cost the mayor of Tunceli his seat. After the PKK accused him of being a "traitor," Mehmet Kocademir fled to the Netherlands and his assistant resigned from his post. No one accepted the position of mayor in the city for several months. For rebel rivalry and its political consequences, see "PKK'dan Partilere Tehdit," *Milliyet*, October 22, 1993; and "Sol Örgütler PKK ile Çatışıyor," *Milliyet*, December 27, 1993.

66. TBMM, *Faili Meçhul Cinayetleri Araştırma Komisyonu Raporu (Taslak)*, 120–181.

67. Öcalan foresaw the threat in these provinces and blamed *Nakşibendi* religious brotherhoods for working as agents of the state. See Abdullah Öcalan, *Din Sorununa Devrimci Yaklaşım* (Köln: Weşanên Serxwebûn, 1991), 65, 91–92, 103, 113–117.

68. As the Volterra-Gause principle states, two organizations cannot feed from the same resource base indefinitely.

69. For a comparative analysis of rebel governance, see Zachariah Cherian Mampilly, *Rebel Rulers: Insurgent Governance and Civilian Life during War* (Ithaca, N.Y.: Cornell University Press, 2011), chapter 3.

70. The military remained the main target. For every police killed in insurgent attacks, the Turkish army lost almost ten soldiers.

71. The share of attacks targeting the military increased from 17 percent in 1984–1990 to 26 percent in 1991–1999, reaching 52 percent in 2000–2008.

72. With its rough terrain and strategic location on the border, the Hakkari province alone accounted for one-third of these incidents.

73. "PKK'dan Yine Mayınlı Tuzak: 2 Şehit, 15 Yaralı," *Hürriyet*, December 6, 2006; "Şırnak'ta 6 Asker Şehit, 10 Yaralı," *Hürriyet*, May 24, 2007; "Yine Hain Tuzak," *Hürriyet*, June 9, 2007.

74. "PKK Karakola Saldırdı: 6 Şehit," *Milliyet*, May 11, 2008; "Türkiye On Beş Şehidine Ağlıyor," *Cumhuriyet*, October 5, 2008.

75. "Kalleş Bomba," *Hürriyet*, May 23, 2007.

76. Öcalan and the Turkish state entered into negotiations in late 2012. The process led to a cease-fire and the partial withdrawal of rebel forces from Turkey. Peace talks stalled in September 2013. For a survey of recent developments and attempts at conflict resolution, see International Crisis Group, "Turkey: The PKK and a Kurdish Settlement," Europe Report no. 219, September 11, 2012, Washington, D.C.; and Cengiz Çandar, *"Leaving the Mountain": How May the PKK Lay Down Arms? Freeing the Kurdish Question from Violence* (Istanbul: TESEV Publications, 2012).

4. Organization

1. Robin Blackburn, "Emancipation & Empire, from Cromwell to Karl Rove," *Daedalus* (Spring 2005): 72–87.

2. Frederick Cooper and Ann Laura Stoler, "Between Metropole and Colony," in *Tensions of Empire: Colonial Cultures in a Bourgeois World*, ed. Frederick Cooper and Ann Laura Stoler (Berkeley: University of California Press, 1997), 1–56.

3. David G. Atwill, *The Chinese Sultanate: Islam, Ethnicity and the Panthay Rebellion in Southwest China, 1856–1873* (Stanford, Calif.: Stanford University Press, 2005), chapter 5.

4. For the dual nature of Ottoman modernization, see İlber Ortaylı, *İmparatorluğun En Uzun Yüzyılı* (Istanbul: Hil Yayın, 1983).

5. For historical origins of this geocentric approach, see Edward J. Erickson, *Ottomans and Armenians: A Study in Counterinsurgency* (New York: Palgrave, 2013).

6. These powers included Great Britain, France, Germany, and Russia.

7. On the Druze-Maronite conflict, see Leila Fawaz, *An Occasion for War: Civil Conflict in Lebanon and Damascus in 1860* (Berkeley: University of California Press, 1994). On French pressure and interest in the Lebanese problem, see John P. Spagnolo, *France and Ottoman Lebanon, 1861–1914* (London: Ithaca Press, 1977); and William I. Shorrock, *French Imperialism in the Middle*

East: The Failure of Policy in Syria and Lebanon, 1900–1914 (Madison: University of Wisconsin Press, 1977). For European-Ottoman consensus on a reform program, see Ussama Makdisi, *The Culture of Sectarianism: Community, History and Violence in Nineteenth-Century Ottoman Lebanon* (Berkeley: University of California Press, 2000). On Ottoman record, Engin Deniz Akarlı, *The Long Peace: Ottoman Lebanon, 1860–1920* (Berkeley: University of California Press, 1993).

8. Andrew G. Gould, "Lords or Bandits? The Derebeys of Cilicia," *International Journal of Middle East Studies* 7, no. 4 (1976): 485–506.

9. Ali Karaca, *Anadolu Islahatı ve Ahmet Şakir Paşa, 1838–1899* (Istanbul: Eren, 1993).

10. On massacres and reform proposals from the British perspective, see Great Britain, Foreign Office, *Correspondence Relative to the Armenian Question, and Reports from Her Majesty's Consular Offices in Asiatic Turkey* (London: Her Majesty's Stationery Office, 1896); Great Britain, Foreign Office, *Correspondence Respecting the Introduction of Reforms in the Armenian Provinces of Asiatic Turkey* (London: Her Majesty's Stationery Office, 1896).

11. Fikret Adanır, *Makedonya Sorunu* (Istanbul: Tarih Vakfı Yayınları, 2001).

12. On Ottoman views, European reform programs, and foreign advisors, see respectively, Sinan Kuneralp and Gül Tokay, eds., *Ottoman Diplomatic Documents on the Origins of World War One*, vol. 4, *The Macedonian Issue, 1879–1912* (Istanbul: ISIS Press, 2011); Steven W. Sowards, *Austria's Policy of Macedonian Reform* (New York: Columbia University Press, 1989); and *Osmanlı Arşiv Belgelerinde Kosova Vilayeti* (Istanbul: T. C. Başbakanlık Devlet Arşivleri Genel Müdürlüğü, 2007), 98.

13. There is documentary evidence on the Eastern Inspectorate. It sheds light on Great Power involvement, its regulatory framework, and the activities of the inspector during his brief tenure. See Fahri Taş, *Osmanlı-Ermeni İlişkileri 1912–1914 (Vilayat-ı Şarkıyye Islahatı)* (Erzurum: Atatürk Üniversitesi Yayınları, 2006); and Fahri Taş, "Vilâyat-ı Şarkıyye Islâhatı ve Genel Müfettiş Nicolas Hoff," *Atatürk Araştırma Merkezi Dergisi* 14 (1998): 923–968. For Ottoman documents on the inspectorate, see Zekeriya Türkmen, *Vilayet-i Şarkiye Islahat Müfettişliği, 1913–1914* (Ankara: Türk Tarih Kurumu, 2006), 111–215.

14. On the activities of inspectorates, see the minutes of inspectors' meetings in 1936 in M. Bülent Varlık, ed., *Umumi Müfettişlikler Toplantı Tutanakları–1936* (Ankara: Dipnot, 2010).

15. The Turkish state feared that the French in Syria and the British in northern Iraq were mobilizing minority groups on the border to destabilize the newborn Republic. These groups were Armenian and Kurdish nationalists in Syria (El-Cezire) and Kurds and Nestorians in northern Iraq. Several administrators of the First Inspectorate concurred with this analysis. See Hüseyin Koca, *Yakın Tarihten Günümüze Hükümetlerin Doğu-Güneydoğu Anadolu Politikaları* (Konya: Mikro, 1998), 230–264.

16. Cemil Koçak, *Umumi Müfettişlikler, 1927–1952* (Istanbul: İletişim, 2003), Part 1.

17. On military pacification, see Jandarma Umum Kumandanlığı Raporu, *Dersim* (1932, repr., Istanbul: Kaynak Yayınları, 2010). For a documentary account of state-led transformation in the region, see Tuba Akekmekçi and Muazzez Pervan, eds., *Dersim Harekatı ve Cumhuriyet Bürokrasisi (1936–1950)* (Istanbul: Tarih Vakfı Yurt Yayınları, 2011).

18. In the eyes of Republican elites, the name Tunceli symbolized the transition from backwardness to civilization, a place where hard-working peasants replaced bandits (*çapulcu*) who preyed on others' property. See Naşit Hakkı Uluğ, *Tunceli Medeniyete Açılıyor* (1939; repr., Istanbul: Kaynak Yayınları, 2007), 193. Similarly, the Indonesian state changed the name of Papua to Irian Jaya (Victory City) after it acquired the island from the Dutch.

19. On trust networks that limit outsiders' access to community resources, see Charles Tilly, *Trust and Rule* (New York: Cambridge University Press, 2005).

20. Dersim presented a set of challenges to the state: It had a distinct identity and occupied a difficult geography. Yet its relatively small size and distance from the border made it a suitable candidate for administrative experiments.

21. M. Hakan Yavuz, "Five Stages of the Construction of Kurdish Nationalism in Turkey," *Nationalism and Ethnic Politics* 7, no. 3 (2001), 1–24.

22. This bureaucratic irregularity was called *mücavir*, which gave legal rights to local authorities in areas adjacent to their jurisdiction.

23. Ardahan, Kars, and Iğdır and cosmopolitan cities such as Mersin and Adana were put under the responsibility of coordinator governors. Minister of the Interior Nahit Menteşe justified this move by emphasizing its advantages for collecting intelligence and coordinating counterinsurgency operations. *Ayın Tarihi*, December 21, 1993.

24. On special zones where state of exception is the norm, see Giorgio Agamben, *Homo Sacer: Sovereign Power and Bare Life* (Stanford, Calif.: Stanford University Press, 1998), chapter 7; and Giorgio Agamben, *State of Exception*, trans. Kevin Attell (Chicago: University of Chicago Press, 2005), chapter 1.

25. Emergency regions were established to address security threats as well as to manage economic downturns and natural disasters. Special rule practices that served security goals presented major challenges to the state, whereas economically minded administrative arrangements did not contribute to zone making.

26. For the full text of the government decree, see *T.C. Resmi Gazete*, No. 19517, July 14, 1987, 1–4. *T.C. Resmi Gazete* is the Official Gazette of the Republic of Turkey.

27. On government decree 430, see *T.C. Resmi Gazete*, No. 20727 December 16, 1990, 1–4.

28. This clause was later repealed. See M. Sezgin Tanrıkulu and Serdar Yavuz, "İnsan Hakları Açısından Olağanüstü Hal'in Bilançosu," *Sosyal Bilimler Araştırma Dergisi* 5, no. 6 (2005): 493–521.

29. See the transcript of Tunceli representative Kamer Genç's speech in the TBMM in *Tutanak Dergisi* 18/46 (May 23, 1990), 24. *Tutanak Dergisi* is the TBMM's journal of record (1961–).

30. "Süper Valilik'te "Süper Yetki" Erozyonu," *Milliyet*, October 29, 1991.

31. Some governors would not go without a fight. Bolat Bolatoğlu, the governor of Mardin, publicly complained that the new military commander (*asayiş komutanı*) who was responsible for internal security was not under his control. Kozakçıoğlu, the first OHAL governor, raised similar concerns about the establishment of the Gendarmerie for Internal Security. "Güreş, Vali ile Tartıştı," *Milliyet*, December 9, 1991; "Halkın Devlete Güvene Sağlanmalı," *Milliyet*, June 25, 1987.

32. The new governor's long list of recommendations included tax-exempt status for the region, cheap energy, industrial parks, and subsidies for machinery. *Ayın Tarihi*, May 26, 1996.

33. İbrahim Yılmazçelik, *Dersim Sancağı* (Kripto: Ankara, 2011), 86–99.

34. *Sancak* was an Ottoman administrative unit between a province and a district and can be defined as a subprovince.

35. The Ottoman Provincial Law (1864) had geopolitical origins. It was the document that created a large province (Tuna) in the Balkans by incorporating Niş, Vidin, and Silistre. The goal was to prevent European intervention. For the full text of the law, see Mehmet Seyitdanlıoğlu, "Bir Belge: Yerel Yönetim Metinleri III: Tuna Vilayeti Nizamnamesi," *Çağdaş Yerel Yönetimler Dergisi* 5, no. 2 (1996): 67–81.

36. It should also be noted that there were cases in which political or economic incentives guided redistricting efforts. While the former primarily had served right-wing populism since the 1950s (for example, Osmaniye), the latter helped a region to recover from massive dislocation. For instance, Düzce and Yalova were elevated to provincial status after a major earthquake hit Turkey in August 1999.

37. This approach resembled the Chinese imperial vision that put frontier regions of Inner Mongolia and Tibet under special rule. See Justin Tighe, *Constructing Suiyuan: The Politics of Northwestern Territory and Development in Early 20th Century China* (Leiden: Brill, 2005), 5.

38. Saygı Öztürk, *Kasadaki Dosyalar* (Adana: Ümit Yayıncılık, 2003), 29.

39. On the incorporation of the *sancak* of Alexandretta into Turkey, see chapter 3, note 58.

40. On the Third Inspectorate, see Erdal Aydoğan, "Üçüncü Müfettişliğin Kurulması ve III. Umumi Müfettiş Tahsin Uzer'in Bazı Önemli Faaliyetleri," *Ankara Üniversitesi Türk İnkılâp Tarihi Enstitüsü Atatürk Yolu Dergisi* 33–34 (2004): 1–14. For the legislation that created the Third and Fourth Inspectorates, see TBMM, *Zabıt Ceridesi* 5/7 (December 12, 1935): 96–104. *Zabıt Ceridesi* is the TBMM's journal of record. The Second Inspectorate, which was established in eastern Thrace, served a similar purpose. In late Ottoman times, Thrace was a cosmopolitan region with strong connections to the Balkans. With the departure of Jews in the 1930s, most of the economic capital also left the region.

41. *Genelkurmay Belgelerinde Kürt İsyanları*, vol. 1 (1972; repr., Istanbul: Kaynak Yayınları, 2011), 193–194. Several decades later, after the PKK's first successful attacks in Eruh and Şemdinli, the military commander of Eruh was also forced into retirement. "Devlet Üç Beş Çapulcuya Pabuç Bırakmaz," *Milliyet*, October 3, 1984.

42. Hakkari (Çölemerik) was downgraded to a district. Previously, it had faced several attacks from Kurdish tribes. Most notably, Şeyh Molla Barzani and his 500 men launched an assault on the Oramar region in the summer of 1930. M. Kalman, *İngiliz ve Türk Belgelerinde Botan Direnişleri* (Istanbul: Med Yayınları, 1996), 151–152.

43. On the 1926 legislation, see TBMM, *Zabıt Ceridesi* 2/25 (May 29, 1926): 605–615, 622–624; and TBMM, *Zabıt Ceridesi* 2/25 (May 30, 1926): 629–630, 674–676.

44. See chapter 3 for Şırnak's centrality in guerrilla warfare.

45. TBMM, *Tutanak Dergisi* 18/45 (May 16, 1990): 239–270.

46. There was also a similar proposal in the 1940s to move the provincial center of Bingöl to Genç, and incorporate Lice and Kulp districts into its borders. Ironically, the Genç-Lice-Kulp triangle became a major insurgent sanctuary in the 1990s. Tuba Akekmekçi and Muazzez Pervan, eds., *Doğu Sorunu: Necmeddin Sahir Sılan raporları, 1939–1953* (Istanbul: Tarih Vakfı Yurt Yayınları, 2010), 6, 85, 133.

47. Norman N. Lewis, *Nomads and Settlers in Syria and Jordan, 1800–1980* (Cambridge: Cambridge University Press, 1987), chapter 2.

48. In an interview, the governor of Ardahan, Kutluay Öktem, confirmed the security logic; see "Sorunlarımız daha da Çoğaldı," *Milliyet*, June 14, 1995. For the full text of the legislation, see *T.C. Resmi Gazete*, No. 21247 Mükerrer, June 3, 1992, 1–29.

49. See chapters 3 and 6 for a more detailed discussion of the rivalry between the PKK and Hezbollah.

50. On the forced dislocation of Armenians from Muş and the Turkish demographic engineering attempts, see Fuat Dündar, *Modern Türkiye'nin Şifresi* (Istanbul: İletişim Yayınları, 2008), 282–286, 460; and Fuat Dündar, *İttihat ve Terakki'nin Müslümanları İskan Politikası* (1913–1918) (Istanbul: İletişim Yayınları, 2001). The Indonesian state tried to block the geographical expansion of the GAM with a similar administrative move; it divided the central and eastern districts of Aceh to strengthen their status as buffer zones. Central Aceh in particular hosted north Sumatran migrants as well as the Gayo ethnic group.

51. Imperial Russia shared the same vision in creating the Kholm Province in Poland. The goal was to consolidate Russian interests and communities against Catholic Poles. See Theodore R. Weeks, *Nation and State in Late Imperial Russia* (DeKalb: Northern Illinois Press, 1996), chapter 9.

52. Şırnak is a case in point. Despite its centrality in the 1980s, the Şırnak-Eruh corridor lost its vitality over time. Note the decreasing share of Şırnak, Eruh, and Pervari districts in the universe of insurgent violence in the early 1990s.

53. Tunceli governorship implemented food rationing in the province and allowed individuals to possess food only with proper documentation (1994–1998). The public became aware of this human tragedy after a group of parliamentarians visited the province in 1996. *Ayın Tarihi*, February 27, 1998; "Tunceli'de Çocukların Çifte Dramı," *Milliyet*, October 26, 1996.

54. The Ottoman sultan exiled fifty-five chiefs and religious figures to Rhodes (1892–1895) for collaborating with the rebellious imam. See Caesar E. Farah, *Sultan's Yemen* (London: I. B. Tauris, 2002), 177.

55. On relocation of Dersim tribes, which are estimated to include no less than 18,000 people, to the west of the country, see Hüseyin Aygün, *Dersim 1938 ve Zorunlu İskan* (Ankara: Dipnot, 2010), 169–246.

56. The most extreme counterinsurgency repertoire that aims at cutting civilian support is mass killing. See Benjamin Valentino, Paul Huth, and Dylan Balch-Lindsay, "'Draining the Sea': Mass Killing and Guerrilla Warfare," *International Organization* 58, no. 2 (2004): 375–407.

57. Hacettepe University Institute of Population Studies, "Türkiye Göç ve Yerinden Olmuş Nüfus Araştırması," unpublished report, Ankara, 2006.

58. Supergovernors acknowledged on several occasions (July 1989, August 1993) that there were roughly 12,000 administrative units in the countryside. While 7,000 of them were villages, the rest were hamlets. According to official statistics, more than 3,432 units were depopulated.

59. Hamlets are small rural settlements that typically have a population of less than 150. They are attached to villages and do not possess legal personality. The Turkish state viewed them as "outmoded units" and failed to penetrate them with its bureaucratic structure. Joost Jongerden, *The Settlement Issue in Turkey and the Kurds* (Leiden: Brill, 2007), 126–127.

60. For official province data, see "CHP'nin OHAL Raporu: 36 Bin Ölü, 18 Bin Yaralı," *Milliyet*, January 19, 2004.

61. The hamlets of Tunceli, which featured a dispersed settlement pattern and woody areas, became the main targets. Accordingly, more than one-third of all depopulated hamlets were located within the boundaries of the Tunceli province. For evacuations from Tunceli, see Jabob van Etten, Joost Jongerden, Hugo de Vos, Annemarie Klaasse and Esther C. E. van Hoeve, "Environmental Destruction as a Counterinsurgency Strategy in the Kurdistan Region of Turkey," *Geoforum* 39 (2008): 1786–1797.

62. The first village evacuations took place in Hakkari province in October 1984 following a cabinet meeting of the Turkish government. "Eşkıya için 6 Acil Önlem," *Milliyet*, October 13, 1984; "3 Köy Boşaltıldı, 50 Köy Boşaltılacak," *Milliyet*, October 19, 1984.

63. While 40 percent of evacuees had to leave in less than a week, only half were given a verbal warning, Hacettepe University Institute of Population Studies, "Türkiye Göç ve Yerinden Olmuş Nüfus Araştırması," 78, 106–110.

64. After years of promises, the Turkish government finally announced a plan in 1994 to collapse 79,000 rural units into 4,329 villages. This colossal task would be administered by a new institution, the Rural Settlement Administration (Kırsal Yerleşme İdaresi). The OHAL region would be given priority. However, the government plan failed from the start. European agencies refused to grant loans for the project since it would encourage forced migration. For details, see "Göçenlere Merkez Köy Projesi," *Milliyet*, November 29, 1994; "20 Merkez Köyün Parası Bulundu," *Milliyet*, December 4, 1994; "Avrupa Merkez Köy Projesine Destek Vermedi," *Milliyet*, March 16, 1995.

65. For the Turkish state's resettlement initiative, its historical lineages, and contemporary failure, see Jongerden, *The Settlement Issue in Turkey and the Kurds*.

66. Turkish Institute of Statistics, "Population Censuses of 1985, 2000." Available at http://tuikapp.tuik.gov.tr/nufusmenuapp/menu.zul. Last accessed on October 7, 2014.

67. The majority of Kurdish migrants settled in the Dağlıoğlu, Gülbahçe, 19 Mayıs, Denizli, Kiremithane, Barbaros, Anadolu, Hürriyet, and Yenibey neighborhoods of Seyhan. The municipal population increased from 642,321 in 1990 to 807,934 in 2000.

68. Less than 12 percent of migrants returned to their homes. The 118,000 returnees were mostly from rural areas.

69. The restitution rights of migrants became a major issue since the second half of the 1990s. Convoluted bureaucratic procedures have delayed decision making. As of May 2006, restitution

commissions had resolved only 27,011 of 195,463 applications. See TESEV, *Zorunlu Göç ile Yüzleşmek: Türkiye'de Yerinden Edilme Sonrası Vatandaşlığın İnşası* (Istanbul: TESEV, 2006), 79.

70. Ibid., 221. See also Erdem Yörük, "Welfare Provision as Political Containment: The Politics of Social Assistance and the Kurdish Conflict in Turkey," *Politics and Society* 40, no. 4 (2008): 517–547.

5. Ideology

1. King captures the issue: "Acquiring the power to define a hegemonic discourse about a conflict is a goal self-consciously pursued by belligerents." Charles King, "The Micropolitics of Social Violence," *World Politics* 56, no. 3 (2004): 452.

2. For a discussion of close affinity between a state's cognitive framework and political repression efforts, see David Pion-Berlin and George A. Lopez, "Of Victims and Executioners: Argentine State of Terror 1975–1979," *International Studies Quarterly* 35, no. 1 (1991): 63–86. More generally, for a tool kit view of culture that treats culture as a realm of narratives that social actors use to inform, legitimize, or challenge policy actions, see William H. Sewell, *Logics of History: Social Theory and Social Transformation* (Chicago: University of Chicago Press, 2005), chapter 5.

3. On path-dependent processes leading to inefficient outcomes, see the classic article: Paul A. David, "Clio and the Economics of QWERTY," *American Economic Review* 75, no. 2 (1985): 332–337.

4. The division of Kurdish areas in this way creates an organizational problem because it does not conform to M or U forms of political hierarchy. For a conceptual discussion, see Alexander Cooley, *Logics of Hierarchy: The Organization of Empire, States and Military Occupations* (Ithaca, N.Y.: Cornell University Press, 2005).

5. Mesut Yeğen, *Devlet Söyleminde Kürt Sorunu* (Istanbul: İletişim Yayınları, 1999).

6. "Özal: Kimseden Korkumuz Yok," *Milliyet*, August 27, 1986.

7. On urban partners of the late Ottoman state in Syria, see Philip S. Khoury, *Urban Notables and Arab Nationalism: The Politics of Damascus, 1860–1920* (Cambridge: Cambridge University Press, 1983).

8. Yakup Kadri Karaosmanoğlu, *Yaban* (1932; repr., Istanbul: İletişim Yayınları, 1983).

9. The classic formulation is seen in Şerif Mardin, "Center-Periphery: A Key to Turkish Politics?" *Daedalus* 102, no. 1 (1973): 169–190.

10. Ernest Gellner, *Muslim Society* (Cambridge: Cambridge University Press, 1981).

11. The roving-bandits model refers to a historical situation where multiple actors compete for resources and power in the absence of a centralized authority. See Mancur Olson, "Dictatorship, Democracy and Development," *American Political Science Review* 87, no. 3 (1993): 567–576. For a discussion of the Ottomans' retreat from the Arabian Peninsula, see Hasan Kayalı, *Arabs and Young Turks-Ottomanism, Arabism and Islamism in the Ottoman Empire, 1908–1918* (Berkeley: University of California Press, 1997), 144–173, 196–200; Eugene L. Rogan, "Bringing the State Back: The Limits of Ottoman Rule in Transjordan, 1840–1910," in *Village, Steppe and State: the Social Origins of Modern Jordan*, ed. Eugene L. Rogan and Tariq Tell (London: British Academic Press, 1994), 32–57; and Mary C. Wilson, *King Abdullah, Britain and the Making of Jordan* (Cambridge: Cambridge University Press, 1987), 25–38.

12. On Armenian insurgent groups, see Louise Nalbandian, *The Armenian Revolutionary Movement* (Berkeley: University of California Press, 1963). On biographies of Armenian revolutionaries, see Hratch Dasnabedian, *History of the Armenian Revolutionary Federation Dashnaksutiun, 1890–1924* (Milan: Oemme Edizioni, 1990). Contrast this pattern with the background of Armenians in the Ottoman bureaucracy; see Mesrob K. Krikorian, *Armenians in the Service of the Ottoman Empire, 1860–1908* (London: Routledge, 1978). The literature on Macedonian contention emphasizes regional involvement and the role of the Macedonian Revolutionary Organization

(MRO). For a comprehensive treatment of Greek activities in Macedonia, see Douglas Dakin, *The Greek Struggle in Macedonia, 1897–1913* (Salonica: Institute for Balkan Studies, 1966), 117–145, 198–287, 360–374. On the rise and fall of the MRO, see respectively, Keith Brown, *Loyal unto Death: Trust and Terror in Revolutionary Macedonia* (Bloomington: Indiana University Press, 2013); and Duncan M. Perry, *The Politics of Terror: The Macedonian Liberation Movements, 1893–1903* (Durham, N.C.: Duke University Press, 1988), 194–212. On violence and nation-building in Macedonia, see İpek K. Yosmaoğlu, *Blood Ties: Religion, Violence and the Politics of Nationhood in Ottoman Macedonia, 1878–1908* (Ithaca, N.Y.: Cornell University Press, 2013).

13. Halil İnalcık and Donald Quataert, eds., *An Economic and Social History of the Ottoman Empire*, vol. 1 (Cambridge: Cambridge University Press, 1997).

14. Initially, Village Institutes were designed to bring education to villages. Later, they also included teachers' colleges to expand educator ranks. The architect of the institutes was İsmail Hakkı Tonguç, who viewed them as an instrument for transforming villages from within. He believed that a social universe built around the village would be the source of wealth and progress. For the latent purpose of Village Institutes, see İsmail Hakkı Tonguç, *Canlandıralacak Köy* (Istanbul: Remzi Kitabevi, 1947), 1–38; and İsmail Hakkı Tonguç, *Mektuplarla Köy Enstitüsü Yılları, 1935–1946* (Istanbul: Çağdaş Yayınları, 1976), 102–112. For a faithful attempt to understand the rituals and organization of the village, see İsmail Hakkı Tonguç, *Köyde Eğitim* (Istanbul: Devlet Basımevi, 1938). Overall, twenty-one Village Institutes were established, two of which were located in Diyarbakır and Van.

15. Bureaucratic correspondence of the 1940s about Tunceli is a case in point. The reports highlighted the abusive practices of tribal leaders and religious figures (*seyits*). See Tuba Akekmekçi and Muazzez Pervan, eds., *Dersim Harekatı ve Cumhuriyet Bürokrasisi (1936–1950)* (Istanbul: Tarih Vakfı Yurt Yayınları, 2011), 5, 141, 143, 233, 240, 257, 299–300.

16. On Kurds and citizenship, see Mesut Yeğen, *Müstakbel Türkten Sözde Vatandaşa* (Istanbul: İletişim Yayınları, 2006), 47–88; and Tarık Ziya Ekinci, *Vatandaşlık Açısından Kürt Sorunu ve bir Çözüm Önerisi* (Istanbul: Küyerel Yayınları, 1997), Part 4.

17. On the civic origins of the Turkish citizenship model, see Karen Barkey, "Thinking about Consequences of Empire," in *After Empire: Multiethnic Societies and Nation-Building: The Soviet Union and the Russian, Ottoman and Habsburg Empires*, ed. Karen Barkey and Mark von Hagen (Boulder, Colo.: Westview Press, 1997), 99–114.

18. Jewish leadership reacted similarly to Palestinian claims in the 1920s; see Hilel Cohen, *Army of Shadows: Palestinian Collaboration with Zionism, 1917–1948*, trans. Haim Watzman (Berkeley: University of California Press, 2008), chapter 1.

19. For an overview of this position, see Turkish Democracy Foundation, *Fact Book on Turkey: Kurds and the PKK Terrorism* (Ankara: Turkish Democracy Foundation, 1996).

20. Leaflets distributed by the Turkish military stressed the same point in both the 1930s and the 1980s. The latter compared the glamorous lifestyle of leadership with the rank and file who barely survived in the mountains and promoted military messages with verses from the Quran. "Eşkiya'ya Son İhtar," *Milliyet*, January 14, 1986.

21. In 1993, the director of Turkish Religious Affairs (Diyanet) claimed in a press conference that the source of PKK terrorism was its atheism and that the actions of the insurgents were similar to reprisals taken by Armenians. He went on to argue that Muslim Kurds could not commit violence. Nonetheless, government officials decided to send traveling ulema (*irşad ekibi*) to enlighten the masses as early as 1986. *Ayın Tarihi*, October 24, 1986; *Ayın Tarihi*, October 30, 1993. On the Ottoman origins of this practice, see Emine Evered, *Empire and Education under the Ottomans* (London: I. B. Tauris, 2012), 115–120.

22. This had been evident in the political evolution of the Kurdish nationalist party since the 1990s. As the party penetrated urban towns and cities, it expanded its political claims. It now claims to speak in the name of the Kurds and demands political autonomy.

23. For a detailed account of the political repression of Kurdish civilian unrest in the 1990s, see chapter 6.

24. These surveys were conducted by Piar-Gallup in 1992 and 1994, and by Konda in 1993 and 2006. While the Piar-Gallup surveys relied on small samples, the Konda surveys concentrated exclusively on Istanbul and/or tackled issues of identity. All of these surveys were published in *Milliyet*. For details, see "Güneydoğu Sorununda Yeni Eğilimler Anketi," *Milliyet*, September 6, 1992; "Kürt Sorunu Ağırlaşıyor," *Milliyet*, November 16, 1994; "Kürt Sorununa Çözüm," *Milliyet*, March 3, 1993; and "Biz Kimiz: Toplumsal Yapı Araştırması," *Milliyet*, March 19–26, 2007.

25. Loyalty tests were used in Indonesia to eliminate the civilian base of the GAM insurgency. These activities included distributing new ID cards, screening civil servants, and staging public ceremonies in support of the Indonesian state. See Kirsten E. Schulze, "Insurgency and Counter-insurgency: Strategy and the Aceh Conflict, October 1976–May 2004," in *Verandah of Violence: Aceh's Contested Place in Indonesia*, ed. Anthony Reid (Singapore: Singapore University Press, 2006), 225–271.

26. On perceptions of weakness among the Ottoman-Turkish elite and its dramatic political consequences, see Maurus Reinkowski, "Hapless Imperialists and Resentful Nationalists: Trajectories of Radicalization in the Late Ottoman Empire," in *Helpless Imperialists: Imperialist Failure, Fear and Radicalization* (Göttingen: Vandenhoeck & Ruprecht, 2013), 47–67.

27. For this angle, see Salahi Ramadan Sonyel, *Gizli Belgelerde Osmanlı Devleti'nin Son Dönemi ve Türkiye'yi Bölme Çabaları* (Istanbul: Kaynak Yayınları, 2009). For a discussion of Western involvement in the Kurdish issue, see Bilal N. Şimşir, *Kürtçülük*, vol. 2 (Ankara: Bilgi Yayınevi, 2007), Part 1.

28. On British liberals' support for the Armenian cause, see Eugenio F. Biagini, *British Democracy and Irish Nationalism, 1876–1906* (Cambridge: Cambridge University Press, 2007), 317–326.

29. For the Ottoman Empire's official position on the issue, see *Ermeni Komitelerinin Emelleri ve İhtilal Hareketleri* (1916; repr., Istanbul: Kaynak Yayınları, 2006). The likely author of this text was the highly educated Polish-born Ahmed Rüstem Bey (Alfred Bilinsky), who later converted to Islam and served as the Ottoman ambassador to Washington. Similar views were expressed in his autobiographical work; see Ahmed Rüstem Bey, *Cihan Harbi ve Türk Ermeni Meselesi* (1918; repr., Istanbul: Bilgi Kültür Sanat Yayınları, 2005).

30. On non-Muslim economic intermediaries, see Elena Frangakis-Syrett, "The Economic Activities of the Greek Community of Izmir in the Second Half of the Nineteenth and Early Twentieth Centuries," in *Ottoman Greeks in the Age of Nationalism*, ed. Dimitri Gondicas and Charles Issawi (Princeton, N.J.: Darwin Press, 1999), 17–44. For cultural interlocutors, see Ussama Makdisi, "Rethinking American Missionaries and Nineteenth-Century Historiography of the Middle East," in *From the Syrian Land to the States of Syria and Lebanon*, ed. Thomas Philipp and Christoph Schumann (Beirut: Orient Institute, 2004), 209–224. For the changing perceptions of Europeans, see Aslı Çırakman, "From Tyranny to Despotism: The Enlightenment's Unenlightened Image of the Turks," *International Journal of Middle East Studies* 33, no. 1 (2001): 49–68.

31. Nation-state building efforts in the region had homogenized domestic populations by the 1930s. This had taken place through war making, population exchanges, and communal deportations since the 1870s. For the big picture, see Rogers Brubaker, "Aftermaths of Empire and the Unmixing of Peoples," in *After Empire: Multiethnic Societies and Nation-Building: The Soviet Union and the Russian, Ottoman and Habsburg Empires*, ed. Karen Barkey and Mark von Hagen (Boulder, Colo.: Westview Press, 1997), 155–180.

32. For a survey of political developments in the Young Turk period (1908–1918), see Stanford J. and Ezel K. Shaw, *History of the Ottoman Empire and Modern Turkey*, vol. 2 (Cambridge: Cambridge University Press, 1977), 273–372.

33. On the decision of the League of Nations and the Turkish position, see League of Nations, Council, *Decision Relating to the Turco-Iraq Frontier Adopted by the Council of the League of*

Nations, Geneva, December 16, 1925 (London: His Majesty's Stationery Office, 1925); and Turkey, Hariciye Vekaleti, *Frontier between Turkey and Iraq. Letter and Memorandum from the Turkish Government* (Geneva: Hariciye Vekaleti, 1924). Turkey insisted on a plebiscite to decide about the province's future and stressed ethnographical, historical, and economic reasons for maintaining Turkish sovereignty.

34. "Federasyon, Sevr'dir," *Milliyet*, August 15, 1993.

35. *Ayın Tarihi*, August 5, 1996.

36. According to Şemdin Sakık, Öcalan met with an Armenian delegation in February 1992. The overlapping borders of Kurdistan and Armenia became an issue. In October 1992, the PKK's representative was unable to secure a meeting with government officials in Yerevan. In his testimony to the State Security Court (DGM) of Ankara in February 1999, Öcalan stated that the rebel group had a representative in Armenia and published a journal there.

37. In an authoritative account on Turkish-Iranian relations in this period, Olson suggests that the major issue between two countries was the politics of northern Iraq. Iran supported Talabani and the PKK to create a counterbalance to Turkey's growing ties with Barzani. See Robert W. Olson, *The Kurdish Question and Turkish-Iranian Relations from World War I to 1998* (Costa Mesa, Calif.: Mazda Publishers, 1998), 77–87; and Robert W. Olson, *Turkey-Iran Relations, 1979–2004: Revolution, Ideology, War, Coups and Geopolitics* (Costa Mesa, Calif.: Mazda Publishers, 2004), 1–19.

38. Turkish diplomats who had served in Iraq prioritized the unity of Iraq, periodically referred to the Ottoman past, and treated Kurdish leaders with suspicion or as junior partners. See Gül İnanç Berkay, *Türk Diplomasisinde Irak (1978–1997)* (Istanbul: Türkiye İş Bankası, 2008), 32, 35–40, 54–56, 82–83, 108–109, 115. For a former minister's criticism of Barzani, see Hasan Celal Güzel, *Kuzey Irak: Kürtçülük ve Ayrılıkçı Terör* (Istanbul: Timaş Yayınları, 2007), 91–100, 123–128.

39. The Syrian perspective is discussed in Suha Bolukbasi, "Ankara, Damascus, Baghdad, and the Regionalization of Turkey's Kurdish Secessionism," *Journal of South Asian and Middle Eastern Studies* 14, no. 4 (1991): 15–36.

40. The Japanese and Chinese states made similar attempts. See Kenneth Pomeranz, "Imperialism, Development, and 'Civilizing Missions,' Past and Present," *Daedalus* 134, no. 2 (2005): 34–45.

41. For a collection of state proposals that sought to civilize Kurds and transform the region, see Saygı Öztürk, *Kasadaki Dosyalar* (Adana: Ümit Yayıncılık, 2003); and Belma Akçura, *Devletin Kürt Filmi: 1925–2009 Kürt Raporları* (Istanbul: New Age Yayınları, 2009). For the performance of the state in Bingöl and Tunceli in the 1940s, see several reports prepared by local bureaucrats and Sılan, who represented both provinces in the TBMM. Tuba Akekmekçi and Muazzez Pervan, eds., *Doğu Sorunu: Necmeddin Sahir Sılan raporları, 1939–1953* (Istanbul: Tarih Vakfı Yurt Yayınları, 2010), Part 1.

42. On Turkish counterinsurgency efforts, see the two-volume military text published by the Turkish General Staff: *Genelkurmay Belgelerinde Kürt İsyanları*, 2 vols. (1972; repr., Istanbul: Kaynak Yayınları, 2011).

43. The Settlement Code of 1934 facilitated this process by promising to populate Kurdish areas with Turkish immigrants from the Balkans. Despite the incentives the state offered, the demographic solution did not materialize. For demographic engineering attempts in the interwar period, see İsmail Beşikçi, *Kürtlerin Mecburi İskanı* (Istanbul: Komal Yayınları, 1977). For no-entry zones in Sason, see the secret gendarmerie report prepared by Major Lütfi Güvenç in Necmeddin Sahir Sılan, *Doğu Anadolu'da Toplumsal Mühendislik: Dersim-Sason, 1934–1946* (Istanbul: Tarih Vakfı Yurt Yayınları, 2010), 313–422.

44. On the Ottoman experience in the Gulf, Najd, and Yemen, see Frederick F. Anscombe, *The Ottoman Gulf: The Creation of Kuwait, Saudi Arabia and Qatar* (New York: Columbia University Press, 1997); Zekeriya Kurşun, *Necid ve Ahsa'da Osmanlı Hakimiyeti* (Ankara: Türk Tarih

Kurumu,1998); and Jon Mandaville, "Memduh Pasha and Aziz Bey: Ottoman Experience in Yemen," in *Contemporary Yemen*, ed. B. R. Pridham (London: Croom Helm, 1986), 20–33.

45. For Ottoman centralization attempts in the Druze Mountain, see Kais M. Firro, "The Ottoman Reform and Jabal al-Duruz, 1860–1914," in *Ottoman Reform and Muslim Regeneration*, ed. Itzchak Weismann and Fruma Zachs (London: I. B. Tauris, 2005), 149–164. The historical evolution of Republican tactics and discourses on Dersim is available in official military documents and government reports; see Jandarma Umum Kumandanlığı Raporu, *Dersim* (1932; repr., Istanbul: Kaynak Yayınları, 2010); and Faik Bulut, *Belgelerle Dersim Raporları* (Istanbul: Yön Yayıncılık, 1991).

46. For the pedagogical role of education, see Fortna and Somel who suggest that new-style schools in the late Ottoman Empire served the state's agenda because of their moral content and emphasis on social discipline. Benjamin C. Fortna, "Islamic Morality in Late Ottoman 'Secular' Schools," *International Journal of Middle East Studies* 32, no. 3 (2000): 369–393; and Selçuk Akşin Somel, *The Modernization of Public Education in the Ottoman Empire, 1839–1908* (Leiden: Brill, 2001), 271–277. For the role of these schools in molding the Iraqi ruling elite, see Reeva Spector Simon, *Iraq between the Two World Wars*, updated ed. (New York: Columbia University Press, 2004), 15–16.

47. Several bureaucrats, including prime ministers, visited the region in the interwar era and prepared reports that addressed issues of underdevelopment. Finance Minister Celal Bayar was one of them. See Celal Bayar, *Şark Raporu* (Istanbul: Kaynak Yayınları, 2009). For a study that examines the reports of the State Planning Organization (DPT) targeting the region since the 1960s, see Semih Yalçın, *Doğu Anadolu'ya Yapılan Kamu Harcamaları (1960–1980)* (Ankara: Berikan, 2009).

48. Albertine Jwaideh, "Midhat Pasha and the Land System of Lower Iraq," in *Middle Eastern Affairs*, ed. Albert Hourani (London: Chatto and Windus, 1963), 106–136. The irony of land reform in Turkey is the persistent gap between interventionist discourse and the limited application of policies. For a collection of proposals, see Doğu Perinçek, *Toprak Ağalığı ve Kürt Sorunu* (Istanbul: Kaynak Yayınları, 2010), esp. 79–84, 93–106, 116–122, 155–164.

49. First, the Turkish government sealed the long Syrian border. Starting from Nusaybin district, the border was mined and protected by barbed wire fence, watchtowers, and new lighting. However, this strategy did not work on the mountainous Iraqi border. For an early recognition of the last point, see "Apo'nun Maskesi," *Milliyet*, October 3, 1985.

50. A detailed account of Turkish counterinsurgency efforts is available in Ümit Özdağ, *Türkiye'de Düşük Yoğunluğu Çatışma ve PKK* (Ankara: 3 Ok, 2005).

51. There were almost no asphalt village roads across the region in 1985. As of 2000, one-third of all village roads were asphalt in Mardin. Still, the issue remained in Şırnak, Van, and Hakkari. Devlet İstatistik Enstitüsü, *İl Göstergeleri, 1980–2003* (Ankara: DIE, 2004), 90.

52. "Demirel: GAP'a Laf Ettirmem," *Milliyet*, July 19, 1992. The GAP is a massive regional development project that cost 32 billion dollars. The project invested heavily in developing infrastructure and water resources (most importantly dam construction) in order to increase productivity and employment in the rural sector. For a detailed discussion of the GAP's objectives, see Republic of Turkey, State Planning Organization, *GAP: The Southeastern Anatolia Project Master Plan Study: Final Master Plan Report*, 2nd ed. (Tokyo, Japan: Nippon Koei Co.; Ankara: Yüksel Proje, 1990).

53. A two-time prime minister, Bülent Ecevit viewed the Kurdish problem as a regional issue. He was suspicious of Western imperialist plans and did not trust local intermediaries in Turkey and beyond (village guards, the "feudal" class, and Kurdish leaders in northern Iraq). He worked tirelessly to cut a deal with Baghdad in the early 1990s and refused to align himself with tribal leaders in domestic politics. The political cure for the Kurdish issue, he believed, was regional economic transformation.

54. Eastern and southeastern Anatolia continued to rank at the bottom of the development index. Their GNP per capita was the lowest in the country and there was significant capital flight from these regions. In addition, the GAP did not deliver local benefits; instead, it mainly sup-- ported industrial development in western Turkey. For growing regional inequality after the 1960s as a result of industrialization policies that favored western parts of the country, see Mustafa Sönmez, *Doğu Anadolu'nun Hikayesi* (Ankara: Arkadaş Yayınevi, 1990), 150–190. In the 1990s, the "East" continued to lag behind other regions in terms of individual income, capital accumulation, credit, and tax revenue; see Mustafa Sönmez, *Bölgesel Eşitsizlik: Türkiye'de Doğu-Batı Uçurumu* (Istanbul: Alan Yayıncılık, 1998), 274–288, 295–296.

55. Similar to the Chinese frontier vision, the Turkish view on eastern Anatolia vacillated between the two extremes as a liability or as an undeveloped asset. For the Chinese position on eastern Tibet, see Xiuyu Wang, *China's Last Imperial Frontier: Late Qing Expansion in Sichuan's Tibetan Borderlands* (Lanham, Md.: Lexington Books, 2011), chapter 5.

56. On boundary making and identity formation, see Fredrik Barth, ed., *Ethnic Groups and Boundaries: The Social Organization of Cultural Difference* (Boston: Little, Brown, 1969).

57. For the evolution and failures of the Ottoman conscription system, see Eric Jan Zürcher, "The Ottoman Conscription System in Theory and Practice," in *Arming the State: Military Conscription in the Middle East and Central Asia, 1775–1925*, ed. Eric J. Zürcher (London: I.B. Tauris, 1999), 79–94.

58. On legislation regarding the regiments and their tribal composition, see Bayram Kodaman, *Sultan II. Abdülhamid Devri Doğu Anadolu Politikası* (Ankara: Türk Kültürünü Araştırma Enstitüsü, 1987), 21–66. For a more recent treatment, see Janet Klein, "Power in the Periphery: The Hamidiye Light Cavalry and the Struggle over Ottoman Kurdistan, 1890–1914" (PhD diss., Princeton University, 2002).

59. On the pro-state record of *Nakşibendi* religious order in the region, see Butrus Abu-Manneh, "Salafiyya and the Rise of the Khalidiyya in Baghdad in Early Nineteenth Century," *Die Welt des Islams* 43, no. 3 (2003): 349–372; and Itzchak Weismann, *Taste of Modernity: Sufism, Salafiyya, and Arabism in Late Ottoman Damascus* (Leiden: Brill, 2001), 52–54.

60. On the cultural politics of Abdulhamid II, see Selim Deringil, *The Well-Protected Domains: Ideology and Legitimation of Power in the Ottoman Empire, 1876–1909* (London: I. B. Tauris, 1998).

61. As of 1994, there were more than 232,668 *ronderos* in Peru. See James F. Rochlin, *Vanguard Revolutionaries in Latin America* (Boulder, Colo.: Lynne Rienner, 2003), 69. On *rondas*, see Orin Starn, "Villagers at Arms: War and Counterrevolution in the Central-South Andes," in *Shining and Other Paths*, ed. Steve J. Stern (Durham, N.C.: Duke University Press, 1998), 224–257.

62. In the Algerian civil war, self-defense groups were established in connection with political parties and regional associations; see Luis Martinez, *The Algerian Civil War, 1990–1998*, trans. Jonathan Derrick (New York: Columbia University Press, 2000), 151–153.

63. Abuses by village guards were documented in an unpublished special report by the Diyarbakır branch of the Human Rights Association; see İnsan Hakları Derneği, *Ocak 1990-Mart 2009 Döneminde Köy Korucuları Tarafından Gerçekleştirilen İnsan Hakları İhlallerine İlişkin Özel Rapor* (Diyarbakır: İnsan Hakları Derneğİ, 2009). Bedran Akdağ, a former village guard, gave similar testimony. In the Kızıltepe and Derik districts of Mardin, ex-militants and special teams detained civilians for monetary gain in the 1993–1996 period. See (Korucu) Bedran Akdağ, *Dağın Ardındaki Gerçekler* (Istanbul: Ozan Yayıncılık, 2012), 70–112.

64. Major tribes, including Tatar, Alan, Jirki, and Batuhan, were represented in these meetings. After drawing attention to the growing power of the PKK and the Kurdish nationalist party in the region, they asked for greater shares from village guard ranks and demanded permanent status. "Emniyet'te Gizli Toplantı," *Milliyet*, November 23, 1993; "Böyle Seçim Yapılırsa, PKK Kazanır," *Milliyet*, November 24, 1993.

65. The local heads of the National Action Party (MHP), the RP and the DYP as well as the mayor of Şırnak province were members of the Tatar tribe. "Şırnak'ta Akrabalar Yarışıyor," *Milliyet*, November 17, 1994.

66. The RP became powerful in the OHAL region after the municipal elections of 1994. As one party candidate put it, the key to its success was resisting political repression without necessarily opposing the state. The party also successfully blurred the lines between Islamic solidarity and Kurdish-Islamic identity. See Ruşen Çakır, *Ne Şeriat ne Demokrasi: Refah Partisini Anlamak* (Istanbul: Metis Yayınları, 1994), 150–160. A similar political process was at work in Indonesia. The Indonesian state began to emphasize Islam in order to reconnect with Acehnese society. See Edward Aspinall, *Islam and Nation: Separatist Rebellion in Aceh, Indonesia* (Stanford, Calif.: Stanford University Press, 2009), 213.

6. Strategy

1. Timothy P. Wickham-Crowley, "Terror and Guerrilla Warfare in Latin America, 1956–1970," *Comparative Studies in Society and History* 32, no. 2 (1990): 201–237.

2. Jason Lyall, "Does Indiscriminate Violence Incite Insurgent Attacks?," *Journal of Conflict Resolution* 53, no. 3 (2009): 331–362.

3. Note that the relationship between counterinsurgency method and the type of violence is not given. While the former refers to tactics, the latter is about targets. Any tactic can lead to indiscriminate or selective violence independent of its intensity or the technology it employs.

4. Matthew Adam Kocher, Thomas B. Pepinsky, and Stathis N. Kalyvas, "Aerial Bombing and Counterinsurgency in the Vietnam War," *American Journal of Political Science* 55, no. 2 (2011): 201–218.

5. Paul K. MacDonald, "'Retribution Must Succeed Rebellion': The Colonial Origins of Counterinsurgency Failure," *International Organization* 67, no. 2 (2013): 253–286.

6. Laleh Khalili, "The Location of Palestine in Global Counterinsurgencies," *International Journal of Middle East Studies* 42, no. 3 (2010): 413–433.

7. John A. Nagl, *Learning to Eat Soup with a Knife: Counterinsurgency Lessons from Malaya and Vietnam* (Chicago: University of Chicago Press, 2005).

8. Patricio N. Abinales, *Images of State Power: Essays on Philippine Politics from the Margins* (Quezon City: University of the Philippines Press, 1998); Alfred W. McCoy and Francisco A. Scarano, eds., *Colonial Crucible: Empire in the Making of the Modern American State* (Madison: University of Wisconsin Press, 2009); Julian Go and Anne L. Foster, eds., *The American Colonial State in the Philippines: Global Perspectives* (Durham, N.C.: Duke University Press, 2003).

9. We observe that the location of rural operations shifted from administrative units (such as villages) to inaccessible geographical locations (such as mountains) after 1993. A comparison with the 1984–1992 period confirms this trend. The share of these geographical spots as the sites of military encounters almost doubled, reaching 60 percent in the 1993–1999 period. For a detailed discussion of administrative units and geographical categories in the countryside, see the Appendix.

10. The Turkish army conducted its first large-scale operation at Cudi Mountain in August 1989. Several villages located on the mountain were evacuated and became provisioning centers for the army. While the operation had some success (twenty insurgents were killed in the clashes), security forces could not establish a permanent presence in the area because of its indefensible position.

11. One thousand nine militants surrendered to the state in 428 separate incidents. Surrenders reached a peak as the conflict escalated in the 1992–1994 period and declined substantially after 1999. The number of surrenders was not significant in the 1980s.

12. Repentance Laws in 1985 and 1993 promised to pardon those who joined the rebel organization but did not participate in acts of violence. Only twenty-five insurgents benefited from the first series of legislative acts in 1985–1986.

13. Unaccounted rebel deaths refer to fatalities (commonly found buried) with no direct evidence of how and when the individual died. Four hundred forty-eight bodies were discovered on eighty-two separate occasions; most of which belonged to rebels who had died during a military encounter.

14. "PKK Savaş Açtı," *Milliyet*, March 23, 1992.

15. Compared to insurgent casualties, security losses increased at a much slower pace between the two periods, rising from 1.7 to 2.9 on average in counterinsurgency operations. A similar trend was observed for security deaths during insurgent attacks although the figures were slightly higher, increasing from 2.4 to 3.3 on average.

16. James D. Fearon, "Why Do Some Civil Wars Last So Much Longer Than Others?," *Journal of Peace Research* 41, no. 3 (2004): 275–301.

17. On the coordination between the military and civil authority, see Daniel L. Byman, "Friends Like These: Counter-Insurgency and the War on Terrorism," *International Security* 31, no. 2 (2006): 79–115

18. With one exception, these bureaucrats later pursued political careers in Prime Minister Tansu Çiller's DYP. While some of them were elected to the TBMM, a more ambitious one, Mehmet Ağar, built a political career as a right-wing party leader.

19. "Güreş: Riskli Dönemdeyiz," *Milliyet*, July 7, 1992.

20. On Kundakçı's military record, see Hasan Kundakçı, *Güneydoğu'da Unutulmayanlar* (Istanbul: Alfa Yayıncılık, 2007).

21. For a survey of similar efforts by Russia in Chechnya, see Mark Kramer, "The Perils of Counterinsurgency: Russia's War in Chechnya," *International Security* 29, no. 3 (2004–2005): 5–63.

22. The security forces consisted of 110,000 troops in the OHAL region. In addition to commando and gendarmie units, 17 percent of the troops were stationed on the border. The state also increased the scale of its military presence by replacing batallions with regiments in border districts to defend military posts. "PKK Liderlerine Sürek Avı," *Milliyet*, November 11, 1993.

23. "Özel Tim Suç Rekortmeni," *Milliyet*, September 29, 1996. Special teams were formed in 1986 under the newly established terrorism unit, Terörle Mücadele ve Harekat Daire Başkanlığı. They were not allowed to enter villages or operate in the mountains. Their numbers reached 1,587 after the OHAL administration was established in 1987. In 1993, Çiller decided to use them against the ERNK in urban areas, and by 1996, their numbers had increased to 7,000. There were complaints about them, especially in Tunceli, for destroying property and mistreating civilians. Two thousand eight hundred and seventy-six members of special teams were transferred or fired.

24. In most situations, civil wars redefine the organizational boundaries of state coercion and bring in new agents who are commissioned to wage violence in the name of the state. Privatizing security may effectively mean giving allies who might be interested in pursuing personal gain (mercenaries) and/or resolving preexisting conflicts in their favor. In the Colombian conflict, paramilitaries (later the AUC—United Self-Defense Groups of Colombia) evolved into criminal gangs who became heavily involved in drug trafficking. Another interesting outcome might be the consolidation of power in a single institution within the state. The Secret Service of Pakistan (ISI) became "a state within a state" during the civil war in neighboring Afghanistan. On paths of military development in the Third World, see Ariel I. Ahram, *Proxy Warriors: The Rise and Fall of State-Sponsored Militias* (Stanford, Calif.: Stanford University Press, 2011).

25. The most successful military operation in this period was conducted in Nusaybin district in April 1988. Based on a lead, security forces engaged a large number of rebels who had recently crossed the Syrian border and entered Turkey. The clash took place close to Dibek Mountain. It was long and bloody: Twenty insurgents were killed, as were four members of the security forces, including a lieutenant and a major. Another thirteen were wounded. A helicopter also

went down. "20 PKK'lı Öldürüldü," *Milliyet*, April 2, 1988. From an operational standpoint, it is also worth mentioning the success of insurgent attacks in the 1980s. Until March 1990, the PKK lost no more than four militants in any single attack.

26. "Şam ve Tahran Gözaltında," *Milliyet*, February 16, 1992. Previously, the Turkish government leased Puma helicopters from France in 1987. *Ayın Tarihi*, December 1, 1987.

27. Lyall and Wilson rightly argue that mechanization can decrease a state's military effectiveness by creating an information starvation problem. However, air power in general and helicopters in particular were instrumental in the battlefield victories of Turkish forces. See Jason Lyall and Isaiah Wilson III, "Rage against the Machines: Explaining Outcomes in Counterinsurgency Wars," *International Organization* 63, no. 1 (2009): 67–106.

28. The key was the increasing number and strength of ties between insurgents and security forces, which refer to the coverage and depth of counterinsurgency operations respectively. On network terms, see Mustafa Emirbayer and Jeff Goodwin, "Network Analysis, Culture and the Problem of Agency," *American Journal of Sociology* 99, no. 6 (1994): 1411–1454.

29. U.S. strategy in Vietnam relied on similar tactics, specializing in "clearing," "search and destroy," and "securing" operations. For a detailed military account, see John H. Hay Jr., *Tactical and Materiel Innovations* (Washington, D.C.: Department of the Army, 1989).

30. Erdal Sarızeybek, *Şemdinli'de Sınırı Aşmak* (Istanbul: Pozitif Yayınları, 2011), 101.

31. Military encounters took place in 114 districts in 1993, covering, on average, ninety-four districts per year in the 1991–1994 period. Contrast this pattern with the 1980s and post-2000 period, when military operations were limited to twenty-five districts.

32. In 1995, the territorial jurisdiction of the Gendarmerie for Internal Security was scaled down to three provinces (Van, Şırnak, and Hakkari). See "Asker OHAL'ı Şeklen Kaldırdı," *Milliyet*, November 25, 1995.

33. The four major sanctuaries were responsible for only one-third of military encounters in 1992, Tunceli accounting for only 3 percent of such encounters.

34. Note the change in the annual share of military encounters in these districts in the 1990s. Cizre and Silopi: 10 percent in 1992, 4 percent in 1995–1997, and 2 percent in 1998–1999; Uludere and Çukurca: 4 percent in 1992, 8 percent in 1995–1997, and 2 percent in 1998–1999; Yüksekova and Şemdinli: 1 percent in 1992, 10 percent in 1995–1997, and 8 percent in 1998–1999.

35. More than 8 percent of all military encounters happened in the central district of Şırnak in 1998 through 1999. Although Şırnak became the single spot with the highest number of insurgent fatalities throughout the conflict, the average number of fatalities per operation in the district was relatively low (4.2).

36. During this operation, security forces lost twelve men and another ten were wounded. *Ayın Tarihi*, April 14–19, 1998; "Operasyonlarda 86 PKK'lı Öldürüldü," *Cumhuriyet*, April 20, 1998.

37. An unprecedented increase in armed encounters ensued in neighboring districts of Şırnak. These districts were Beytüşşebap, Çatak, and Gürpınar, which suffered 10 percent of all military encounters in 1998 through 1999. The numbers of insurgent fatalities in these encounters were high. For example, in two separate operations in September and October of 1988 that were conducted in the Faraşin Valley of Beytüşşebap and the Kato Mountain of Çatak district, the rebels experienced no fewer than 100 casualties.

38. Almost one-fifth of armed encounters took place in Genç, Kulp, and Şırnak in this period (1998–1999).

39. This was Operation Sparrow, which was conducted with 10,000 troops in April 1996. Security forces destroyed rebel camps after bloody clashes that left 126 insurgents and thirty-nine security forces dead. The rebel camps, which housed more than 150 militants, were located at an elevation of 10,000 feet. They had separate living quarters and a classroom for educational training as well as generators and satellites. "Şok Operasyon," *Milliyet*, April 9, 1996. For detailed

coverage, "Ateş Çemberi," *Milliyet*, April 10, 1996; "Yavaş Yavaş İmha," *Milliyet*, April 11, 1996; "Raktepe 16.30," *Milliyet*, April 12, 1996; "Bölgede Nokta Operasyonu," *Milliyet*, April 13, 1996.

40. "24 General ile Son Temizlik," *Hürriyet*, April 30, 1998.

41. See chapter 3 for details on Tunceli.

42. *Ayın Tarihi*, December 2, 1994; "71 PKK'lı Öldürüldü," *Milliyet*, April 3, 1995; *Ayın Tarihi*, September 7, 1995

43. "Tunceli'de Operasyon," *Milliyet*, September 25, 1996.

44. The Turkish army entered northern Iraq from Uludere and Çukurca in October 1992. With the support of tanks and helicopters, it targeted Hakurk, Haftanin, and Zap camps. According to military sources, the PKK lost 40 percent of its manpower in this operation. Meanwhile, the number of security casualties was around 153. "Harekatın Bilançosu," *Milliyet*, October 30, 1992.

45. Direct attack strategies favor the strong actor in wars. Rebels have a greater chance to win guerrilla wars when they adopt opposite approach interactions. Ivan Arreguin-Toft, "How the Weak Win Wars," *International Security* 26, no. 1 (2001): 93–128.

46. Interview with Oral Çalışlar. Oral Çalışlar, *Öcalan ve Burkay'la Kürt Sorunu* (Istanbul: Pencere Yayınları, 1993), 21.

47. There were nineteen cross-border operations in this period, including Operation Steel (1995), Operation Slap (1996), Operation Hammer (1997), and Operation Dawn (1997). The most important ones came after the military conducted sweeping operations in Turkey. For the motivations behind the code names of military operations, see Gregory C. Sieminski, "The Art of Naming Operations," *Parameters* (Autumn 1995): 81–98.

48. "Siirt'te İki Bölücü Ölü Olarak Yakalandı," *Milliyet*, July 16, 1985.

49. Security forces located 2,431 PKK shelters in a fourteen-month period (January 1994–February 1995). More than half were located in insurgent strongholds. For a detailed breakdown of shelter locations, see "Güneydoğu'nun Altı Sığınak Gibi," *Milliyet*, February 26, 1995.

50. The PKK assigned certain individuals the task of providing food supplies in bulk quantities. For example, we learn from one arrest incident in Pervari district that key supplies were distributed to the rebels in the mountains by individuals who were responsible for provisioning. This system seemed to work well, as most PKK shelters had ample food supplies that would have lasted for months.

51. The exception was the 1996–1999 period, when security forces were able to capture disorganized and fleeing insurgents in the OHAL region. Most of the arrests took place around sanctuary districts, where there were spillover effects, and in "safe locations" in the region that had kept a low profile throughout the conflict.

52. "Bismil'e PKK Yine Saldırdı," *Milliyet*, March 16, 1992.

53. Tribal allies of the state were mostly located in Zone 1. Among others, these tribes included Tatar, Jirki, Batuyan, and Goyan (all in Şırnak); Pinyaşi (in Hakkari); and Izdinan, Alan, Geraviyan, Piran, Şerefhan, Halilan, and Kasuran (all in Van).

54. The state would vent its rage on a village when it could not locate insurgents. For example, several villages were burned to the ground in counterinsurgency operations during the interwar period. Similarly, Chechen and Indonesian forces held the families of insurgents accountable.

55. When they crossed the border, refugees first lived in mountain camps such as Bihere, Seraniş, and Besive. Later in the 1990s, under UN administration, Camp Mahmur became the only protected site for refugees from Turkey. The camp is still open today and hosts 12,000 people.

56. *Ayın Tarihi*, August 14, 1993. A curfew was later enforced. The district governor, Özcan Bademli, pointed fingers at the PKK for provoking violence. However, witnesses blamed special teams for the violence and claimed that the casualties could have been much higher if the gendarmerie had not intervened. Meanwhile, the Kurdish nationalists, the DEP, brought the issue to the attention of the TBMM for investigation. TBMM, *Tutanak Dergisi* 19/40 (October 5, 1993), 299–301; TBMM, *Tutanak Dergisi* 19/40 (October 6, 1993), 12. "Çiller, Güreş ve Gazioğlu'nun İstifası İstendi," *Cumhuriyet*, October 6, 1993.

57. Two hundred forty-six civilians died in ninety-seven separate counterinsurgency incidents. Almost half of these incidents occurred in the countryside, especially when peasants were mobilized to protest gendarmerie action.

58. In 1992, protestors gathered in front of the Kümbet Mosque, which was located on the outskirts of the town. They chanted "Down with fascism in Kurdistan." When villagers from Hasretpınar breached the police barricade, security forces opened fire on the crowd. One man was killed and a woman was injured. For detailed coverage, see "Kanlı Saldırı: 4 Ölü," *Cumhuriyet*, August 17, 1992; "Güneydoğu'da 5 Ölü Daha," *Milliyet*, August 17, 1992; "Korsan Gösteride 3 Ölü," *Milliyet*, August 16, 1993; and "Digor'da Ölenlerden 5'i Terörist Çıktı," *Hürriyet*, August 16, 1993.

59. The only exception was the city of Batman, which previously had been a district of Siirt.

60. There has rarely been an overlap between the political identity rebels promote during civil wars and the self-identification of the target population. In the Turkish context, this mismatch found its best expression in geographical terms. Zone 1, which was previously an empty niche, was dramatically transformed into a stronghold by the insurgency. Zone 2, which covered most of eastern Anatolia, remained under the hegemony of Sunni Islam despite heavy Kurdish presence. Here, confessional identity (Sunni versus Alevite) was instrumental in boundary making. In Zone 3, outside the OHAL region, national (Turkish) identity prevailed and the ethnic project could not find enough followers.

61. Military courts concluded that those who gave logistical support to insurgents or provided guidance should be considered as members of the rebel organization with a special mission. "PKK Kılavuzuna 15 Yıl," *Milliyet*, August 6, 1990. On Torumtay's comments, see "Silah Çeken Düşmandır," *Cumhuriyet*, August 18, 1989.

62. As Kalyvas has rightly noted, the identification problem hurts the incumbent most. Stathis N. Kalyvas, *The Logic of Violence in Civil War* (New York: Cambridge University Press, 2006), 90.

63. In fact, half of all arrest incidents in the Transition Zone took place at these four sites.

64. For example, Süleyman Anık, the local head of the Dargeçit branch of the incumbent party (Motherland Party), was detained with other party members. *Ayın Tarihi*, September 2, 1991.

65. Fifty-two percent of arrests were reported in district centers in this period. In the second half of the 1990s, the screening efforts of the security forces would shift to large cities.

66. On these operations, see "PKK'ya Darbe," *Milliyet*, August 1, 1988; "PKK'lılara Yeni Darbe," *Milliyet*, August 17, 1988; and "1'i Ölü 22 PKK'lı Ele Geçirildi," *Milliyet*, September 23, 1989.

67. Almost half of all successful counterinsurgency operations against urban safe houses were reported in the city of Diyarbakır and in Nusaybin, a district of Mardin. In addition to their unique advantages such as dense population and proximity to the border, both locations were major centers of civilian unrest.

68. "PKK Köy Bastı," *Milliyet*, February 21, 1994.

69. Aydın was the regional commander of gendarmerie forces in Diyarbakır. During the clashes, eight civilians and five insurgents were killed and the town was severely damaged. While the OHAL governor attributed this to the PKK's show of force, Nazmi Balkaş, the mayor of Lice, argued that it was the state forces that burned down the buildings. Kani Yılmaz, the head of the ERNK in Europe, denied responsibility for the assasination. After Aydın's death, the minister of interior was replaced and a new anti-terror law was outlined in a MGK meeting. "General Şehit," *Milliyet*, October 23, 1993; *Ayın Tarihi*, October 26, 1993; *Ayın Tarihi*, November 22, 1993.

70. Although civilian unrest continued after 1994, the window of opportunity for the PKK was clearly missed in the early 1990s. With one exception, one had to wait until 2005 to find another incident with a civilian fatality after 1993. Hence, the wave from 1989 through 1993 remained the most politically significant chapter in civilian unrest.

71. There were two local networks of civilian unrest, one centered in Cizre and the other in Diyarbakır. Both were located in the Transition Zone.

72. In an interview, the father of the deceased militant, Yusuf Dündar, suggested that the special teams turned a peaceful ceremony into a violent one. For a credible account of the incident, see the reporting by Namık Durukan: "Nusaybin'de 300 Gözaltı," *Milliyet*, March 16, 1990; and "Nusaybin'de Durum Gergin," *Milliyet*, March 17, 1990.

73. Forty-nine civilians were arrested in connection with the Cizre incident. "Teröristler Durmuyor," *Cumhuriyet*, March 26, 1990; "Derik'te 100 Gözaltı," *Milliyet*, March 26, 1990.

74. This figure accounted for two-thirds of all incidents that took place within the OHAL boundaries.

75. For details, see *Ayın Tarihi* for July 11–14 and July 19, 1991. A similar pattern was observed in March 2006, when a funeral in Diyarbakır resulted in an almost identical number of arrests, imprisonments, and casualties and fueled demonstrations in several towns in the Transition Zone. See "PKK Cenazesinde Olay," *Hürriyet*, March 28, 2006.

76. On Hezbollah's own account of its rivalry with the PKK, see M. Hüseyin Yılmaz, *Hizbullah Ana Davası: Savunmalar* (Istanbul: Dua Yayıncılık, 2011), Part 3.

77. The city of Diyarbakır, the northern districts of the province (Silvan and Bismil), the city of Batman, and Nusaybin were hit especially hard.

78. The number of unsolved political murders to the east of Cizre was rather small. On the competitive nature of adjacent identities, see William P. Barnett and Michael Woywode, "From Red Vienna to the Anschluss: Ideological Competition among Viennese Newspapers during the Rise of National Socialism," *American Journal of Sociology* 109, no. 6 (2004) 1452–1499.

79. Political repression led to an escalation of civilian unrest from 1989 to 1993 and then deterred it from 1994 to 1996. The long-term political outcome was not what the rebels or the state intended. On the escalatory nature of indiscriminate violence, see Stathis N. Kalyvas, "The Paradox of Terrorism in Civil War," *The Journal of Ethics* 8, no. 1 (2004): 97–138.

80. In Zone 3, the security forces tried to contain the PKK threat in the provinces that were adjacent to the OHAL (Ağrı, Urfa, Adıyaman, Malatya, Erzincan, and Erzurum). Accordingly, 42 percent of all military encounters in Zone 3 took place in these spots.

81. In 1995, 55 percent of all arrests in the country took place in four major cities that had recently received Kurdish migrants (Istanbul, Adana, Mersin, and İzmir). This figure represents a twofold increase from 1992.

82. The number of districts where arrests were made increased from forty-eight in 1991 to seventy-three in 1992. This was made possible by the rising intensity of counterinsurgency operations. Arrests increased sixfold between 1984–1988 and 1992, and almost doubled from 1992 to 1993. In fact, close to half of all incidents were reported between 1992 and 1994.

83. "PKK Kana Doymuyor," *Milliyet*, June 27, 1992.

84. The suspects included the head of the ERNK in Istanbul, seven district heads, and campus organizers. "PKK'nın Istanbul Sorumlusu Yakalandı," *Hürriyet*, October 27, 1992.

85. A typical example would be the story of Abik brothers. On August 1995, an explosion was reported in a low-income neighborhood of Istanbul, Siyavuşpaşa. The Abik brothers died, while the wife of Nizamettin Abik and his two children survived the explosion. Nizamettin, who had been born in Şenyuva village of Mazıdağı district in Mardin, was 24. He and his brother were members of the Metropole Revenge Teams (MİT), had received technical training in Greece, and had been involved in bombings in the city. "Hücreevinde Patlama: 2 Ölü," *Milliyet*, August 30, 1995.

86. On demographics of these neighborhoods, see "İşte Göç Faciası," *Milliyet*, July 25, 1995. On police action, see "11 PKK'lı Öldürüldü," *Milliyet*, January 8, 1994.

87. A time bomb killed six individuals and injured forty-two. The targets were military cadets who attended the School of Infantry. The MİT claimed responsibility for the attack. "Tuzla'da Hain Tuzak: 6 Ölü," *Cumhuriyet*, February 13, 1994; "Caniler Aranızda," *Milliyet*, February 13, 1994.

88. "İstanbul'da 5 PKK'lı Yakalandı," *Hürriyet*, September 3, 2005.

89. "180 Üniversiteli PKK Kamplarında," *Milliyet*, August 16, 1991.

90. The suspects were captured in Operation Blow, which lasted twelve days. Based on a lead, security forces raided several houses and arrested high-ranking PKK officials, including a teacher, a retired imam, and a university student. "15 PKK'lı Öldürüldü," *Milliyet*, May 15, 1994; "Mavi Trene Yine Bomba," *Milliyet*, May 16, 1994.

91. Two-thirds of these border encounters took place in districts that neighbored a district within the OHAL. With the inclusion of three provinces (Kars, Ardahan, and Iğdır) on Turkey's eastern border, the location of two-thirds of all military encounters in Zone 3 can be accounted for.

92. *Ayın Tarihi*, October 30, 1993; "Tehlikeli Tırmanış," *Milliyet*, October 31, 1993.

93. Not surprisingly, more than half of all the arrests in Zone 3 related to rural logistics were reported in provinces that were adjacent to the OHAL.

94. In its 20-year history, the Kurdish nationalist party failed to garner enough support from Kurds in Istanbul. This was evident in election results. In five national elections held from 1995 to 2011, the party won only five of 361 seats for Istanbul and its vote share ranged between 3.5 and 6 percent of the provincial vote.

Conclusion

1. For a research program on political contention, see Doug McAdam, Sidney Tarrow, and Charles Tilly, *Dynamics of Contention* (Cambridge: Cambridge University Press, 2001).

2. Charles Tilly, *Contentious Performances* (Cambridge: Cambridge University Press, 2008).

3. Denise Natali, *The Kurds and the State: Evolving National Identity in Iraq, Turkey and Iran* (Syracuse, N.Y.: Syracuse University Press, 2005).

4. For a relational understanding of ethnicity, see Rogers Brubaker, *Nationalist Politics and Everyday Ethnicity in a Transylvanian Town* (Princeton, N.J.: Princeton University Press, 2006).

5. On the multiple orders thesis, see Karen Oren and Stephen Skowronek, *The Search for American Development* (Cambridge: Cambridge University Press, 2004).

6. Jeremy Weinstein, *Inside Rebellion: The Politics of Insurgent Violence* (New York: Cambridge University Press, 2007), 23.

7. Zachariah Cherian Mampilly, *Rebel Rulers: Insurgent Governance and Civilian Life During War* (Ithaca, N.Y.: Cornell University Press, 2011), 68, 70.

8. Paul Pierson, *Politics in Time: History, Institutions, and Social Analysis* (Princeton, N.J.: Princeton University Press, 2004).

9. On endogenous change, see Avner Greif and David D. Laitin, "A Theory of Endogenous Institutional Change," *American Political Science Review* 98, no. 4 (2004): 633–652.

10. Elizabeth S. Clemens and James M. Cook, "Politics and Institutionalism: Explaining Durability and Change," *Annual Review of Sociology* 25 (1999): 441–466.

11. Such contingencies can be brought about by exogenous shocks such as foreign intervention, natural disasters, and systemic wars. Domestic developments can also challenge the path, especially when there is new political leadership or decisive military outcomes.

12. On turning points, see Andrew Abbott, "On the Concept of Turning Point," *Comparative Social Research* 16 (1997): 85–105; and Ira Katznelson, "Periodization and Preferences: Reflections on Purposive Action in Comparative Historical Social Science," in *Comparative Historical Analysis in the Social Sciences*, ed. James Mahoney and Dietrich Rueschemeyer (Cambridge, UK: Cambridge University Press, 2003), 270–301.

Appendix

1. Jennifer Earl, Andrew Martin, John D. McCarthy and Sarah A. Soule, "The Use of Newspaper Data in the Study of Collective Action," *Annual Review of Sociology* 30 (2004): 65–80.

2. Jeremy M. Weinstein, *Inside Rebellion—The Politics of Insurgent Violence* (New York: Cambridge University Press, 2007); Ashutosh Varshney, *Ethnic Conflict and Civic Life: Hindus and Muslims in India* (New Haven, Conn.: Yale University Press, 2002); Mark R. Beissinger, *Nationalist Mobilization and the Collapse of the Soviet State* (Cambridge: Cambridge University Press, 2002); Steven I. Wilkinson, *Votes and Violence: Electoral Competition and Ethnic Riots in India* (Cambridge: Cambridge University Press, 2004).

3. Arrest incidents can also be viewed as detentions in the Turkish context, where detainees were typically released from police custody before seeing a judge. That is why in Turkish usage the verb "detain" is used to refer to the act of arrest by law enforcement in civilian unrest cases.

Index